PARK BAGGER

MARLIS BUTCHER

Park Bagger

ADVENTURES IN THE

CANADIAN NATIONAL PARKS

RMB

For information on purchasing bulk quantities of this book, or to obtain media excerpts or invite the author to speak at an event, please visit rmbooks.com and select the "Contact" tab.

RMB | Rocky Mountain Books Ltd.
rmbooks.com
@rmbooks
facebook.com/rmbooks

Cataloguing data available from Library and Archives Canada
ISBN 9781771604789 (softcover)
ISBN 9781771604796 (electronic)

All photographs are by Marlis Butcher unless otherwise noted.

Cover photo Aulavik - Muskox (Marlis Butcher)

Printed and bound in Canada

We acknowledge the financial support of the Government of Canada through the Canada Book Fund and the Canada Council for the Arts, and of the province of British Columbia through the British Columbia Arts Council and the Book Publishing Tax Credit.

For my parents,
who immigrated to this great country of opportunity
to raise their children.

ACKNOWLEDGEMENTS

Special thanks to Parks Canada for preserving significant samples of the varied Canadian landscapes and for making these special places available to us. Also to the Indigenous Peoples of this vast land, for teaching me and sharing the splendour.

I thank everyone who had the faith and confidence in me to explore the farthest reaches of this vast country, and to successfully write this book. Specific thanks to fellow adventurers Paul and Sue Gierszewski, John Borley, Carmen Braund and Blake Sparks, who shared the burdens of getting into those really remote parks. Also Sue Neal and Dr. Anna Dowbiggin for helping see my writing through. I also truly appreciated the encouragement from Stefan Kindberg, my sponsor to The Explorers Club, and from Dr. David Galbraith, my sponsor to the Royal Canadian Geographical Society's College of Fellows.

CONTENTS

PREFACE

Falling down mountainsides, being pinned to cliff faces by driving sleet, paddling kayaks through giant whitewater, ricocheting a canoe through deep canyons and being clotheslined off a mountain bike in a dense forest are some of the consequences of exploring the farthest reaches of Canada's wilderness. But there are also much larger rewards to be experienced, such as the pleasures of strolling through dreamy woodlands, contemplating life while paddling on calm waters, and meditating in the Arctic under the midnight sun. Then there are adventures that can be both daunting and awe-inspiring, like encounters with bears, bison and butterflies. The promise of these experiences is what pushes me to explore Canada's national parks and discover my country.

I was born and raised in Montreal, and my education included Canadian geography, peoples, history and literature. The photographs and stories piqued my interest. The strength of character and resilience of both the Indigenous Peoples and the first Europeans who settled here intrigued me. The challenges they endured contrasted so much with my own secure, cushy, modern Canadian experience. This awareness developed into three driving forces in my life.

First, like many Canadians, I wanted to get to know my country personally, to visit all of the provinces and territories. That quest naturally led me into the national parks. However, I did not originally set out to see all the parks. They were just something to visit when I was in the area; interesting places which helped me get to know the part of the country I was exploring. Only after noticing that I'd been to over half the national parks did I become obsessed with getting to all of them.

Second, Canada has so much wilderness that even as a child I felt I needed to know how to survive should I ever become lost. Not that I was afraid of getting lost, but I expected I would be at some point and I wanted to be prepared for it.

Family vacations in nearby national parks introduced me to basic camping: how to live without the comforts of a modern home.

As a teenager I travelled farther afield with the Girl Guides, learning everything I could about summer and winter camping, canoeing, kayaking, Nordic skiing, snowshoeing, dog sledding, wild edibles, first aid and whatever other survival courses the Girl Guides had to offer. Their motto "Be Prepared" was not lost on me.

Those experiences led me to travelling with outfitters who organize trips for small groups of adults to some of the more remote parks. I became not only familiar with travelling alone to the group meeting points across the country but comfortable enough to go on adventures with just my husband, Martin, and even completely by myself.

Eventually, in order to complete my mission of visiting all the national parks, I had to truly stretch my personal limits. I needed to use all my knowledge, skills and abilities to boldly try things I'd never dreamt of. I had to develop novel ways of getting to and safely exploring the most remote reaches of this enormous country.

A third driving force for me was that I shouldn't ever complain about any hardships while travelling in Canada. I have it so much easier than those who came before. For instance, I don't have to wear long, water-wicking skirts while forging through swamps. I don't have to carry a heavy canvas tent. I don't have to build my own canoe. And I don't have to rely on the availability of wild game for food. I can wear quick-dry pants, backpack ultralight nylon tents, rent a lightweight canoe and survive on store-bought freeze-dried foods. Still, it is nice to know how to build a shelter and forage for food, just in case.

There is of course another driver, and that's the adrenalin rush from venturing out of my comfort zone. The satisfaction of not having remained complacent is matched by that of the personal growth gained by exploring new things and places.

In 2002 someone asked me how many parks I'd been to. I didn't know; I'd never thought to count them. I scanned through my travel journals and found that I'd been to more than half of the 44 national parks that existed at that time. That act of cataloguing my visits suggested a new objective: I had to see them all. Hence I became a "park bagger" – someone who attempts to visit all the national parks of Canada. This quest overtook much of my life, and certainly it superseded my interests in exploring the rest of the world. Even relaxing Caribbean vacations were forfeited to this obsession. Overall, though, I've been fortunate, and I am extremely grateful to have been able to follow my passion.

Having visited so many of the parks, I came to associate myself with Parks Canada's mission. I too wanted to share the parks, and my adventures in them, with everyone. I'd tell my stories to friends and colleagues every time I returned from a park visit. They wanted to know more. They wanted to see my photographs. Some people reacted by reminiscing about their own park visits. Some were inspired to go and visit the parks, while others were happy just to have learned about the wilderness without needing to endure it themselves. Many people suggested that I write a book about my exploits. And so this book was born.

This is the story, or rather the stories, of some of my adventures as a Canadian park bagger. They are sorted from west to east to provide a sense of geographic continuity, rather than chronologically as I hopscotched opportunistically across the country.

I invite you to come with me on my journeys discovering Canada.

INTRODUCTION

Canada is the world's second-largest country by area, spanning some 5500 kilometres from the Pacific to the Atlantic oceans and 4600 kilometres from Middle Island in Lake Erie at the US border to the north end of Ellesmere Island. Despite this vast geography, we are only 38 million residents, and 95 per cent of us live along the southern edge of the country. While a few people do live in the North, 80 per cent of the landmass is uninhabited because it is largely inhospitable. The North consists primarily of buggy forests, deep swamps, rock, tundra and Arctic permafrost. Houses on many of those types of land tend to sink into the ground. As a result, the vast majority of the 10 million square kilometres of the country is preserved in its natural state. Of course, industry does attempt to exploit the land for minerals, oil, gas and even water. Hence our national parks.

Parks Canada's objective is to create at least one park in each of the 39 natural regions it has carved the country into, with the following mandate:

> On behalf of the people of Canada, we protect and present nationally significant examples of Canada's natural and cultural heritage, and foster public understanding, appreciation and enjoyment in ways that ensure the ecological and commemorative integrity of these places for present and future generations.

Unlike the national parks of most other countries, however, many of Canada's are inaccessible by road. Which of course invites a question: How is it a "park" if people can't visit it? Well, people *are* allowed to visit all the Canadian parks; the challenge is how to get to some of them. And that may be okay, because some people (like me) enjoy challenges.

I had to become creative in finding transportation and funding. I became opportunistic in my quest, hooking up with other, similarly minded explorers, going with licensed outfitters, and even taking advantage of Parks's public visitation packages. Visitors, I can confirm, may enter these parks by bicycle, car, truck or small ship as well as by float plane, small plane and helicopter.

I also had to be flexible with how I'd overnight in the parks. Some have five-star hotels, some have comfy rustic cabins, most have campgrounds, and many have backcountry campsites with no road access. There are also parks where you can camp pretty much wherever you wish – just be sure to bring everything you'll need, because there's no easy way to quickly get anything you may have forgotten. And then there are a few small parks where there's no overnighting allowed at all.

The sheer size of the country means there is a great variety in the activities and points of interest in the parks. Although I was surprised by the urban attractions in some of the parks, I have to confess that a spa and first-class dinner are fine things to enjoy after a challenging sojourn in the wilderness. Of course there are playgrounds and beaches in many of the parks, but there are also scenic drives. Then there are the sportier ways of enjoying and getting to know the land. Visitors can partake in walking, hiking, backpacking, snowshoeing, skiing (both Nordic and alpine), cycling, canoeing, kayaking, sailing and on and on. Greedily, I've tried to do it all.

Many of my park experiences included learnings from and about Canada's Indigenous Peoples, the first people to live on and with this land. Recognizing their skills and knowledge, Parks Canada now manages many parks in collaboration with Indigenous Peoples. That co-operation has in turn enabled visitors like me to participate in traditional meals, beading, games, orienteering, sweatlodge bathing, and smudging, and even visit with the spiritual world. These cultures have had a great influence on those like me travelling through this great land: our paths, canoes, kayaks, snowshoes, tents and foods such as bannock and jerky are based on Indigenous ways. They are integral to our Canadian identity, our parks and my own experiences.

What impressed me most, however, were the amazing landscapes.

Each park is so unique. I've found everything from sparkling oceans and inviting beaches, to glaciers and snow-covered mountains, to desolate lands, to friendly forests, to endless prairie grasses. With this diversity comes all sorts of wild animals, some fun to meet, others threatening. I've met up with polar, grizzly and black bears. I've seen wolves, wolverines, martens and beavers. Then there were the bison, sheep and goats, moose, caribou, elk and deer. The smaller critters such as ground squirrels and chipmunks are undeniably cute, but they are also very destructive, I've discovered. Raptors and songbirds are always a welcome sight. And while bees and butterflies are enchanting to watch, insects such as the ubiquitous mosquitos, black flies and horse flies have driven me crazy.

As a result, my escapades in the parks have been as varied as the vast diversity of the parks and their locations. And as my wilderness survival skills developed with experience, I ventured into the remotest of the parks and discovered that they aren't nearly as scary as I once expected. In fact, I have found I can be comfortable, at least for a short time, pretty much anywhere in Canada. Visits to the national parks are at once challenging and stress-free, exciting and calming, entertaining and educational.

So my adventures in the Canadian national parks unfold.

THE NORTHWEST

1

Aulavik

MOSQUITOS AND MUSKOX

Late in June 2017 six of us met with our two Black Feather outfitter guides, Gail and Caleb, in the Parks Canada office in Inuvik in the Mackenzie River delta. I had never met Dave, a serious long-distance hiker, or Terry, a retired judge from Windsor, Ontario, but we'd each travelled with Gail on other trips. Americans Cathy and Ian were new to Arctic canoeing, but were experienced paddlers down south. Heidi, in her 80s, was a retired Swiss ski instructor who was eager to experience the far North before she became too frail to manage it.

Apart from just getting acquainted, the meeting was for the mandatory backcountry camping orientation and polar bear safety instructions before heading into Aulavik National Park on Banks Island. As part of the safety plan for our 13-day trip in this High Arctic park, we were each issued a can of bear spray and a bag of pen-sized explosive flares called bear bangers.

Our objective was to paddle 160 kilometres of the Thomsen River, Canada's northernmost navigable waterway, which runs northward right through the middle of the park. Aulavik makes up just less than a fifth of the 70,000 square kilometre Banks Island, Canada's fifth-largest, at the west end of the Northwest Passage.

Despite the name of the park meaning "place where people travel," the only way to get to Aulavik is by plane, or possibly by boat if the ice on the Arctic Ocean has broken up. We flew. On an unusually calm sunny day, a small Twin Otter propeller plane flew us over the Beaufort Sea to Banks Island. On our way across the water we spotted a pod of pure-white beluga whales, easily distinguishable from the bluish-white ice floating on the dark surface of the ocean. This first sighting of wildlife, although from high up in the sky, marked the start of our adventure.

Almost too quickly travelling 520 kilometres, we arrived at Sachs Harbour. Situated on the south coast of Banks, Sachs is the only settlement on the island. I had been hoping to meet some of the 112 residents, but we only had enough time to refuel, so we couldn't explore the hamlet. With fine flying weather, our pilots were anxious to get us to our destination.

Travelling almost 240 kilometres due north over Arctic tundra, we passengers kept our noses pressed to the windows. We noted several small groups of muskox grazing on what appeared to be, from our altitude, barren ground. We also watched flocks of what looked like white snow geese, flying below us from pond to inky dark pond between the low, rolling hills. I wondered about the evolution of polar animals' camouflage: white might be excellent in the winter, but not so much in the summer when most of the snow has melted. Furthermore, some of these white animals migrate south in winter. How odd.

Our little plane landed in Aulavik National Park on a flattish strip of dirt delineated by old oil drums. Despite having been filled with stones, a few of the drums had been blown over by the wind. A forewarning of conditions to come? From the end of the runway we taxied back along the bumpy terrain to Green Cabin on the west bank of the Thomsen River.

Green Cabin is an old hunting shelter, painted green of course and consisting of just one large room with a few folding tables, plastic chairs and some emergency supplies. We unloaded our gear and watched as the plane left us alone on the tundra. The sky had become grey and it was starting to rain. There was a bone-chilling cold to the air. We watched as the rain dissolved the thick snowbank on the far side of the river. In spite of the prospect of a dreary, miserable canoe trip, I tried to be positive: I had made it to another national park!

Inside Green Cabin, Gail gave priority to warming us up with hot soup, made from vegetables she'd grown in her own garden at home and freeze-dried. We'd need all our strength to manage the tasks necessary to make our days in the park as comfortable as possible. Camping is all about survival work: a continuous stream of jobs without modern-day comforts like insulated shelters, furnaces, hot and cold running water and fully equipped kitchens.

Re-energized, we started setting up our tents in the cold, wind-driven rain. Each of us had been issued a two-person winter tent, except the one couple, who shared a three-place tent. We worked together to hold down the nylon sheets until tent pegs and rocks had been put into place. Unfortunately one tent got away from us and was blown violently down into the fast-running river, where it was immediately snagged by exposed rocks, the strong wind tearing at the thin nylon. Scrambling down the steep, slushy bank, we balanced our way out over the ice-topped river rocks. We managed to catch the escaped tent, but found it was already bulging with gritty river water. The heavy, water-laden tent had been punctured and shredded as it grated over the rough riverbed. Carefully we heaved the mass, wringing the water out of it. Not having netted any fish, we joked about how poor a trawling method this was. As a result of this folly, for the rest of the trip we had to repeatedly patch this tent with duct tape; and we discovered that tape doesn't stay fast in wet weather.

Our next task was to assemble our canoes. We had four folding canoes made of a thick polyester-type fabric that is stretched into shape by a series of hinged aluminum poles and ribs. All we had to do was unroll the skin, unfold and snap the poles and ribs together, and assemble the lot using the supplied rubber mallets. This was easier said than done, though, because the tight-fitting parts needed to be pressed into just the right places. We were lucky to have so many hands helping to put these puzzles together. We were also very thankful for the shelter of Green Cabin, given how harsh the weather outside had become.

Happily, the sun came out the following day. We put our canoes into the water, loaded our gear and set forth. Although we had strong headwinds, as we did most days no matter which direction the crazy meandering river ran, we were happy to be on the water. I paddled with Dave; Caleb and Terry paddled together; Cathy and Ian had their matrimonial boat; and Gail paddled for Heidi. Later in the trip we'd adjust our paddling partners to more comfortable balances of strengths and abilities.

With no trees or other vegetation more than about 15 centimetres tall, we could see for kilometres between the low, green hills. Arctic wolves peeked down from the snow-topped muddy riverbanks, curiously watching us as we paddled downstream. There were muskox, small groups of the big shaggy beasts, grazing on every other hill. We canoed past orange-billed king eider ducks and pure-white gulls. A pair of swans flew overhead. A peregrine falcon eyed us suspiciously from its perch on a rocky cliff hanging over a river eddy where we rested awhile to shelter from the incessant wind.

And oops, on one of those lovely canoeing days, when I was paying more attention to these wondrous sights than to where I was paddling, my canoe got blown up against a gravel bank in the middle of the river. After much struggling and frustration Dave and I managed to get the canoe unstuck, but we had turned away from our intended side of the low, stony island. Unexpectedly, we had found the deep-channel route on the other side of the island. Caleb and Terry accompanied us, the strong current pushing both our boats rapidly downsteam. The other two canoes, which had been in the lead before the island, unfortunately chose the wrong channel. They became grounded in shallow water and had to be hauled over the muddy pebbles. Eventually all four boats safely met up again at the next bend in the river.

The water was dark brown and thick with sediment because of the slumping riverbanks. The permafrost was permanently frozen no longer: the ground was melting, exposing the soil to erosion. We sorrowfully watched as mud banks collapsed into the water like calving glaciers.

When unloading our heavy gear each afternoon that we made camp, we struggled over those thawed riverbanks, occasionally sinking knee deep into the mire. After passing loads of equipment, and then the empty canoes, fire-brigade-style, up to the high, flat plains overlooking the river, I'd climb up myself, covered in mud. Since there are no facilities of any sort other than what we brought with us, I had only the wildflowers to wipe my hands clean on. I resigned my clothing to the filth of the hostile wilderness for the duration of the trip.

Most of the fields above the Thomsen, we discovered, were broken up into a labyrinth of small, squarish plots outlined by narrow water channels. The squares were all approximately three hectares in size. The drier of these plots were covered with wildflowers – that's were we set up our tents – but most were marshy from melted snow. Sandhill cranes waded in the distant wet patches. About a kilometre back from the river, in lower-lying areas, the meltwater overflowed into the squares, creating small, clear ponds. Loons would call from these ponds when we approached to collect drinking water.

Some days, instead of paddling, we went exploring on foot. We'd carefully walk along the narrow, elevated, grassy dikes that surrounded the soggy squares, to get to the distant hills. The gentle slopes were swathed in colourful wildflowers with wafts of the sweetest perfumes. Nature flourishes spectacularly in the few weeks of summer, under the 24-hour sun in the High Arctic. With no trails or paths to follow, we lamented having to tread on the fragile-looking blossoms. However, I happily noted that the flowers, hardy enough to withstand Arctic gales, did not break under our boots.

On top of a hill overlooking the confluence of the Muskox and Thomsen rivers, we arrived at a 1,000-year-old Thule summer campsite. These were peoples who had lived in the Arctic even before the Inuit. We found many tent rings: arrangements of rocks that had been used to hold down round tents. There were piles of large rocks that had been used to cache food. And there were many, many decaying caribou and muskox bones scattered about the place. Researchers had counted approximately 800 muskox skulls on this plateau. Orangey-red lichen covers all of the remains of human activity, attesting to the length of time that has passed since this site was last used by the Thule.

We settled down for lunch on some rocks in the middle of this historic site. Although we were eating crackers with cheese and cured meats, I like to think we were sharing a meal, over time, with some of those ancient travellers who noshed on fresh muskox meat. We were all sitting in this flowered field enjoying food, company and the expansive views of the Thomsen River valley.

On our way back to camp we decided to avoid the low-lying marshy plots for as long as possible, hiking instead over a row of hills. However, we were stopped short of the first summit by a huge muskox that had crested that hill from the other side. Just a few metres above us, the beast stared down at us, letting us know we were not to proceed. Without hesitation, we quietly complied, edging our way down the side of the hill. I stopped every few metres to turn around and take photos. To my surprise, the last time I looked back there were seven of these thick-horned giants watching our retreat, their mean, rough coats billowing in the wind, juxtaposed against the pretty, purple-flowered crest of the hill. The scene was backed by a perfect bright-blue sky. I snapped my last photograph and then left the muskox in peace.

Back down on the plain again, each of us found our own way along the myriad of dikes. Looking down at my feet, watching that I didn't step into the soggy fens, I almost walked onto a small grass-covered pingo. Pingos are round-topped, cone-shaped hills formed by lifting permafrost. The squawk of a jaeger, a huge, gull-like bird that was perched on top of the pingo, made me look up at where I was going. These fierce hunting birds are known to attack people, and this one didn't appear happy with my approach. I altered my course to avoid both pingo and jaeger and found another dry route back to camp.

The following few days were extremely warm, in the high 20s Celsius. The last time we checked the thermometer one day, it was 30 degrees – way too hot for the Arctic! Our neighbouring muskox were lying in patches of leftover snow in the shadowy trenches between the hills, trying to stay cool. A pair of wolves paced the far bank of the Thomsen, scratching and twitching in the midst of a swarm of mosquitos that had risen out of the low Arctic willows that windless day. To us it looked like the wolves wanted to go into the water for relief from the heat and mosquitos but the water was too thick with mud.

That day was also too hot for us to paddle or hike. In the stifling still air the mosquitos invaded our kitchen teepee, attracted to the potential to feed. Our low dome tents, while bug-free, were like bake ovens inside, and there was no shade in this treeless Arctic wilderness. So each of us simply sat dozing outside, in the shadow of our tents.

Despite the heat, I wore my heavy boots, long pants, a long-sleeved shirt and my winter gloves, just to keep the mosquitos from biting. A bug net kept my head safe.

After a few hours of this mind-numbing stillness, the wind finally picked up again and the mosquitos settled down into the weeds. I took advantage of this reprieve and raced along the dikes to the nearest pond. Quickly I stripped off my clothes and ran in. I didn't care that the bottom of the pond was muddy and reedy – I was just happy for the relief. The cool water soothed my itchy, dirty skin. I took a moment to swab myself with my hands, the first body wash I'd had since arriving in the park.

As per standard, respectful wilderness practice, I don't use soap to bathe where there's no water circulation – and the water in these ponds was stagnant. Even biodegradable soaps would have added non-native ingredients to these remote, pristine environments. However, after days of minimal body washing inside my tent, this simple submersion in water felt wonderful.

Unfortunately the mosquitos were waiting for me to come out of my pond. They attacked in full force the moment I sat down on the dike to put on my socks. Hurriedly I pulled on the rest of my filthy clothes. In the process I suffered a few more bites – the itching would start, I knew, the following day.

On the Arctic tundra there is no animal-safe place for human food and "smellies" – toiletries and other nicely scented items. So we kept these items in dense, 60-litre plastic barrels inside the kitchen teepee. We surrounded the kitchen tent with a bear-fence, a simple tripwire that would set off small explosives to let us know when we had visitors. During the day, we disarmed the fence so that we wouldn't accidentally trip it ourselves. Fortunately we never did see any polar bears, and "Bob," the lemming that took shelter under our kitchen at one camp, was too small to set off any alarms.

One bright sunny night when I was desperately braving the clouds of mosquitos to go pee, I noticed there were three adult muskox, one adolescent and two cute kids, grazing alongside our kitchen tent. From my faraway spot, swatting to keep the mosquitos off my exposed buttocks,

I watched these muskox. While muskox are vegetarians and hence wouldn't likely be attracted to the smellies inside the kitchen, there was the possibility that they'd wander too close to the tripwires and set off the explosives. However, the mosquito-safety of my tent outweighed my desire to shoo the muskox away. Also, those beasts, at up to 400 kilograms each, looked rather mean. I took the chance and went back to bed. The explosives never went off and I slept soundly.

From the north, the midnight sun shone brightly through my orange nylon tent. I had to wear eyeshades to simulate darkness so I could sleep. Most nighttimes were quite cold and I snuggled in my winter sleeping bag. However, on a couple of those very hot days I slept stark naked on top of my sleeping bag, feeding the few mosquitos that had followed me into my tent. These extreme temperature fluctuations were unexpected and frustrating. I expected that the wildlife were just as uncomfortable as we were.

Out on the river, even in strong headwinds, was always the best place to be: cool and mosquito-free! We paddled past three very large pingos covered with grass and wildflowers. Only their cone shapes identified these hills as special permafrost formations.

We paused at each of several tributaries that feed into the Thomsen. Into these rocky estuaries Ian cast a line for Arctic char. However, the fish, if they were present in the muddy waters, didn't find the lures. So no tasty char for our lunches.

We usually ate lunch at riverside spots sheltered from the wind, under rocky cliffs or behind flower-covered sand dunes. Unfortunately flies and mosquitos also liked those lees, so we'd scoff down our food and hurry back onto the sanctuary of the swift river as quickly as possible. We really didn't have much time to rest.

The land, however, had many attractions enticing us to put up with the mosquitos. One afternoon, instead of paddling we went on a hike over several hills alongside the river. On the highest hill, overlooking the Thomsen River, was a pre-Dorset site. The pre-Dorset peoples had lived here even before the Thule. We found many lichen-covered tent rings, food caches and some possible graves. This site extended over several hills.

There were pieces of decomposing animal bones, caribou antlers and muskox skulls, most of them partially buried in the ground, every-where. Ironically, over on the next hill were several muskox grazing on the mosses growing between the skulls of their long-dead ancestors. Either these animals didn't recognize their slaughtered family members, or their dead had no meaning to them. We quietly watched as they foraged their way into the far valley out of our sight.

Among the debris were some obviously carved, chipped or cut bones and stones, possibly the remnants of prehistoric tools. I almost stepped on one oddly curved small rock, but instead I stopped and picked it up. The one edge fit nicely into my palm. Turning it over, I saw that the opposite edge had been carefully chip-carved and tapered into a nice, thinly curved blade. This might have been a stone *ulu*, a traditional northern-style knife! I felt the excitement of an amateur archaeologist. We photographed the stone, then properly put it back exactly into the indented soil where I'd found it.

Our group split up on the hike back to camp because Heidi was an extremely slow walker. Caleb stayed back to accompany her. The rest of us were already resting in camp when we heard a bear banger go off, the explosion echoing in the hills. Emergency! Quickly Gail gathered up supplies and gave us instructions to stay in camp to relay a satellite phone call for help if necessary. Just as she was about to leave towards the source of the alarm, Caleb and Heidi appeared in the distance and gave an "all's okay" hand signal. We settled down and waited for their return.

At long last Caleb and Heidi arrived in camp and told us the story of what had happened. After we'd walked out of their sight over a hill, a lone Arctic wolf had appeared and charged at them. From a hidden crag, the animal had likely watched the larger group of us pass, and seemed to have considered our two stragglers to be weak prey. But Caleb and Heidi successfully scared the predator off with the bear banger and then nonchalantly sauntered the rest of the way back to camp. Heidi had even managed to photograph the frightened animal as it ran away. For the rest of our journey, however, we ensured that no one wandered off alone and unseen by the rest of our group.

We tried to travel farther down the river, but the water was running low, as the last of the snow had melted. Finding water deep enough to float our canoes was becoming challenging. The shorelines had turned into wide, muddy flats with no comfortable access between the shallow streams of running water and the dry higher ground. Furthermore the risk of polar bear encounters increased the closer we got to the Arctic Ocean. So we opted to end our journey at the "Back Channel campsite" near where the Thomsen River empties into the south end of Castel Bay, on the Arctic Ocean.

This last camp was on a large gravel island in the river delta. As everywhere along this river, there are no facilities, trails or even hints of where one might set up tents. The Back Channel campsite is simply a flat enough area where small planes may land, so that's where paddlers set up camp.

We wandered about the island looking for a drier spot where we could set up our tents, yet not right on the designated landing strip. The latter we identified by tire tracks left by the last plane that had landed there earlier in the summer. Of course, that landing area was on the other side of the island. So back and forth we walked, portaging all our bags, barrel packs and the canoes, from the muddy riverbank, around a pond and swampy weeds, to the site we'd selected. In the process, everything, including ourselves, became covered with a thick layer of mud.

In addition to our regular daily camp chores, that day we had to pack up the canoes. This meant we had to collect cleanish water from the shallow pond to first wash the mud off of ourselves. Then we collected more water with which to clean the boats. Finally we took the canoes apart and stuffed the pieces into their large cargo bags.

On our final day in Aulavik, before the Twin Otter came to collect us, we had time to explore our gravel island. We spent an hour walking the circumference, noting the numerous goose feathers strewn about the island. Perhaps this had been a nesting site, but we didn't see anything that resembled nests. Whatever the birds had been doing here, they'd long since flown away.

The drone of distant propellers distracted our contemplations, and we hurried back to the landing site, where we'd already piled our bags and equipment. It was time for us too to fly away. Our exploration and travels in Aulavik were complete.

2
Vuntut

THE BRITISH MOUNTAINS
CARIBOU, WOLVES AND GRIZZLIES

Vuntut National Park, in the north of the Yukon Territory, is one of those parks that's almost impossible to get to. There are no roads to this landlocked Arctic park. The southern quarter of the park is made up of much of the Old Crow Flats wetland, a boggy plain filled with small lakes, ponds and streams, which is why the park is named "Vuntut": Gwitch'in for "among the lakes." The northern part of the park, composed of the British Mountains, with their low, crag-topped hills and broad muskeg meadows, has been designated a "Declared Wilderness Area" in order to protect the Porcupine caribou, one of the largest migrating herds in North America. As a result, very few people have visited Vuntut and there are no recommended routes or places to go in the park. And there are no facilities of any sort.

So my first challenge was to figure out how to get into Vuntut National Park, just 50 (barren) kilometres north of the community of Old Crow. And Old Crow is an isolated community itself, with no road access. I considered, and rejected, several possibilities:

- A boat might meander north up the winding Old Crow River. But surprisingly, the actual length of the river is more than triple the straight-line distance to the park due to the many bends in the river. Further challenging the use of this route into the park is the fact that the river is not regularly cleared of debris such as encroaching shrubs and beaver dams.
- A float plane could land on one of those lakes in the Old Crow Flats, but I'd be trapped there in the middle of a vast mosquito-ridden wetland.

- I could fly into the Declared Wilderness Area. The challenge with this option was that to prevent disturbing the wildlife, the territorial government requires a lengthy environmental assessment. As assessments normally require a baseline status for comparison and so few people have visited the park, I didn't expect to receive a favourable assessment on a timely basis.

Working by phone with the park manager based in Whitehorse, I devised yet another way into the park: a helicopter could land just north of the boundary and I could simply step over the "line" into the park. The more I thought about it, the more realistic, though pricey, this plan became.

From the comfort of my home, I scoured Google Earth and topographical maps for mountain passes on the park's northern edge where a helicopter might land. I found a possibility just a few kilometres east of the Alaskan border, but I was afraid such a site might create a perceived international incident with our US neighbours. So I located another couple of passes farther east along the northern boundary of the park. On the maps at least, these sites looked reasonable.

Early in 2018 I received permission from Parks Canada for my team to walk into Vuntut National Park from the northeast and backpack 35 kilometres through the Declared Wilderness Area to the edge of the Old Crow Flats. In July, three of us chartered Canadian Helicopters to fly us 250 kilometres westward from Inuvik, NWT, on the Mackenzie River, with hopes of landing in either of the two passes I'd identified. We were taking a chance, because I couldn't find any information at all about whether the terrain was suitable for landing. But I was optimistic.

Looking out the helicopter windows, we saw dark clouds sweeping over the mountains to the north of Vuntut – a storm was coming in from the Arctic Ocean. To avoid the rain our pilot detoured to the south. This deviation gave us our first view of the Old Crow Flats wetlands. The vast, watery land stretched out below us to the southern horizon. Interesting of course, but we were happy to be heading to the higher, drier land to the north.

When we approached our targeted GPS coordinates, we found that thick rain clouds had already enveloped the mountain chain that delineates the northern boundary of Vuntut National Park. As we couldn't land on the passes I'd selected, our pilot tried to set us down in the valley to the south of the pass. Although the plain looked flat, there was sufficient tilt to possibly cause the helicopter to rollover on the ground. On the third landing attempt our pilot found a sufficiently level spot. He carefully manoeuvred the helicopter so that its skids would settle between grassy lumps of sod in the wet field. Excitedly we disembarked, grabbed our backpacks from the cage on one of the skids and crept away from the helicopter. Our pilot didn't waste any time. He wanted to leave before the storm arrived.

So there we stood, my friends John and Blake, and me. We surveyed the shape of the valley and the mountains to the south and consulted our maps and GPS. These mountains and valleys are mostly nameless open spaces on the charts. Oriented, we found the route I'd traced on the map so many months ago. That's when I realized I had actually made it: I was in Vuntut National Park!

We were in the Arctic, well above the treeline, so there was nothing to obscure the view. We could see for kilometres down the lush green plain to both east and west, to where the valley rose gently up the base of the faraway mountains. A rocky, steep-sloped peak barred our view to the south. We had to circumnavigate that mountain.

First, however, we needed to get out of the muskeg we'd landed in. Muskeg is a field of very lumpy soil, hummocks of soft earth with weeds growing on them, surrounded by water. When stepped on, these hummocks either squish straight down to the water level or, if too narrow, bend over into the water – potential ankle twisters either way.

Each of us had about 27 kilos of supplies in our backpacks. We carried everything we needed to survive for seven days in the wilderness, though we were planning on flying out on the fifth day. In the Arctic one has to be prepared for delays due to unpredictable weather. Intense heat, sun, wind, rain, sleet, snow and cold are all possible in the summer. Therefore we brought layers of clothing, two low-domed tents, a kitchen tarp, winter sleeping bags and pads, freeze-dried foods, two stoves, fuel and water purifiers. We also brought several litres of water with us because I'd heard rumours that the area was quite arid – ha! Our first footsteps had already filled with stagnant water.

We helped each other heave our heavy packs onto our backs and then carefully made our way through the muskeg to the base of the mountain. We found that if we went too high up the slope, we'd be negotiating loose, rocky scree. So instead we constantly sought out the "sweet spots" between the wet valley and the unstable, rocky slopes. As there wasn't any one obvious good route, we didn't hike single file. Each of us found our own way. We tried following the caribou trails that braided the mountainside, but the animals didn't seem to mind stepping into swampy water, through dense shrubs and over large rocks. We less nimble humans had to be content with following their paths for a while but then having to veer around a deep crevasse or some other obstacle. It was slow going.

After a couple of hours of picking our way around the mountain we paused for lunch. The dry bread with cheddar cheese, beef jerky and electrolyte-infused water went down well. We sat on some larger rocks, observing the vast land around us. It seemed unreal. There was a lone caribou trotting along far down the valley. We watched it disappear beyond the horizon. The land stretched out invitingly before us, drawing us to follow that caribou. But the beauty was deceiving. We'd already experienced the inhospitable wet valley bottom. Furthermore, those dark clouds were rapidly coming in behind us. We had to find a place to set up camp, and soon.

The rain started to fall lightly as we rounded the mountain into the next sloping valley. Within another hour we came upon a rather small spot that wasn't waterlogged or rocky and was fairly level. This would be our first camp. We gave priority to setting up the three-man winter expedition tent – this thing was designed for the worst Arctic conditions. Good thing too that we put it up first, because the wind had picked up as we worked.

By the time we were ready to set up the second tent, the rain was blowing sideways. The strong wind lashed at us, tearing the smaller two-man tent out of our wet grasps. It was impossible to get the tent poles in place. Soaked, cold and exhausted, we gave up. We stuffed the small tent, along with our backpacks, into the larger vestibule of the expedition tent. This tent had two vestibules, one a square-metre space under the fly at the back of the tent, the other a half-square-metre under the fly at the front.

The wind was so strong that it had driven the rain right through our waterproof clothing. Each of us had become cold and wet, and hypothermia was setting in. Swiftly we piled into the expedition tent, leaving our soaking jackets and waterlogged hiking boots in the vestibule. Unfortunately our sopping wet inner clothes created huge puddles inside the tent. I noted that the guys were shivering. "Unroll your sleeping pad and bag," I directed Blake. "Strip off all wet clothes and get into your sleeping bag, now." Shocked at my forwardness, Blake just stared at me. I added: "I'll face the other way. Just do it." He did. John, teeth chattering, didn't argue. He stripped down and slipped into his bag. Me next. So there we lay, the two men with me in between, in a space slightly wider than a queen-size bed, settling down for a one-hour nap.

Our winter sleeping bags were cozy and warm. We settled. One hour became two as we stared up at the bright yellow roof of the tent, the nylon billowing under the force of the wind. During that "nap," I was planning ahead: we'd have to eat something hot to avoid going into another physical crisis. But where to boil water? We couldn't risk going out into the storm again. Besides, we'd never get the kitchen tarp up and a stove started in that wind. We had no choice: we'd have to boil water in the small vestibule of our tent.

Shifting around inside the tent required a coordinated effort. The endeavour was made all the more complicated because we were each wearing only underwear and our sleeping bags. Like checkers on a board, only one person could move at a time, and somebody had to get out of their way first. I nudged to the front of the tent to open the small vestibule and pin the flap open away from the wind. John moved to the rear to get his stove, fuel and water bottle from his pack in the large vestibule. Blake sat as close to the side of the tent as he could and passed the equipment forward to me. I set up the single-burner gas stove on the only flat spot I could find under the wind protection of the fly. Then I traded places with Blake and again with John, and then John with Blake, so that I was in the back to get the kettle out of my pack and John was up front to light his stove. I passed the kettle forward, Blake filled it along the way and John placed it on the stove.

But the stove, though tested before the trip, wouldn't start. So I dug out my stove and passed it up to John, who passed his dead stove to me in the back. With relief we got the second stove started!

Blake and I traded places again so that Blake could dig three pouches of freeze-dried dinners out of his pack. John is vegetarian, but he wasn't going to go through the trouble of getting to the back of the tent to get one of his dinners from his pack; he'd put up with meat that evening.

These dinners are designed to be eaten right out of their bags: just add boiling water, stir and wait a few minutes for the precooked food to reconstitute. But we found that the kettle only held enough water for two dinners – we had to go through the whole checkers routine again to prepare the third dinner. Finally the meals were ready, and they tasted oh so good. There were no leftovers that night.

We folded up the empty food pouches into a special "smell-proof" plastic bag and then into one of our bear-proof Kevlar bags in the large vestibule. Yes, we had cooked, eaten and then stored food inside the tent. This was a big "no-no" in the wilderness because the food smells could attract animals. However, we'd have put ourselves in greater danger, of hypothermia, if we'd attempted to get the food outside, away from the tent. The wind was still howling and the rain pelting down when we finally called it a night.

By morning the rain had subsided to a slight drizzle. I waited as long as I could, but eventually I had to go out to pee. The guys would have to move aside so I could get out the door. However, first I had to dress, and my clothing, stuffed into the tent's inside pockets, was still soaking wet. There was nothing I could do about it. I sighed, "Damn, that means I have to put my pants back on." John and Blake burst out laughing – anywhere else such a statement would have had a totally different connotation. That sentence became the running joke each time we had to give each other privacy throughout the trip.

When I got back into the tent I stripped off again and crawled into my warm, dry sleeping bag. Together we went through the crazy checkerboard procedure again, to make coffee and instant oatmeal for breakfast, inside the little tent. The rain ceased while we were cleaning up, and slowly the clouds dispersed. We had bright sunny skies for the rest of our days (and nights) in Vuntut.

We went out to explore our immediate neighbourhood. The creek in the valley bottom had flooded. We couldn't approach it without hip waders, which of course we didn't have. Our intended backpacking route had thereby become cut off. Hence a change in plans: we'd set up a base camp on our little dry spot and explore Vuntut via day hikes. In the gentle breeze we easily put up the second tent. That tent became John's home.

Per standard camping protocol, we removed our four food bags from our tents. Normally we'd suspend our food containers in trees, well out of the reach of bears, but there are no tall trees in the Arctic. I'd planned ahead for this challenge, and devised a method that hopefully would secure our belongings: I had brought along some of the newly developed soft-sided bear-proof bags – the kind that teeth and claws are not supposed to be able to get into. We tied these to low shrubs because bears aren't particularly known to move their food to other locations before eating it. Wolves, however, do take their prey elsewhere to eat, thus the second part of my new system: we tied the food bags together in pairs, the idea being that if a wolf tried to drag a pair of bags away, they might get caught up in shrubs and rocks. Part three was the addition of a bear bell, an "early warning system," to each set of two bags. Should any predators go after our supplies, we'd have to use air horns to try to scare them off. Brave or foolish, it was the best we could do.

A couple of caribou wandering by distracted us as we secured our camp. They pranced about, as though annoyed that our tents should be in their way – not that the valley wasn't wide enough for them to pass safely. Or perhaps they were simply attracted by our presence and approached to find out whether or not we were a threat. The caribou came to within about 50 metres of us. Containing our excitement, we stood stoically in place, taking photographs until they trotted up the valley and out of sight.

Up the hillside from our camp we found a series of ground squirrel burrows. One of these cute rodents peeked out at us, sat up, and sent out its "tsik tsik" warning signal. Further frustrating the critter, we knelt down to photograph it. Bewildered, the tsik-tsik, as they're known in the North, kept popping in and out of its hole. After getting our photographs we left the creature in peace.

We wandered through clusters of lush wildflowers, mostly purples and yellows, and through wet patches of cotton grass, the white puffy seed heads bobbing in the breeze. We carefully made our way through more muskeg at the northern edge of our valley, and over several shrub-lined rivulets. The verdant green valley was vast, we noted: about a kilometre wide and several kilometres long. The mountains rose 250 metres up either side, with exposed rocky cliffs right up to their rugged peaks.

We were happily hiking back to camp when I came to a sudden stop. There was an odd, large beige mass that I hadn't noticed before, about 200 metres beyond the other side of our tents. Suddenly the lump moved. I recognized immediately that it was a blond grizzly bear, and it was heading towards our camp. The bear had noticed us, too. It paused and stood up to sniff the breeze coming from our direction. We, and the bear, went into high alert. Fortunately, this was a "good grizzly": it turned around and ran away. We slowly, cautiously, moved forward to indicate that this was our territory, for now. Every so often the grizzly looked back over its shoulder to confirm that we were still approaching the camp. It continued its retreat. We watched that bear until it disappeared around a mountain two kilometres away. When we arrived at camp we were relieved to find everything still intact. Our bravery, or foolishness, hadn't been tested.

One of our hikes took us towards Mount Clement – the only named mountain on the map. We gingerly stepped through some watery muskeg that enveloped a creek. The creek itself was no more than a metre across, so it was easy to hop over. Then we cautiously climbed up the gentle but rocky edge of the mountain until we reached a large plateau. There we found nesting birds, bees and butterflies amongst a multitude of colourful wildflowers – a remote, pristine alpine meadow. Enthralled by the beauty around us, we ambled towards the other side of the plateau.

We came to an abrupt halt and gasped as we found ourselves at the edge of a very deep cliff. The view was breathtaking: we were looking down into another vast valley. There were large hills down below, and far behind them we could discern Timber Creek with patches of snow in its shaded, undercut banks. Beyond the creek, in the distant haze, the jagged British Mountains reached into Alaska some 65 kilometres away. The expanse of raw, untamed land was overwhelming. It was like we were looking back in time at the Earth before people overran it. We stood there on the brink of the world in complete awe, stunned into silence.

Gradually we came to terms with the enormity of the vista before us. Inadvertently, yet inevitably, we started to impose our humanity on the place: we attempted to capture the scene in photographs. In a bid to provide some sense of scale, we photographed each other in front of this huge landscape. It was as though we were trying to tame the land. Nothing we did, however, could really portray the magnitude of the place. Eventually we gave up, relaxed and ate lunch. Thereafter we lost the desire, or need, to climb the rest of the way to the top of Mount Clement. What more could we possibly have gained from summiting?

We were sated. Vuntut had imposed itself and had overwhelmed us. We had not tamed it at all.

Solemnly we returned to our camp and called Canadian Helicopters, by satellite phone, to arrange for them to meet us the following afternoon. They agreed to pick us up in the pass that was supposed to have been our drop-off point.

The morning of our fifth day in the park, after we'd finished breakfast but before striking camp, we had some new visitors. We had caught the attention of three grey wolves that were passing through the valley. They came to within 10 metres of our camp. Two of them were quickly bored with us and went off to try digging up our tsik-tsik neighbours. The third wolf circled us, sniffing and judging but never threatening.

This predator didn't even display any awareness of or interest in our food bags. We of course busied ourselves with our cameras, though we also had our bear spray and air horns ready just in case.

The two wolves that had gone for our neighbours eventually abandoned their quest and trotted up the valley. The third one, noticing that its companions had left, turned away from us and ran to catch up with the others. All three wolves crested a hill, took a final look back at us, and then loped out of sight. We were ecstatic. What an awesome last encounter in the park!

However, we did have to turn our attention to our work. The tents had to be taken down and our gear repacked, followed by six kilometres to be hiked. We had, after all, a 3 p.m. appointment with a helicopter, and those pilots don't like to be kept waiting. We worked efficiently and hiked a higher route around the mountain, putting up with more loose rock but avoiding most of the muskeg. The route required many detours around deep crevasses, but overall it was quicker than the line we'd taken on our first day in the park. Our experience and familiarity with the terrain were paying off.

We arrived at the original drop-off point with a few hours to spare. All we had to do was cross a kilometre of wet valley floor and climb up to the saddle between the two mountains to the north. But again our plan had to be modified, this time because up there on the right side of the mountain were hundreds of dark-brown specks. We peered through binoculars and the longest camera lenses we had, and were stunned by what we saw.

The Porcupine caribou herd had arrived at the park boundary on its way back south from the calving grounds around the Porcupine River at the Beaufort Sea! At approximately 200,000 animals, this is one of the largest migrations in North America. And at 2400 kilometres round trip each year, it is also the longest mammalian voyage on the planet. And we were there to witness this phenomenon!

Adults and calves, too many to count, dotted the top and sides of the mountain. They weren't advancing. They were grazing. They were staying on the high ground to minimize the mosquito menace. Eventually, as the weather becomes colder, killing off the bugs, the caribou come down into the valleys. But not that day – it was too hot. We in the valley wore T-shirts and protective netting to keep the bloodthirsty mosquitos at bay.

The three of us climbed up the south side of the mountain, just to where the scree starts. We found dry rocks to sit on to wait for the helicopter and watch the caribou. Finally, at about 3:30 we heard the beating of rotors. Grabbing our packs we hurried down to the sort of flat, wet valley floor where we hoped the pilot could land. The chopper arrived, but it hovered over the saddle where we were supposed to be. We jumped up and down madly waving our arms in the air, trying to get the pilot's attention. He ought to be able to see us colourful specks so out of place on the treeless valley floor, we reasoned. Finally, the helicopter came over to us, touching down so close that we had to drop to our knees and sit down in the muskeg. Yup, the pilot had seen us right away, but he too had wanted to view the caribou on the mountain.

We loaded our packs into the cage mounted on one of the helicopter's runners, then climbed aboard. Donning our headsets – everyone has to wear ear protection in these noisy machines – we were surprised to hear music: CCR. Okay, we were switching back into civilization mode, and it was good, fun music.

But before heading back to Inuvik, we hovered over the caribou, watching and photographing them as they grazed unperturbed by our presence. From the air we saw that the herd extended down the north side of that mountain as well. As we flew eastward we passed over another mountaintop with hundreds more caribou on it. There were so many animals wild and free. I contemplated that this was how North America might once have been before human beings arrived, and perhaps how this land should continue to be: with no people.

We interrupted our flight to hover over a plateau with 12 muskox on it. There were two large bulls circling each other and butting heads. Farther east we paused again to observe a female grizzly with two cubs foraging in the brush. We felt so privileged and lucky to be able to witness these natural wonders that we wanted to laugh and cry at the same time. We were overcome with emotion.

Our helicopter flew us over marvellous crested mountains, hoodoos, and lush green (we now knew this meant "wet") valleys as we exited the park. There are no markers separating the park from land that's not protected, and there are no physical differences. This place is so remote that there simply is no human development. And even if there had been, from up above, where we were flying, it would have looked like just a pinprick on the vast landscape.

Back in Inuvik Blake went for dinner with some family friends of his. John and I ate in our shared hotel suite. Although the sun was still bright in the sky, it was getting late and I was ready for bed. Blake gave us a phone call, asking us to meet him in the bar. So for the last time on this trip I uttered the words "damn, now I have to put my pants back on!" and got dressed to go out drinking with the guys.

PINGO LANDMARK

TUK AND THE ARCTIC OCEAN

With limited vacation time, Blake flew home directly after our unique visit to Vuntut National Park. John and I had more time available to us, and there were three more Arctic attractions we wanted to see. So after bidding farewell to Blake, John and I rented a large SUV in Inuvik and drove north, to the end of the road – to the Arctic Ocean.

The new Highway 10 to Tuktoyaktuk had just been opened the previous year and we were eager to try it out. Prior to 2017 the only way to drive to "Tuk" was via an ice road, open only in the winter. The new 138-kilometre all-weather road has permanently replaced the ice road. Highway 10 is the only road in North America that leads to the Arctic Ocean.

We allowed 2½ hours for the drive, and intended to camp overnight in Tuk. The highway, we discovered, is a two-lane dirt road running atop a couple of metres of gravel. There are no shoulders to pull off onto – the edges of the road simply drop steeply down to the tundra. Occasionally there is a third lane to allow for trucks to pass. There were few other vehicles on the road the day we drove it.

The tundra stretched out flat on both sides of the highway, and was swathed with low shrubs, grasses and colourful wildflowers all the way to the horizon. There were innumerable ponds and creeks: part of the Mackenzie River delta, I assumed. A few clusters of scraggly pine trees dotted the landscape outside of Inuvik. The farther north we drove, the fewer trees we saw, and eventually there were none at all.

The road is far from straight, however, and although the land appeared to be flat, it actually undulated. The road seemed to slip down into shallow valleys where it meandered in such odd ways that it showed up again in unexpected places on the highlands. Looking north into the distance, we saw only a series of disconnected, unaligned segments of the road. Occasionally there'd be a dust cloud following a dot on a far-away piece of the road, and we'd know that in about five minutes or so we'd be passing another vehicle.

John and I could see the two giant pingos, the second attraction of our journey, about half an hour before we arrived at the small turn-off to a dirt parking lot. These two solitary hills near Tuktoyaktuk are part of the Pingo Canadian Landmark. Pingo is Canada's first and only "Landmark" because just after its designation, Parks Canada decided to discontinue the Landmarks program.

Arriving at the Landmark, we stepped out of the car to take some photographs and were immediately swarmed by mosquitos. The cloud of bloodsuckers went crazy for us, driving us to total distraction. Frantically we dug through the trunk of our car to find our bug jackets, inadvertently letting hundreds of the pests into the car – we'd regret that for the rest of our road trip.

At about 53 metres high, the two largest of the eight pingos in this Landmark are some of the biggest of their kind in North America. Basically, pingos are round-topped, cone-shaped hills on the Arctic tundra. Despite being the only hills on this vast landscape, these grass-covered mounds look rather unspectacular. It's how they were created that really makes them special. Water from nearby rivers or ancient lakes seeps underground, beneath the frozen tundra, and forces the permafrost to lift, perhaps two centimetres a year, eventually forming these hills. Exposure to wind, rain, freezing and thawing causes the rounded pinnacles to cave in, crack and erode, giving them the appearance of giant ruined Bundt cakes.

Just a few kilometres farther up the road, Tuktoyaktuk, a hamlet of fewer than 1,000 people, was the third attraction of our road trip. Right in the middle of town is another, smaller pingo. John and I walked up a rough, muddy footpath that zigzagged amid long grass and brilliant wildflowers to the top of the pingo. From there we could see all of the hamlet and the end of the highway at the Arctic Ocean.

Highway 10 becomes the main street through Tuk, weaving its way around subdivisions, between ponds, waterways and of course the pingos, to where the Mackenzie River delta meets the Beaufort Sea. There's a gravel parking area on a small headland protruding into the Beaufort, on the Arctic Ocean, and that's where the camping area is.

John and I drove over to the campground, hoping to find a place to set up our tent. Several camper trailers were already parked beside the picnic tables. With our personal clouds of mosquitos following us, John and I walked around the camp. We weren't thrilled about setting up our tiny nylon tent on the jagged gravel, exposed on the little peninsula to potentially harsh polar winds. We agreed that a warm, mosquito-free hotel in Inuvik was preferable – or perhaps after our time in Vuntut National Park, we were just tired of roughing it. A leisurely drive back to Inuvik, in the very long hours of daylight, was appealing.

The long summer day was sunny, warmish and windless, so John and I clambered down the rocky ledge to the water and stuck our toes in, just so we could say we'd touched the Arctic Ocean. And yes, the water was cold, icy cold, as one would expect of an ocean named Arctic. Oddly, I had no interest in going for a swim. My mosquitos made me want to remain fully dressed.

John and I considered renting a canoe and paddling through the maze of small islands to the two giant pingos. We were told that the trip, one way, might take us an hour. What, I worried, would happen if the weather suddenly changed and we became stranded alone in that Arctic delta? We asked people at the campsite if they might like to join us, so that we'd at least have some security in numbers. Unfortunately we had no takers, so we reluctantly gave up on the idea. Both of us were experienced enough to know that Arctic weather is nothing to be tri-fled with.

Instead we joined the other tourists wandering the town. We walked around the schooner *Our Lady of Lourdes*, the ship that once provided supplies to the isolated Arctic communities, now displayed on blocks in Tuk. We stopped to visit the re-creations of some traditional sod houses set low into the permafrost. Our slight disappointment at not being able to enter the building that day was completely offset by our delight at the reason: a group of elders were holding a meeting inside. The sod house was not just a tourist attraction, but was actually being used in a traditional manner.

We walked over to a canvas tent-kiosk where a very industrious young man had set up a barbecue and was selling muskox burgers and stew. My extra broad bugnet hat came in very handy because there was enough room inside it for me to hold and eat my lunch – I didn't have to expose my face and hands to my cloud of mosquitos.

John and I made one last stop before driving our mosquito-infested suv back south to Inuvik. We had to take photos of the sign marking the north end of the Trans Canada Trail, the 24,000-kilometre Great Trail. Now that would be a long hike! Perhaps someday …?

3
Ivvavik

THE BEAUFORT SEA
WHITEWATER AND WOLVERINE

I'd always wanted to follow in the footsteps of some of the great explorers of North America. In 2004 I found an opportunity to do so with Canadian River Expeditions. CRE guides rafting trips on the Firth River through Ivvavik National Park, paddling 130 kilometres to the Beaufort Sea. Ivvavik is located at the very north end of the Yukon Territory, adjacent to Alaska and the Arctic Ocean. This is the land that Alexander Mackenzie explored in the late 1700s, and it was Sir John Franklin's target when he tried to sail though the Northwest Passage in 1845.

My adventure started at Pearson airport in Toronto, and it had repercussions that affected the entire trip. I tried out the proffered luggage shrink-wrapping service. The service made sense, as it would secure my oddly shaped backpack with its straps, tent, new down sleeping bag, self-inflating mattress and a brand-new camera tripod bulging out in all directions. Unfortunately, the resulting tightly wrapped bundle was just too small – it made the 2700-kilometre flight to Edmonton fine, but there it was overlooked by airport personnel. So it wasn't transferred with me on the 2000-kilometre flight north to Inuvik via Yellowknife and Norman Wells. I arrived in Inuvik, NWT, with only my day pack. This calamity confirmed why I always pack my well broken-in hiking boots and essential toiletries in my carry-on. The airlines promised me that my pack would be delivered to me the next day.

Someone later commented to me that, had it been their luggage lost, they would have been extremely angry and complained loudly upon arrival at Inuvik. They were surprised I didn't make a big fuss. But I knew that shouting couldn't help the situation and would only stress everyone out, myself included. So, not being able to do anything further about my missing pack, I resigned myself to the situation. I reminded myself to be thankful I had allowed for an extra day in Inuvik – for just such an emergency.

We were 12 adventurers on this trip. When I learned that the other 11 people all belonged to the same family or were close friends thereof, I was worried that I'd feel left out. I didn't know their history, stories and inside jokes. However, the challenges we were to face together on this trip quickly made me part of the group. We became a team on the very first day. Our guides were the three J's (James, Johnny and Joel) and Andy, our Inuit interpreter from Inuvik. Andy's dog, Blue, was our four-legged mascot.

In the lobby of our hotel in Inuvik, James informed us that the Twin Otter that was to fly us to the Firth River the following day was being commandeered by the military to exchange personnel on an icebreaker. As a result, we'd be flown to the Firth immediately after dinner this day. My spare-day contingency plan had been quashed, and I was left with exactly two hours to scavenge, beg and borrow everything I would need to survive 12 days in the Arctic wilderness. My adventure thus started much earlier than I'd anticipated.

Two ladies of our group rushed with me to the Northern Store, the one clothing shop in town. There we discovered that only cotton summer clothing was available in the women's department. The anxiety I'd managed to suppress to that point started to surface. I hurried through random aisles trying to find anything that might be of use to me. I found long johns and windproof pants – size small – in the men's department. A boy's size large long-sleeved shirt sort of fit me. I also became the proud owner of a pair of meatpacker's gloves, the only warm, waterproof gloves we could find. I purchased underwear, shirts, photographic film, water bottle, toiletries and bug-dope, all courtesy of the airline, which eventually reimbursed me.

I borrowed a spare tent, sleeping pad and rain gear from Canadian River Expeditions. Eventually I would also borrow at least one item from each person on our trip: warm hat, fleece jacket, eye-shades, shorts, sunscreen and even a magazine to read. Stuffing all my acquisitions into a couple of large garbage bags, I became the bag lady of the Arctic.

This mad rush to replace my carefully selected equipment with makeshift gear was done in unusual summer heat. Inuvik was experiencing a record-high heat wave, with temperatures around 28°C – hotter than what I'd left in Toronto. I was exhausted, dehydrated and totally stressed out by the time we boarded our Twin Otter.

The little plane took us 275 kilometres west to just outside the Alaskan border. En route we had wonderful views of the crazy labyrinth of the Mackenzie delta that glowed like rivers of gold under the bright sun. We watched the shadow of our plane float over the low, barren hills, and observed the storm clouds in the mountains ahead of us. Our expert pilots flew us around the rain and over iced-up Margaret Lake, and made a smooth landing on the pebbly bank of the Firth. Johnny and Joel were already on the river, having arrived earlier to get our three large, black rubber rafts inflated and stocked with communal gear and food. We added our personal packs and my garbage bags.

The plane took off, and we were left alone. Completely alone. When we could no longer hear the drone of the engines, I was overcome by a feeling of smallness, of insignificance, of solitude in the unending vastness of our planet. Our tiny group was like an isolated prehistoric tribe migrating over an unknown land. I was part of this small band of people standing alongside a wide river in a very broad, treeless valley. High mountains buffered the edges of the wide valley. With no distance or size references around us, I wondered: Where do "I" end, and where does "everything else" start?

Twenty-four hours of daylight further confused our senses. We ate breakfast just before noon or whenever we got up; dinners were eaten near midnight. Hikes to explore our surroundings were sometimes done after dinner, when the day was a bit cooler. Eyeshades were helpful to cut the light in the bright-yellow tents so we could sleep more soundly. The stress of getting ready for the flight, and all these new and unaccustomed sensations, had triggered a migraine in me.

For the first few days on the river I blindly concentrated on my paddling, distracting my mind from the throbbing pain in my head. When on land I tried to rest in my tent, out of the bright sun. The nurses in our group spent three days figuring out how to cure me. As much water as I drank to rehydrate, I immediately purged, along with anything else I tried to ingest. The ladies devised all kinds of remedies to try out on me. They finally found the solution: cola, not my favourite beverage. My body accepted the concoction of chemicals which included electrolytes and sugars. I was finally rehydrated and the pain disappeared – the migraine cycle had stopped! I went into an emotional frenzy of gratitude to the nurses who'd cured me, and for finally having gained the ability to appreciate the trip. Cola became my drink of choice.

Yes, there were cans of pop stashed in the cool bottoms of the rafts. With my head intact, I discovered that there was an allotment of one beer per person per day, and there were bottles of wine for every dinner down there too! We were also carrying folding camp seats and a large dining tent with insect screens. There was even a privy tent. We were definitely not roughing it on this trip! This wasn't at all what I'd expected on such a remote wilderness adventure. Not only that, these indulgences were so incongruous with the garbage bags I was living out of – but then, everything about this trip was strange. I wasn't going to complain, though. I decided that from then on, I was going to enjoy everything that came my way.

From past wilderness trips, I was quite accustomed to switching to a diet of freeze-dried staples by about day three. On this trip, CRE provided meat dishes and fresh vegetables every single day. Even on our last day, we celebrated with steaks, baked potatoes, mini carrots, coleslaw and a large bottle of sparkling wine! The food had been stored and well preserved in the bottom of the rafts, under our personal and camping gear. The thin rubber hull did not provide much insulation against the ice-cold water we were floating on, and the result was a natural refrigerator effect. I'd never have guessed that we'd enjoy such luxuries on a wilderness trip.

The wide river valley where we landed that first day was like a rocky pasture with clumps of green grasses and splashes of purple, yellow and white wildflowers. A few clusters of stunted trees dotted the hills. We walked up to the craggy rocks at the top of one hill to obtain a panoramic view of the world around us. I had straggled behind, but was happy I'd made the effort. Shading my eyes with my hands, I looked around. The view was awesome! The river snaked below us, through the tundra, to Franklin's sought-after Beaufort Sea, somewhere out there beyond the hazy horizon.

The next day, we paddled our flotilla of rafts downstream. Or rather, we floated. The swift current carried us along. We only paddled in the rapids in order to help control our descent. The three J's steered. The rafts turned sideways and even backwards, bouncing off the walls and rocks like bumper cars through the low canyons. In some places where the river was too broad and shallow, the bottoms of the rafts would scrape on the riverbed. In other places we would glide silently over deep dark holes. We passed easily over Class II rapids, our rafts smothering wave trains that would have provided exhilarating rides for canoeists. We scouted for the most favourable routes through Class III and IV, intermediate and advanced rapids. Their fanciful names: Sheep Slot, Sheep Horn, The Ram, and Wrap-Around Rock, were as entertaining as the rides were exciting.

The Firth winds its way through steep canyon walls carved out of lifted and twisted sedimentary rocks with beautiful layers of purple, yellow, blue and grey. The strata were still horizontal in a few places, but mostly the millennia of geologic forces had pushed them diagonally, vertically, and sometimes into ridiculous curves falling back on themselves. The intriguing geography would sometimes distract us from watching out for the sharp rocks in the river.

The first raft went over a pointy boulder and of course was torn open. As the air fizzled out of the bottom chamber of that raft, the second one followed suit, getting punctured by the very same rock. Fortunately these boats were made with several independent air chambers, so that if one deflated, the craft wouldn't sink. However, damaged boats become very unstable and awkward to steer. Deftly we managed to beach the shrinking boats without too much water flooding in. The third raft managed to stay safely clear of that hazardous rock.

While Johnny and Joel glued patches over the cuts in the bladders of the rafts, our dog, Blue, raced around rocks and trees, sniffing out whatever excited him, fascinations that were beyond our ability to detect. Most of us just lazed in the sun, swatting at mosquitos. Blue seemed disappointed in our lack of enthusiasm.

Some of the guys took advantage of the long delay while the glue was drying the boat patches into place: they went fishing. They caught way more grayling than we were allowed to take, so most of the salmon-like fish had to be released. The ones we kept became a delicious dinner and leftovers went into lunch sandwiches the next day.

There were no specific campsites along the river, no signs, no anything civilized. We camped wherever there happened to be an appealing flat area, whenever we were ready to stop paddling. We set up camp at some traditional sites such as Joe Creek, Wolf Tors and Red Hill, where circles of rocks have been available for centuries to hold down tents. In the sandy soil, tent pegs alone were no match for the strong winds. Wherever we camped, we were also careful to keep the tents zipped shut, to keep the cute but nosy ground squirrels out. They were everywhere despite Blue's efforts to keep them out of his (their) territory.

Upon returning from one hike, we found a wolverine snooping around our campsite. Wolverines are much smaller than bears, but are notoriously more vicious and extremely strong. Apprehensively, we kept at what we hoped was a safe distance, but we couldn't keep Blue from tearing after the beast. Perhaps because there were so many of us, the wolverine decided not to fight. It hastily vacated our campsite, but not before giving Blue a terrible fright. The poor dog came scuttling back to us, its hairs bristling.

One morning, just as we were getting up, two F18 fighter jets from Inuvik raced through the sky above us, with an ear-splitting boom. They circled around and passed over us a second time. The military is not supposed to train over the national park, because the noise would disturb the wildlife, especially the calving caribou. Out of frustration at the second pass, one of our guides (I won't say which) gave them the finger. One of the pilots must have seen this, because he came back a third time, flying low through the river valley. Directly above us, he turned vertical, shot straight up, and disappeared into space – his way of giving us the finger in return. We felt the heat and smell of his exhaust, he'd been so low. Not nice. Since the jets didn't return after that incident, I guessed that the pilot was satisfied that we weren't criminals escaping to the Beaufort Sea.

There are no paths in the park, but during our hikes we often followed caribou trails so that we could avoid treading on the vegetation that stubbornly clung to life in this harsh climate. Life up there was condensed and accelerated in the 24-hour sunshine of the short summer season. At one o'clock one morning, we hiked up to the craggy top of a low mountain. From that vantage point we could see the sun peeking out over the horizon line beyond the North Pole – the sun was in the south on the other side of the Pole. With the sun low in the sky all night, the photographers' "golden hour" was greatly extended, softening the fields of yellows, purples, blues and whites. The land was covered in wildflowers. There was even a bumblebee buzzing through the blossoms! White fluffy mountain goats specked the nearby cliffs. Golden eagles soared above. We were in an Arctic Garden of Eden, God's rock garden.

We went on some long hikes. However, as I'm a relatively poor climber, becoming exhausted very quickly, I was always the last one to arrive at the top of the 700-metre-high mountains. Once on the plateau, I could outpace most others, hopping from rock to rock. We followed along from one rugged ridge to another and another, always keeping the river in sight. We were aware that by wandering too far away from this landmark we could easily get lost. Other than the river, there was nothing around to suggest where our camp was.

On the top of one plateau we found an ancient caribou fence: many piles of rocks set in rows along the steep mountain embankment. Andy explained that Inuvialuit women and children would set up fires between the piles, funnelling the caribou towards the waiting hunters. Several years ago, researchers had painted the rocks white so that the shape of the "fences" could be seen from the sky. To the chagrin of subsequent hunters, permanent paint had been used, so the markings, like graffiti, still remain to this day.

As we paddled, we saw several caribou on the riverbanks. These animals belonged to the Porcupine herd, which does not always migrate in unison. They break up into sub-groups, often following one dominant female, in a single file. There are groups that break off and rejoin each other, and there are the odd individuals who wander about on their own. The caribou generally follow ancient routes that seem to meander over the landscape. Cliffs, fast and icy rivers, wolves and bears might force detours along their routes, but they are always drawn forward again, as if by compass. They go to their summer calving grounds at the north of Ivvavik National Park. "Ivvavik" is Inuvialuktun for "place for giving birth." Some of the animals don't make it: we saw a dead calf that had been born before the cow reached her destination. We saw another abandoned young caribou wandering along the riverside – it hadn't been able to get up the steep bank with the rest of the herd.

Downstream, the canyon walls were lower, eventually petering out so that the land we passed through was flat and hummocky. There were no more trees; that is to say, nothing higher than the knee-high Arctic willows. The grasses and wildflowers grew denser here than in the highlands we'd come from. In the light breeze, vast pastures of wild blue lupine swayed like waves on the ocean.

I woke up one day to the smell of smoke. Fire! Quickly I stumbled out of the staleness of my tent and looked around. The air was thick with smoke but I saw no flames or reddened skies. The J's were already up and on their satellite phones, asking the park wardens in Inuvik what was going on. We were informed there were major forest fires threatening Dawson City, 600 kilometres to our south. Officials were considering evacuating the town of 2,000 people. The strong, warm south winds were blowing the smoke towards us. For now, we were safely outside the danger zone, so we continued our northbound trip down the river and prayed for everyone's safety.

We stopped to investigate an abandoned, broken-down komatik, an Inuvialuit sled, on the riverbank. That was one of the few signs of civilization we'd come across. It reminded us that while we were alone passing through this seemingly forlorn place, others had travelled here before us. This land is well known to mankind, yet the wilderness has not been destroyed.

Near the mouth of the river, the big whitewater gave way to swift-moving currents. The river had become braided with channels, and there was no way of knowing which routes were deep enough for us to pass through. Everyone donned hip waders so that we could quickly jump out, shove the rafts over the shallow spots and then hop back in again. We did a lot of pushing and pulling. We worked hard to keep ourselves moving forward, northward.

Off in the distance – I had no way of knowing how far – was a lone hill: "New Mountain." Someone suggested we hike across the extensive plain to climb that hill. We did, and from that slight elevation we were able to see our destination: the Arctic Ocean. The Beaufort Sea was within our reach! My dream of following the route of those first explorers was coming true.

From the top of New Mountain we also saw our first muskox. We silently watched these thick, shaggy Arctic goats amble by. I was amused by their stubby white legs, which I thought resembled socks sticking out from under their dark brown, woolly coats. They took no notice of us. When we descended the hill, we stopped to inspect their giant hoof prints – comparable to a men's size 12 boot. On our way back to our rafts we also found wolf prints, caribou antlers and a fox den (no one was home).

The temperature had become noticeably colder in those last few days. We no longer felt the warm southern, smoky wind. We paddled wearing our fleeces and jackets, and I was grateful for those meatpacker's gloves! There were patches of snow and ice clinging to the shady side of the river. A short distance farther downstream we found ourselves carefully navigating past huge slabs of ice that threatened to block our way through the river delta. We were thankful we didn't encounter any obstacles that needed portaging around or, worse, retreating upstream against the current in order to find another way to the sea.

The next day, we were camped on Nunaluk, a long sandspit on the Beaufort. The fabled sea was free of ice and perfectly calm when we arrived. Jaegers, terns and other seabirds circled above us.

57

It seemed as if we had landed on a Caribbean beach. Only the palm trees were missing.

We walked in ones and twos, exploring the strand, scrutinizing oddly stacked collections of driftwood, poking at seashells and collecting colourful pebbles. While we were exploring, a north wind had picked up, pushing slushy ice into the bay, reminding us that we were actually in the Arctic. This new wind was cold and clear, refreshing. We trusted that it would make its way south and benefit the people of Dawson City.

After a couple of hours of beachcombing along the length of the spit, I went back to the wind shelter of my tent. Out through the mesh door, I watched a lone caribou prance all over our campsite, seemingly happy to have some company. The midnight sun was shining down on us, and I contemplated this marvellous world I had the privilege to visit.

CRE had one last surprise for us: our Twin Otter "hopped" us to Herschel Island, just about a kilometre away. We had a few hours to explore this territorial park while the plane shuttled our rafts and gear back to Inuvik.

A hundred years ago, Herschel was used as a whaling station. Today, an old, weathered store, warehouse, church and cemetery are all that remain. A small museum inside one of the buildings tells of the harsh existence of those Arctic whalers.

An eider duck eyed us suspiciously from its nest beneath the doorway of a trapper's cabin. Another caribou, relatively tame, walked up to us and posed for pictures. We also took photographs of our returned plane, parked next to a billboard which read, "This Beach is Not a Designated Airstrip." The driftwood and rocks that littered the island had been removed from a stretch of land to create a "runway" on which planes landed despite the warning sign.

On our flight back to Inuvik, we pressed our noses to the windows, gazing at the pods of pure-white belugas, not at all camouflaged against the dark sea. I supposed they wouldn't be visible in the midst of an ice floe. Wondering what else was down there, hidden in the vast water and land we were flying over, I knew I'd have to go back to explore the Arctic some more.

Too soon we were back in Inuvik and had to adjust to social norms. Our first priority was a hot shower – our first in over a week. I had sponge-bathed out of a dish pan a few times while in the park, but nothing beats a hot shower and well-shampooed hair! As my backpack with clean clothes had still not arrived from Edmonton, I donned the cleanest clothes I had: the ones I'd worn on my flight from Toronto.

Once civilized again, our little group went out for a celebratory dinner. In a hotel restaurant, we sat properly in high-backed chairs at linen-covered tables. Having become accustomed to sitting on a folding camp chair and eating from a plate on my lap, I could only hope my table manners were still intact.

While we waited for our dinner orders, I provided a bit of entertainment: I had discreetly brought along one of my garbage bags containing the items I had borrowed from my fellow adventurers. With exaggerated ceremony, I pulled the items out one by one. As I returned each item to its owner, I gave thanks. Someone feigned surprise that I hadn't borrowed any briefs – I replied by way of pulling out the pair of shorts I'd borrowed from one of our guides. Yup, I'd borrowed it all. I'd been very resourceful in obtaining all I needed to not only survive but also enjoy our wilderness adventure. I also incidentally proved that modern equipment is still not needed for outdoor adventures (though it sure does make life easier).

My backpack arrived at our hotel the following day, in the car that came to return us to the airport for our flight home. As I didn't need the pack anymore, all I could do with it was check it back in with the airline and hope it arrived home with me. This time, it did.

4
Kluane Reserve

THE ST. ELIAS MOUNTAINS
ZOOMING AROUND MOUNT LOGAN

In August 2002 Martin and I flew to the Yukon to explore the region. We had a few objectives, including getting to know Kluane National Park, backpacking through the Chilkoot Trail National Historic Site and learning about the Yukon gold rush.

With a station wagon we'd rented in Whitehorse, the territorial capital, we drove 150 kilometres westward along the Alaska Highway to Kluane National Park and Reserve. Marking the westernmost point of Canada, the park is the home of the Kluane First Nations people, the name being derived from the Indigenous words for big, or whitefish, lake country. The park has also been designated by the UN as a World Heritage Site.

Our first stop was at the visitor centre in the village of Haines Junction, to check in to the park. As the place was jam-packed with tourists travelling on luxury trips between Alaska and Whitehorse, we didn't stay very long. We wanted to be outside, on the land. So we drove on to the park campground to set up our base for the next few days.

The site was packed full with recreational vehicles and trailers, but we had a tent and there was lots of room for those. In fact, our little three-man dome tent was the only one in the forested camp that day. If we ignored our car parked next to the tent, we might have imagined we were wilderness camping. Late that night, though, and every night thereafter, other tents appeared. People arrived on motorcycles, on bicycles, in trucks, and on foot, but all would disappear again each morning. Everyone, it seemed, was just passing through.

On our way to the campsite that first day, we had shopped for camp-stove fuel in the village general store and discovered they had bison steaks. Forget the freeze-dried stews I'd brought along from home; we were having steaks for dinner! I barbecued the lean bison meat and baked the potatoes on a wood fire in the pit by our tent that evening. These, accompanied by a fresh Caesar salad and some wine from the liquor store, made for a very fine camp meal.

To get an initial feel of the park, Martin and I walked the easy 5.5-kilometre Dezadeash River Trail. The sky was blue, the evening warm. The sun glistened off the ice-capped mountains on the other side of the river. A cooling wind rustled in the aspens along the riverbanks. There were no other sounds. Despite the beautiful day, none of the people we'd seen in town or in the RV park were on the trail. We had the place to ourselves. We almost felt lonely in that immense valley.

The following day Martin and I set out for some real exercise. We drove to Kathleen Lake to climb up to King's Throne: five kilometres, gaining 550 metres altitude, to a cirque at 1280 metres above sea level. We were told to allow five hours for the round-trip hike. I noted the time when we set out and began waymarking our route with my GPS. In our heavy hiking boots, with hiking poles and carrying daypacks full of emergency gear, we started our adventure. We followed a short, marked trail through a flat aspen forest. As the trail started to ascend we found ourselves walking on a spongy path of needles in an evergreen forest. The footpath ended at the base of a steep scree slope. From that point on, the line on our map did not translate into a line on the ground. There was nothing but a steep expanse of loose rocks above us. Up is where the map directed us, so up we climbed.

We clambered up that rocky field, trying to select the least menacing-looking route. To minimize the height of our upward steps, we each walked in a zigzag fashion, creating our own personal switchbacks. When the blood throbbing in our ears became too deafening, we stopped for a few breaths. We joked that we were just pausing to drink water and take photographs of the view behind and below us.

The view was in fact truly awesome: we could see that Kathleen Lake, at 34 square kilometres, was really very large. There were several more lakes far off in the distant valley, all surrounded by spruce and poplar forests and snow-covered mountains. The wilderness looked vast and serene.

The higher we climbed, the colder the air became. We stopped in the wind shelter created by a large boulder, put on extra layers of clothing and ate our lunch. With binoculars we could see cars far below, parked at the trailhead. Above us we could see the cirque – the King's Throne – but there were dark clouds creeping over the mountaintop. Stoically we continued upwards. After another 20 minutes of climbing we were lost in a storm. Those menacing clouds had overtaken us. The wind was howling and sleet lashed at our faces. The beautiful views we'd enjoyed for the last few hours had become completely obscured. We had no idea whether we had summited the mountain or just crested the cirque. Time to head downhill!

Of course, by the time we were off the mountain, drying ourselves in the warming hut at the trailhead, the sun had come out. Two other hikers joined us – they had gone farther than we had, turning back only because they had been unprepared for snow at the summit. Martin and I rued the fact that had we persevered an hour or so longer, we would have been enjoying the summit view with these other hikers. As it was, however, all we could do was shrug. We'd done the right, safe thing. We couldn't have known that the storm would clear so quickly.

The good weather lasted for the rest of our explorations of the park. Martin and I stopped at several of the scenic lookouts alongside the Alaska Highway, which borders the park. We enjoyed beautiful views of Kathleen Lake, the St. Elias mountains and Kluane Lake, on the way north to Sheep Mountain.

A short dirt road from the highway brought us to the Sheep Creek trailhead. Our objective was a gentle 450-metre climb over five kilometres and return. The trail followed a couple of old mining roads along the Slims River, through a spruce-beetle-devastated forest and out onto a plateau. There we had our first vista of the day: the creek sparkling in the sun, framed by ice-topped mountains. Silver ribbons of water from hidden glaciers ran down the grey mountain faces, disappeared into the forests and then reappeared as they flowed into Sheep Creek below.

We continued to follow the trail through another forest, which thinned as we gained elevation. Eventually we passed through the treeline and onto the open scree. That's when we saw them: a whole herd of 22 Dall sheep balanced on the opposite mountainside facing us. We were amazed they were finding enough to graze on along that barren-looking slope.

Our trail levelled out as it wound around Sheep Mountain. The bear bells Martin had tied to our hiking poles jingled as we went. The noise was intended to prevent us from surprising any grizzly bears we might come upon. Since we never saw any bears, we'll never know if the bells worked or not. However, as we hiked, we heard the tinkling of other bells approaching, though we couldn't see them around the curve of the mountainside. Martin jested: "That's a bear with a belly full of hiker bells approaching us." Some 250 metres farther we came across the other hikers – no bear. They too had noticed the odd sound effect of our mutually approaching bells. We shared a good laugh and relief at not having encountered any grizzlies.

Martin and I made it all the way to Forty-eight Pup Creek, where we stopped for lunch. We sat ourselves down on the ground, leaned back against some boulders and enjoyed the picturesque view before us. Beyond the silent, forested valley below us, up between the distant grey, snow-peaked mountains, gleamed the Kaskawulsh Glacier. Blanketed with dark sediments, the icy mass seemed to be asleep in its mountain crib. The world was at peace. What a perfect picnic site we'd found.

Our lazy respite was interrupted by a bold little ground squirrel. The creature scurried up to us and started licking the strap of my hiking stick. My hands had obviously been sweating salt. Leery that this cute, though wild, little animal might become used to human handouts, I shooed it away. We carefully packed up our leftovers and garbage and backtracked down the mountain to our car.

I drove us farther north, through the ashen remains of a forest burnt down in 1999, to the community of Burwash Landing, just outside the park. There, "the world's largest gold pan" stood on edge, marking the entry to the townsite. This town hosts the Kluane Museum of Natural History. Martin and I got a close-up view of mounted samples of each of the local animals and chunks of various local minerals. We also saw and learned about traditional Indigenous tools, clothing and artifacts. Very interesting!

On our last day in the park, I took a flight to see Mount Logan. At 5959 metres, this is the highest peak in Canada. Martin refused to get into the little five-person, single-propeller Cessna. So I went with three Italian tourists, and I got the co-pilot's seat!

We flew northward, low over the trees on the smaller mountains around Kluane Lake, and then turned west. I watched for but didn't see any moose or bears in the forest below. As we flew into the higher mountain ranges along the Kaskawulsh River, we saw Dall sheep. We followed the river to its source, the glacier Martin and I had seen from afar.

Our pilot flew us up the grey-striped glacier tongue to Canada's largest ice fields. An infinite number of giant white pyramids stuck out of the ice before us. These were snow-covered mountaintops as far as the eye could see. Who knew how far down under the ice the mountains went, or how thick the blanket of ice was? In the middle of it all was Mount Logan, looking pretty much like all its neighbouring mountains, except perhaps a bit taller.

There is no way to get to Mount Logan other than to fly or to traverse the ice field. Due to the many crevasses and unstable surfaces that year, there was no hiking over the glacier, and our plane could not land on it. As a result, I had to be satisfied with only flying past Canada's highest peak.

Our pilot decided to have some fun with us: he took us into an ice-filled cirque, then at the last moment veered off between the twin peaks of the mountain. He flew us low, following the undulating waves of a glacier, like a roller coaster. Then over a series of deep blue crevasses at what seemed like lightning speed. The plane banked and followed the curve of another dark debris-striped glacier. Suddenly we were flying over a field of gigantic black ice cubes spilling off the glacier, and then we were over the wide, braided mud flats in front of it. We'd passed over Lowell Glacier and then the Alsek River! Back into the treed mountains we zoomed, rounding so close to the rocky cliffs that I wondered if the wingtip on my side would graze the walls! Over the Alaska Highway we raced, and then we were back on the airstrip, safely on the ground. What a ride! And I was so very grateful I'd taken anti-motion-sickness pills before the flight.

I was still on the adrenalin high when I described to Martin what I'd experienced. Forget hiking, backpacking or climbing; flying was the way to see mountains!

KLONDIKE GOLD RUSH
INTERNATIONAL HISTORICAL PARK
CHILKOOT TRAIL
RACING HYPOTHERMIA

Two days after exploring Kluane, Martin and I joined a hiking group in Whitehorse. The eight of us, including two guides from Sea to Sky, loaded into a van and drove 176 kilometres along the meandering South Klondike Highway to Skagway, Alaska. We were going to back-pack in the Chilkoot Trail National Historic Site. Yes, flying may be easier, but nothing beats backpacking for getting to know a place.

The 53-kilometre trail follows through the Chilkoot Pass, starting near Skagway, crosses the US/Canadian border and ends at Bennett Lake, British Columbia. This traditional Indigenous trade route was adopted in 1897 by prospectors going to the Yukon to search for gold. In just two years, approximately 25,000 people made their way up the Chilkoot Pass to the gold rush.

To minimize winter disasters (i.e., deaths due to starvation, freezing and "lawlessness"), the North-West Mounted Police had implemented a law requiring that each person entering Canada via the Chilkoot Pass have one ton of supplies with them. This requirement led to a variety of results: shrewd entrepreneurs building and charging for use of ice steps on the steepest sections of the route, a tramway, a tele-graph cable and whole towns quaintly labelled "camps." Entire for-ests were cut down not only for cooking and heating fires but also for buildings and, at the top of the pass, for boats to get the gold seekers to the Klondike.

In 1898–99 a railway was built from Skagway through the neighbouring White Pass to meet up with the Chilkoot Pass at Bennett Lake. The railway rendered the Chilkoot Trail irrelevant, and everything on the Chilkoot was abandoned. Much of what was left behind, if not decayed, is still there under a fully regrown forest. This is why, in both the USA and Canada, the Chilkoot Trail is designated as the Klondike Gold Rush International Historical Park.

In 2002 we weren't required to bring a ton of goods with us, but we did still have to carry all our camping gear, food and equipment, plus emergency supplies, for the five-day trek on the Chilkoot Trail. As this was Martin's first ever backpacking trip, he balked when I insisted we train for six weeks on the Bruce Trail near our home. We had to become comfortable carrying heavy loads. I showed him many of the tricks of the trade for reducing as much weight as possible: bring a cup and a bowl (no plate), a small spork instead of a fork and spoon, a small hand towel instead of a bath towel, a child-sized toothbrush, a sliver of hand soap in a tiny plastic bag, sample-size instead of regular-size toiletries, layers of lightweight clothes, a lightweight down sleeping bag and so on. I also cut all the tags off our clothing. And as much as possible, everything we chose to carry should have more than one use, because every fraction of a gram added up to weight we'd have to carry on our backs.

The Chilkoot trailhead is in Dyea, 16 kilometres down a dirt road from Skagway. Dyea is one of those townsites that no longer exists other than on maps. Trees have regrown where they'd once been cut down for buildings. Pretty flowers were blooming in the 100-year-old town cemetery when we arrived, evidence that someone still tends some of the graves.

For the first two days, we hiked along a relatively flat or gently inclining trail following the Taiya River valley through dense coastal rainforest. I stopped often to admire the cascading river and its many waterfall tributaries. The humidity trapped under the forest canopy, and the heat we were generating carrying our heavy loads, compelled us to hike in shorts and with our sleeves rolled up. We maintained a slow but steady pace.

The forest floor was carpeted with a thick green moss. The tropical-looking leaves of devil's club draped over red mushrooms and luscious ferns. In this forest of alder, hemlock, cottonwood and spruce, many old, fallen trees had become "nurse trees" on which the next generation of plants grew. As I walked along, I indulged in sampling the grape-like twisted-stalk berries, the red highbush cranberries and the sweet black currants.

At Finnegan's Point, a designated campsite, we stopped for lunch: bagels with cream cheese, sliced cucumbers and tomatoes, and red peppers. That meal took some weight out of our packs and gave us the energy to continue on to Canyon City. By the end of that day we'd backpacked a total of 12.5 kilometres.

After helping to set up the tents in the designated campsite, I sat back to relax in a huge rocking armchair that had long ago been carved out of a single tree. I almost rocked back onto a mouse's tail – it squeaked in terror as I leaned back. "Sorry," I apologized. I'd have to be more careful how and where I relaxed in this forest.

The remains of Canyon City are on the other side of the Taiya River, accessed from the campsite by a very swingy hanging bridge. We walked through the site, past remnants of a farm, a rusted iron stove, broken dishes, tin cans, saw blades, a huge old rusted boiler and various unidentifiable objects. This was all junk, human garbage that hadn't decomposed in the last 100 years. As we were examining these artifacts, someone whispered "Bear!" We looked up to see a black bear in the bush nearest us. Quietly we backed away, out of its territory, and back over the river to our camp.

We woke up to a light drizzle the next morning. After a quick breakfast we packed up for a wet hike through the forest. We passed by a live tree whose trunk had grown into a donut-shaped loop – very odd. We walked up eight kilometres of trail, gaining about 300 metres of elevation. Even with our rain gear layered over sweaters, we noticed that the air was becoming cooler.

We lunched at Pleasant Camp, in an emergency shelter recently built by the park services. The drizzle had become rain when we continued our hike. We passed rotting telegraph poles and old glass insulators, the bare wire lying partially buried alongside the trail. There was an old wash basin, a heavy iron frying pan and miscellaneous pieces of lumber – all stuff that had been deemed too heavy to be worthwhile to remove when the trail became obsolete.

The Canadian park warden in Skagway had told us that due to heavy rains that year, much of Sheep Camp had been washed out. As a result, the number of backpackers allowed on the trail this year had been very limited – we were lucky there was space for our group. The approach to Sheep Camp was very soggy. Where the trail became completely obscured by running water, red flagging tape had been tied to the trees to mark the rest of the route into camp. At one point the trail was nothing but a torrent of rushing water – the Taiya had overflowed its banks. The pass had become a flood plain. To preserve our hiking boots we removed them and waded the last 250 metres through knee-deep, ice-cold water in our socks. Five bufflehead ducks swam nonchalantly by as we slogged upstream.

We arrived at Sheep Camp to find the emergency shelter bobbing in the water, chained to a tree so it wouldn't float away downstream! The trail crew had built a temporary dike of rocks and fallen trees, so there were still a few high and dry spots for tents. I changed into warm, dry wool socks and put on my hiking boots: ah, happy feet again! Then I took time to visit the interpretive centre, a cabin still high and dry, with its artifacts and photographs of life in the pass a hundred years ago.

Our third day had started off well enough, with a slight breeze and a mist in the air. "No problem," we thought. We had raincoats and pack covers and were eager to continue our adventure.

While Sheep Camp was in a dense forest, the trees became smaller as we climbed the Long Hill out of the flood plain. The ground became sandy and rocky. The formal trail seemed to peter out, so we opted to walk along the drier route of the old tramway, a few visible broken-down towers marking the way. The going was good until we arrived at a cliff of jagged rocks – the Golden Stairs.

No steps have been cut into the snow-covered precipice since the winter days of the gold rush. Now there's just a rocky 800-metre cliff to climb. The trail map told us the slope is a 45° incline, but after having completed the route, I think that was just the average angle. There were times when we were climbing a near vertical wall, hand over hand, without ropes.

The Canadian border is at the top of the Golden Stairs. The base of the cliff is called the "Scales" because in the late 1890s the Canadian government set up a post there to ensure that every prospector had one ton of winter supplies before climbing up into Canada. Nothing remains of the checkpoint anymore, though we did find tons of rusted, discarded stuff at the site where the North-West Mounted Police weigh-stations used to be.

There is no trail up the "Golden Stairs." We tried climbing up the loose scree at the edges of the cliff, as prescribed by our map. But that route had become unviable, a case of "two steps up, one step down." We found we could make more headway up the middle of the cliff face, clambering hand and foot over the massive rocks.

A heavy fog rolled in as we started our ascent. Eventually we couldn't see more than a metre above or below us. Between the fog and the large boulders, we often couldn't even see each other. All I knew was my direction: upwards. At some point the wind picked up and we were hit with a rainstorm. The slippery, wet rocks quickly became too treacherous for us to attempt a retreat. All we could do was continue our climb.

No one spoke, or if they did no one heard for the din of the incessant wind. Several times the squalls were so strong that they pinned me to the rock face – I had to wait for the gales to subside before I could move again. The wind drove the rain right through our pack covers and into our packs. Anything that wasn't encased in plastic bags became soaked. This meant we were also carrying the additional weight of the rainwater in our backpacks. Onwards and upwards we pushed, slowly, very slowly.

I stopped behind a car-sized boulder, out of the wind, to catch my breath and drink some water. However, standing still, soaking wet, I began to shiver violently. My teeth chattered uncontrollably. I had no choice but to continue climbing: I had to keep moving to generate enough heat to avoid hypothermia. At the summit, someone pointed at the cairn that marks the international border, but we were too dangerously cold to stop for photographs. The rain had turned into sleet.

We made it to the emergency shelter on the plateau. Dropping our wet packs on the stoop, we pulled out dry fleece jackets and piled into the tiny cabin. A few minutes later, another group of backpackers joined us in the shelter – we hadn't even known anyone was behind us in the pass. With so many people crammed into the hut, and so much wet clothing hanging from the rafters, the room became steamy warm very quickly. We made hot soup on our camp stove and stuffed ourselves with peanut butter and jelly sandwiches. We settled.

But we had to move on to the next designated site, Happy Camp, just few kilometres farther. With renewed energy we bravely set out into the storm again.

I made a quick stop at a latrine precariously balanced at the edge of the precipice behind the emergency shelter. The howling wind threated to blow the outhouse over. Only a very uncomfortable necessity drove me to go in there, and I didn't linger.

The wind was still driving the icy rain as we walked along the plateau. We couldn't look back at each other without being pelted in the face with ice. Forward! If there had been a trail up there, it was gone, washed out. We couldn't avoid treading through the expansive pools of rainwater and slushy snow. Water overflowed into my boots until no more could flow in – they were full. That water became warm as my boots acted like a neoprene wetsuit. Or perhaps my feet had become too numb to feel anything anymore. In any case, I didn't care. Like the others, I just walked straight through the endless puddles, streams, and rivers on our way to Happy Camp. No one spoke. My one thought: "tomorrow will be a better day."

Happy Camp is situated at the forested edge of the rocky plateau. As a result of all the rain, the camp had become a mudhole. We dropped our packs and set up the tents: four people holding up rain flies to keep the other four more or less dry as they set up the tents underneath. Rocks were piled on top of the tent peg loops to keep the shelters from being blown away. When we got to putting up Martin's and my tent, I complained it would get soaked in the muddy depression. As soon as those words were out of my mouth I realized I was losing my composure – mental exhaustion was setting in. I shut up and silently helped with the rest of the tents. When we were done, everyone crawled into their warm, dry sleeping bags for a desperately needed nap. I was so grateful for the break.

An hour later my mind was settled again. I put on my muddy, wet "waterproof-breathable" jacket and trod through the rain to the camp's emergency shelter. There I found our two guides setting up for dinner. I apologized to them for my earlier unwarranted outburst. They in turn confessed that they too had been very concerned that we wouldn't make it up the Golden Stairs in that storm. Like me, however, they had been aware that we had no choice but to push on. It had taken us 12 hours to hike 10 kilometres that day. Our guides were relieved that we made it safely to the campsite, even if Happy Camp was a mudhole. I helped make dinner.

As their strength returned, each person wandered into the shelter. Only Elizabeth, the other woman in our group, refused to leave the sanctuary of her tent. She had been struggling more than the rest of us up the Golden Stairs, and one of our guides had been helping her much of the way. She was exhausted. I finally coaxed her to leave her warm sleeping bag and walk through the cold rain to refuel with some hot food. She, like the rest of us, began to recover as the hot, thick stew did its work. As soon as we finished only the most necessary chores – cleaning up and bear-proofing the kitchen stuff – we all went to bed.

The rain continued all night, but exhaustion quickly brought on a very deep sleep.

That sleep helped us recover the physical and mental strength necessary to pack up our wet, muddy camping gear and continue hiking the next day. Our boots and outer clothing were still soaked. I had a slight migraine, I presume brought on by the stormy weather. Stubbornly, I hiked on, slower than the others. We had only nine kilometres to backpack, slightly downhill, to our next camp at Lindeman City. I didn't care that it was still drizzling.

Relative to what we'd experienced the previous day, this was a great hike. Despite the extra-heavy packs (due to their wet contents), we chatted and stopped often to examine more artifacts. We passed horse-shoes, individual boots and shoe soles, and shovels. We stopped to look at the ribs of abandoned boats meant to be used to get to the gold fields. I snacked on blueberries that I picked alongside the well-defined trail. By midday the skies had cleared and we were in good spirits again.

There was a rainbow over Lindeman Lake when we arrived, and we set up camp in the sun. The wind, still very strong, quickly dried our tents as well as the clothing we'd draped over bushes around the camp-site. A wood fire burning in the stove in one of the emergency shel-ters helped dry out the clothing we'd hung in the rafters. The shelter became very hot, damp and smelly as dirty clothes and boots dried.

We had time to visit Parks Canada's interpretive centre: a tradition-al canvas prospector tent filled with interesting displays, photographs and artifacts of life on the Chilkoot, from the time of the Indigenous trade route to the gold rush stampede. We browsed the small library of books about the area.

That evening we sat outside in the sun, eating our crab and pasta din-ner and our chill-set cheesecake dessert. Camp life had returned to normal. Today was a better day.

As the sun set and the temperature dropped, I moved into the warm, stinky shelter. Alone, by candlelight, just like people did a hundred years ago, I wrote in my journal. I caught up on the last two days of our crazy adventures, and wondered at how much I could endure. I reflected on the even more extreme hardships those gold rushers had endured; how bad their alternatives must have been that they were willing to put up with this. I thought of the women at the time, hav-ing to do this trip in long skirts, hems heavy with mud from dragging through the dirt. And those awful shoes they had to wear. Worse yet, they had to repeat the trip multiple times in order to get all of their ton of supplies over this pass. I realized I had no reason, or right, to complain.

We had more rain that night, and our guides' tent and sleeping bags became soaked. Everyone was grateful for the warming and cheering effect of the morning sun, which dried us out yet again. At least we wouldn't have to carry heavy wet gear.

On this, the final day of our trip, we had time to explore the remains of Lindeman City. While nothing of the wooden buildings remains, we were amazed at how much junk was lying about. There were old tin cans everywhere. Lines of broken glass delineated where tavern walls had once stood. Even the cemetery was strewn with ancient litter. One of our guides took it upon himself to straighten the weathered fence around the graves.

With relief, I noted that the clear-cut landscapes we had seen in the 100-year-old photographs had become completely reforested, though with debris still rusting away between the trees. Stumps of spruce had suckered to produce new trunks which had since become full-grown trees again. Nature had taken back its own.

The last 11 kilometres of the trail took us through ancient trapping grounds, and by the campground and helicopter landing pad at Bare Loon Lake. We passed the decaying timbers of an old cabin. The path was broad and easy to walk along, so we could enjoy the scenery rather than watching where we put our feet. There were wooden bridges over the creeks and boardwalks over the marshy sections, making our last few kilometres "a walk in the park." The only permanent resident along the route, an 80-year-old lady who lives in a sod-roofed cabin, was attending to her garden. She didn't take much notice of us as we passed.

Eventually the ground became sandy. Through the trees we got glimpses of One Mile Rapid, the dangerous water route many gold-rushers had attempted in order to avoid carrying their loads along the sandy trail. We sympathized with them as we struggled with our own heavy packs, each footstep sinking deep into the soft hillside.

Bennett Lake marked the end of our backpacking trip. We set up our tents on the beach. Sparkling in the sun, the sand contained many tiny fragments of glass – remnants of the townsite that had once stood here. The usual scattering of rusty cans, horseshoes and other metal leftovers of the gold rush were further reminders of the area's storied past.

There is not much left of Bennett the townsite. A dog barked at us from one cabin, letting us know the summer occupants were nearby. The main attraction in town was a church, its walls made of small strips of wood, put together like a quilt – very pretty. In the nearby graveyard many of the wooden markers had long since decomposed, though a few gravestones survived and were still tended. The lonely site overlooked the mountain lake, surrounded by silent forests. The scene was restful, picture-postcard perfect.

We visited with the park warden, primarily to formally check out of the trail. We ended up staying in her cabin for a while as she regaled us with stories and photographs of the Klondike. Through a window, the warden pointed out landmarks which looked so very different from the scenes of the bustling townsite in the century-old pictures.

The White Pass and Yukon Route train arrived in Bennett the next day, bearing passengers from the cruise ships in Skagway. Those tourists were on a day trip to see something of the Klondike. Dressed in white shorts, sundresses and sandals, they greatly contrasted against us in our muddy, smelly clothes. We hadn't showered during those last five days on the trail. Despite our repulsive appearance, many of the tourists were very interested in us and our adventures. We became part of the tourist attraction!

We loaded our packs into the freight compartment of the train and boarded the last car. Other backpackers who had arrived that day joined us on the return trip to Skagway. We joked that because we smelled so bad, we weren't allowed to mingle with the posh passengers up front. The true reason was to enable the conductor to easily identify those of us who only had one-way tickets back to Skagway.

The brown and green wood-trimmed antique train rumbled along the narrow-gauge railway, pulled by green and yellow engines. The rail line, built in 1898, descends 1000 metres over the 109-kilometre journey from Carcross, Yukon, through British Columbia and down the White Pass to Skagway, Alaska. We had joined the rail journey in British Columbia where the Chilkoot and White passes merge. The train passed over bridges, through two long tunnels and around very tight turns on trestles suspended on cliff faces. Looking forward in those curves, we could see the trestles supporting the front end of the train, but straight below us it seemed there was nothing holding up our own carriage. We could only see the deep rocky valleys below.

The White Pass is longer, wider and not as steep as the Chilkoot Pass.

But because we had hiked the Chilkoot in a heavy storm, we hadn't appreciated how narrow that pass was, or the beauty of the cliffs, forests and snow-peaked mountains around us. So I was grateful for the clear day to enjoy the amazing scenery.

Back in Skagway we checked into the fancy campground, took long hot showers and put on the clean clothes we'd left behind for our return. We went out for dinner and toasted our accomplishment! We had had an awesome experience.

5
Qausuittuq

THE CENTRAL HIGH ARCTIC
BACKPACKING WITH PEARY CARIBOU

Qausuittuq, pronounced cow-soo-'ee-took, meaning "a place where the sun doesn't rise," became a national park in 2015. At 11,000 square kilometres, the park makes up almost two-thirds of Bathurst Island in the Canadian High Arctic, 3600 kilometres due north of Ottawa. The park is one of the most challenging to get to, the nearest access point being the hamlet of Resolute Bay on Cornwallis Island, just east of Bathurst.

Early in 2016 a couple of people, Paul and Sue, who were visiting all the major parks in Canada, heard about my being a park bagger. They contacted me to ask if I would join them to be the first visitors to explore Qausuittuq National Park. I jumped at the opportunity. We hired Dave Weir of Ice Blink Expeditions to organize the trip for us, to look after transportation to the park as well as emergency, camping and cooking equipment, and food. Paul took on the job of ensuring that all the legalities such as contracts with airlines and our expense agreements were in order. As a nurse, Sue would provide emergency medical knowledge. I arranged the physical training for the trip, which would entail seven days of backpacking over uncharted tundra.

Paul and Sue lived close by me in southern Ontario, so it was easy to include them in my usual backpack training regime. Eight weeks before the big trip, I introduced them to the Bruce Trail. We did our first hike with just a bit of weight in our backpacks. Every weekend thereafter, we hiked with gradually more weight. Paul and Sue introduced me to the trails in their neighbourhood, thereby broadening the scope of my trail network. As we hiked, we got to know each other. It was crucial that we understood and respected each other's abilities and limitations, because we would be completely dependent on one another in the park.

We received permission from Parks Canada to fly to the northwestern tip of Qausuittuq, but because the agency itself had not yet explored that area, they decided to send someone with us. Mark, a trails specialist, was tasked with locating points of interest or places where trails might be laid. Mark met up with us in Ottawa on our way to the park.

Travelling in the Arctic takes patience. Weather, sea and ice conditions dictate when and where you will go. Our plan was to fly 2100 kilometres north from Ottawa to Iqaluit, the capital of Nunavut. From there we'd fly 1600 kilometres more to Resolute. After an overnight in Resolute, we'd hop onto our 270-kilometre chartered flight into the park. This travel plan was to be executed in two days.

Our adventure began in Ottawa: after an hour delay our flight to Iqaluit was cancelled because of heavy fog in the Arctic. A break in the fog the following day finally allowed us to fly. We cheered when the captain announced our descent into Iqaluit. Barely half an hour later, though, he let us know our approach was being abandoned due to high winds and fog again. We were rerouted to faraway Goose Bay, Labrador – the closest airport large enough for our jet to refuel. I had another drink on board as our three-hour flight became seven. Slightly intoxicated, I laughed at our long detour back to Ottawa. Oh, and then, when we couldn't get another flight to Iqaluit for two more days, we had to spend a night in each of two different places in Ottawa because no hotel had rooms available for consecutive nights.

As we all understood that being grounded was the norm when travelling to the Arctic, we decided to make the most of our extra days in Ottawa by touring the museums and the Parliament buildings. To offset the costs of our extra hotel nights, we broke into our camp food supplies and cooked our freeze-dried dinners at a picnic table in a warm, sunny city park. I also spent some time visiting with family near Ottawa.

On travel day five we finally made it to Iqaluit! However, due to all the cancelled and rerouted flights in the Arctic, we couldn't get seats on the connecting flight to Resolute that day. We were stuck in Iqaluit, on Baffin Island, for the night. Again we took the delay as an opportunity to explore.

We managed to get three rooms at a beautiful bed and breakfast overlooking the Arctic Ocean. From the picture window in the huge sunken living room, we saw a large iceberg grounded at low tide. We clambered down the rocky shoreline to explore this mass of ice left behind on the muddy sea floor. Baffin Island has some of the largest tides in the world, so the water floods back fast. Within half an hour of arriving at the berg, we were forced to quickly retreat to higher ground. The incoming tide also floated that iceberg towards the shoreline, but like us, the ice became grounded again.

So we explored the land and the hills that rise up behind the town. Being far north of the treeline, Baffin Island has no trees over a few inches tall. We walked over shrub-like Arctic willows and through fields of wildflowers. There were masses of fuchsia fireweed, purple saxifrage, bluebells, yellow Arctic poppies and tufts of white cotton grass everywhere. I felt like I was wandering through a low, wildly overgrown garden – an Arctic Garden of Eden.

From a high vantage point near Lake Geraldine, we looked out over the town of some 8,000 inhabitants. All the buildings are made of imported wood, some with metal siding, and most just a couple of storeys high. Many buildings are painted bright blue, yellow or red. Even the old airport was bright Lego yellow. The citizens' pride showed in the amount of public art: a row of nine huge inukshuks arranged in diminishing size; a slender tower of more than 30 large, round rocks stacked in a single column; and several massive carvings of Arctic animals.

There were two large ships out in the bay. One of them was a barge making its annual delivery of fuel that is used by the community to generate electricity, heat their homes and fuel vehicles and equipment. The other ship was a cargo vessel from which a small barge was shuttling crates of goods – almost everything this community would need until next year. Everything has to be delivered by ship or plane because there are no roads to Baffin Island.

The following day we were happily seated in our 42-passenger turboprop on our way to Resolute. We made our scheduled stop at Arctic

Bay, at the north end of Baffin Island, 1200 kilometres north of Iqaluit. There we were to spend 25 minutes to drop off five passengers and refuel. However, a new wave of fog had rolled over Resolute, impeding our plane's ability to safely land there. We were stuck in Arctic Bay while First Air decided what to do. So again, the five of us explorers went for a short hike.

We walked the long road from the airport to the town proper, admiring the picturesque red cliffs and enormous hoodoos that ensconce the fiord in which Arctic Bay is situated. About 800 people, mostly Inuit, live in the hamlet. We noted that the only hotel in town was booked solid with construction workers – we'd have to camp if we were stuck here overnight. But there were also no rooms available for our pilots, the flight attendant and the other three people on our flight. Three hours after arriving in Arctic Bay we were told that the fog in Resolute had not yet cleared and we were flying back to Iqaluit.

We spent another two nights in Iqaluit, waiting to be able to fly to Resolute. Our group split up to different hotels and different rooms each night as rooms became available. We joked that so far none of us had spent more than one night in any one bed on this trip. And that was when Parks Canada pulled the plug on Mark's trip: the cost of the many hotel rooms had become too much. Sadly, our team was reduced to just four people.

Our next flight to Resolute was again supposed to stop in Arctic Bay, but during our descent we didn't see any of the awesome mountains we were expecting. The place was completely flat, not a cliff in sight. Where in the world were we, and why? we wondered. Painted diagonally across the entire wall of the small terminal building next to the runway we had just arrived on were the words "Hall Beach." Consulting a map, we discovered that Hall Beach was a hamlet near the northern tip of mainland Canada, 500 kilometres south of Arctic Bay. We were told we were there to refuel. I surmised, correctly we later learned, that Arctic Bay had run out of jet fuel. Just another detour in our best-laid Arctic travel plans.

I had become overwhelmed by my blatant inability to control anything about this trip. As our flight took off again for Arctic Bay (we still had to go there to drop off other passengers) I gave in to fate and spent the rest of the flight laughing helplessly. I got strange looks from Dave and Paul, who were still frantically trying to control our destiny. We finally arrived in Resolute Bay, seven days late.

I'd been to Resolute many years before, and the impression of the place I got then still held true: Cornwallis Island is like a giant gravel pit. If it were economical to transport gravel, the 250 or so people living in Resolute could make a living exporting it, their most abundant natural resource. Fortunately transportation costs in the short ice-free season are prohibitive, and the island has therefore not been disassembled one shipload at a time.

Our overnight stay in Resolute gave us time to reassess the prospects of this trip. Key decision factors included the availability of the Twin Otter plane that was to fly us to and from Qausuittuq National Park. We were told we could be flown back within one or two days of arriving in the park, but thereafter the plane would only be available after five or more days. And all of these potential flight times would of course be weather dependent. We had enough freeze-dried food to last seven days, so we knew we could manage some delays. Dave and I had no issues extending the entire length of our adventure. Paul and Sue, however, had just received an email about a family emergency, so they were anxious to return home to deal with that. Also, none of us wanted to forfeit all the time and money we'd spent getting this far. So we opted for the safest bet: we booked Twin Otter flights that would give us just 24 hours in the park, 48 if we got "lucky" with a weather delay. At that point, bad weather sounded good because it would give us more time to explore the park.

On the eighth day of our journey we finally boarded the Twin Otter to fly in to the north end of the park. Our target was an airstrip built 40 years ago when geologists were looking for oil or gas deposits. Though they had found some, there wasn't enough to profitably extract and ship south, so the project was abandoned. The corporations had cleared away most of their operations, and no one has ever recorded being on that end of Bathurst Island since.

Our pilots took us to the coordinates of that airstrip, but found only deep puddles and crevasses. In fact, we could see no trace of any human activity – no airstrip, roads, trails or buildings. Mother Nature had taken back her own. We had to look for somewhere else to land.

During our "flight seeing" for another landing place, we traced the path the North Magnetic Pole had migrated over in the mid-1970s. The magnetic pole is what compasses point to, but that point is unstable and has been moving northwards towards the true geographic North Pole. For that reason, aircraft and ships now navigate using a global navigation system based on satellites and the fixed location of the geographic North Pole.

From the windows of our plane we watched the landscape – it matched exactly the topographic maps spread open on our laps. We passed over the Polar Bear Pass National Wildlife Area, easily identifiable by the very long, narrow waterways leading from the west across the island. Although we were flying low, we saw no polar bears, which was fortunate for the walrus we did see. The overgrown seal looked like a huge old, soggy fur coat floating in the sea. We also saw a small herd of muskox in the shadow of a low mountain. Excitedly we pressed our noses to the windows, hoping to see more wildlife.

We flew alongside almost the entire 74-kilometre length of May Inlet – the entire island is only about 185 kilometres long. And that's where we saw several small groups of Peary caribou! They were everywhere, grazing in groups of two to eight animals. There were cows with calves, and bulls. This was the reason for the park: the preservation of the endangered Peary caribou.

While we were distracted by the caribou, our pilots had found a place where they thought they might be able to set down the plane. They made three passes over a relatively flat area, first testing the ground with a slight touch of the big fat wheels, and then going back to see what the ground looked like where the wheels had touched, before finally landing.

We stepped out of the plane and froze in place. A group of four caribou had wandered over a hill towards us. Their velvety antlers glowed in the bright sunshine; their flanks flashed white as they scampered across the plains. They were foraging on the few bits of greenery amongst a seemingly never-ending field of rocks. We were mesmerized by the sight of these rare animals. Fortunately I had a camera with a built-in 60x zoom, wide-angle and macro lens, so I didn't have to mess with changing lenses to capture the caribou in photos before they disappeared out the far end of the valley.

Our pilots, who had waited patiently for the animals to wander far enough not to be disturbed by the sound of the plane, flew off, leaving the four of us explorers behind. As we stood alone in the silent tundra, I realized we had completed our objective. We were the first tourists in Qausuittuq National Park!

And then the reality of our situation set in: there were key tasks we had to do to minimize the risks we might face. First off was to check our polar bear protection. Dave ensured that all of us knew how to access and use his shotgun, and then strapped it to the back of his pack. We were each issued a can of bear spray and a set of 12 bear bangers – pen-sized explosive flares. We tested two of the bear bangers. The sudden explosions of thunder accompanying the bright flashes of light was a shocking disturbance to the peaceful tundra. When the uproar subsided, the silence that resettled over the land was absolute. We could hear our own breathing.

Not wanting to cause any further disturbance, we spoke in hushed tones. In fact, with no background din, raised voices weren't necessary. I theorized that this was why Inuit voices are so tranquil.

We tested our satellite phone, our only form of communication to the rest of the world, with a whispered 30-second call: we phoned Mark to gloat that we'd finally arrived in the park, and of course to let him know that we were sorry he couldn't be with us.

It was time to start exploring the park. We heaved on our heavy backpacks and hiked out of the gravelly plain where we had landed. We slogged through some shallow, snow-melt-soggy muck at the edge of the valley and up onto higher, drier ground. There wasn't much by way of vegetation: mostly just lichens, mosses and the odd clump of Arctic grasses. We did not even encounter the usual Arctic flowers such as pink pillows of moss campion or low fuchsia fireweed. There were no trees, not even the ubiquitous, diminutive Arctic willows. The land looked barren.

We set up our two low dome tents and kitchen tarp on a high plateau. We secured our camp by surrounding it with a bear fence, a simple tripwire attached to explosives that would warn us if a bear were to enter our campsite.

Our camp was near a clear-running stream in a pretty field of yellow Arctic poppies. To be precise, the poppies grew through the cracks of a dried mud plain, each plant blooming a few feet away from its neighbour. However, in a place so devoid of life, a plateau dotted with bobbing colour was a major attraction.

On a broader scale, the land was undulating yet generally featureless. Ravines and boulders were scarce, perhaps a kilometre or two apart. The implication of this for human needs was that when nature called, the rest of the group had to turn away to provide a person with some privacy. The other unusual impact of the Arctic environment on our toilette was an extremely slow rate of decay. This meant we had to use the unique Arctic "smear" method of managing our personal waste: by using rocks to spread out our feces so that the cold wind would freeze-dry it and blow it away. I always made sure to stand with my back to the wind and work quickly so I too wouldn't freeze. In the Arctic, social norms give way to basic survival requirements.

From our camp we could see in the distance the low, rounded mountains of the Stokes Range. From far away those hills looked gentle and easy to climb. But as we negotiated our way up one 350-metre rise, we discovered that the hills were strewn with huge flat boulders interspersed with jumbles of sharp-edged rocks that threatened us with cuts and sprains. There were patches of shale shards which slid out from under our feet, and sand blowouts in which we found chunks of clear quartz. A few mounds of snow still clung stubbornly to the shady side of rocky alcoves, We wondered whether these remnants of last winter would melt before the end of this summer.

From the top of the mountain we looked out over the national park. The other valleys between the Stokes Mountains looked just as broad and barren as the one we were camped in. Despite the lack of points of interest, there were wide bands of colour across the landscape: the stretches of various minerals and lichens seemed to meld into one another, like a delicate mirage of earth tones. The yellow- and brown-striped vista was actually quite spectacular.

Turning back towards our camp, we couldn't help but notice how our bright-orange and blue tents stood out like the beacons they were meant to be. Small as they were, they would be visible in case an emergency evacuation became necessary.

The wind had picked up when we arrived back in camp. We cooked a freeze-dried stew and huddled underneath the billowing kitchen tarp. Along with cups of steaming tea, the food was hot, filling and comforting. We were okay, alone on this vast, barren land.

The very long day of travel and exploration had worn us out. Paul and Sue retired to their tent. I crawled into the other, changed into my thermal long underwear, snuggled into my mummy bag and pulled the drawstring tight around my face to keep the icy air out. I had strapped on eye shades to block out the bright sunlight filtering into the tent – the sun was still shining at midnight. I fell asleep just as Dave crept into the tent for the night. I was reassured by the thought that I was in the same tent as the shotgun. Dave took the shotgun everywhere.

When we awoke the sky was clouded over and the temperature had fallen below freezing. A thin layer of ice frosted the tops of our tents. After going for my morning constitutional inadequately dressed, I rummaged through my pack for extra layers. My down-filled jacket was just the right thing. A breakfast of lots of hot cereal and coffee helped too.

While we ate, Dave pulled out the satellite phone and made a call to confirm what time the plane was coming to pick us up. Late in the afternoon, he was told. That meant we had time for only one more hike without our heavy backpacks.

We hiked towards the distant ice-filled Arctic Ocean. We could see the next island over to the northwest: Ile Vanier, also part of Qausuittuq National Park. We watched for polar bears that might be hunting on the ice floes in between, but fortunately saw none – we were safe.

The terrain was relatively flat, so we kept warm by walking quickly. We hiked over a slight rise to a small lake we'd initially taken for a small sea inlet. There was a large, white, triangular stone, standing out of place amongst the black boulders lining the lake. We took a GPS reading in case that stone turned out to be a place marker. I clambered down the rocky embankment to explore, and found what may have been two old lichen-covered food caches and a stone kayak cradle. These might have been built by Dorset Palaeo-Eskimos who were known to have travelled and lived here between 500 BCE and 1500 CE, before becoming extinct. Or perhaps the subsequent Thule people built them. Or maybe these were creations of my own eager imagination. Whatever they were or weren't, I reported my findings to Parks Canada after we left the park. The park archaeologists will have to figure it out.

We had spent too much time exploring, so we had to hurry back to break up camp and get to the landing site before the plane arrived. Pilots don't like waiting around in uncharted wilderness.

As we carried our heavy backpacks down from the plateau, a couple of male caribou wandered down a rocky slope towards us. They stopped and stared at us, and evidently decided we weren't a threat as they continued on their way right across our route. They were grazing as they went, just a few metres ahead of us. On our part, we too stopped and stared, back at the caribou. We silently watched in awe, respecting their space.

Such beautiful animals. At only approximately 91 centimetres tall at their shoulders, Peary caribou are small compared to their southern cousins, the woodland and tundra caribou. Their petite stature belies their extreme hardiness, being able to comfortably cope in the harsh Arctic environment. Temperatures in the few weeks of summer go up to only around 5^{0}c on Bathurst Island, and there is so little precipitation that the island is considered to be part of a polar desert. The area we'd seen consisted mostly of small rocks and dried mud flats, with very little by way of plant life. As there's not much for vegetarians like the caribou to live on, their existence is tenuous.

We went crazy with the cameras, photographing these two caribou. Sue propped me up as I struggled to keep my long lens steady – I hadn't wanted to create a disturbance by taking off my backpack to access my tripod. Eventually the caribou wandered over the next rise. Only when they were safely out of our sight did we remember that we had a plane to meet. We'd have to hurry to make up the time we'd lost. Hurrying with 25- to 30-kilogram backpacks was challenging, but no one complained. Had we been tardy, we had the best excuse ever: Peary caribou!

During the flight over the Bathurst Island back towards Resolute, each of us was lost in contemplation. We exchanged just a few words, and we seemed to agree that our original schedule of seven days in Qausuittuq may have been too much given how monotonous the landscape was. However, it would have been nice to have had another day or two in some other part of the island, just to see if there was anything different. And perhaps to see more of those caribou!

My final impressions were that despite the apparent desolation, our little group of explorers discovered that in Qausuittuq National Park of Canada, the sun doesn't rise in the summer because it never sets; and the sun shines brightly on the now protected home of the Peary caribou.

Oddly I did visit Qausuittuq again. The following year, on a small expedition ship with Adventure Canada, I sailed with 200 passengers through the Northwest Passage and we made a stop at Bathurst Island. It was September and there was already a dusting of snow on the ground as we stepped onto the frozen beach on the southern edge of the park. A layer of ice enveloped every rock on the shore. The sky was grey. The frigid wind was persistent. Winter had already set in.

Some 25 of us spent the afternoon hiking along a high ridge above the shoreline. The landscape looked like a pencil sketch in shades of black, grey and white. However, unlike the northern interior I'd explored the previous year, here were masses of Arctic willow trees, although they were already dormant for the winter. Their three-centimetre-wide trunks and narrow, leafless grey branches were spread out low over the permafrost. Their ragged pussy-willows had been blown out by the relentless wind.

Scanning the land to our north we spotted the dark mass of a musk-ox lumbering in a distant grey valley. Two hours later we saw a single Peary caribou trotting off between the desolate hills. There really wasn't much happening on this island anymore – everything had already settled down for the winter.

Although the sun had appeared over the horizon, the temperature was well below freezing. It was 6 p.m. and my time in Qausuittuq was running out again. In groups of two and three we clambered down off the steep icy ridge. The other tourists had already abandoned the frosty beach. A single inflatable boat had been left behind, waiting to shuttle the last of us back to the warmth of our cozy little ship.

6
Tuktut Nogait

THE ARCTIC TUNDRA
PRIMEVAL CAMPS AND GRAVES

Tuktut Nogait is a very large, remote national park at the north end of the Northwest Territories, on the Amundsen Gulf of the Arctic Ocean. For years I'd been looking for a way to get there. No one I know had ever heard of this park, and I only knew about it from the list on Parks Canada's website. One western Canadian outfitter had listed a backpacking trip in Tuktut Nogait, but for lack of awareness, there had never been the minimum three people applying to make the trip feasible. Although I annually placed myself on the waiting list, eventually the trip was dropped off their brochure. "Opportunity lost," I thought. How was I ever to get to this park?

Then, in late winter 2014/2015, a miracle happened: Parks Canada placed a notice on their Facebook site advertising trips into Tuktut Nogait and Ivvavik national parks. "It's time to make your #ArcticDream come true. Parks Canada can help you experience a place that many dream about but few ever visit." Yes indeed – this was my time! I immediately emailed Parks Canada to apply.

Ah, but the details: Parks was chartering a float plane that limited each person's baggage capacity to 60 pounds. Parks therefore recommended that people go in groups to share the weight of tents and cooking equipment. Being a solo traveller, I asked whether Parks could pair me up with another solo traveller, so to share the load. "No, they couldn't help with that." Parks responded. However, there was to be a conference at the camping site in the park in the previous week; they would leave a tent there, reserved for me. Wow, I was impressed, and thrilled. I was going to Tuktut Nogait!

The logistics for this trip were to include the flights between Inuvik and the park, a bear-safe camping area with toilet facilities, and daily warden-led hikes to the key points of interest in the Park. However, in mid-June Parks sent me an email apologizing that, due to lack of participants, they would have to make some adjustments to the plans. Parks hoped I wouldn't mind that they were going to fill the remaining seats with media people to create publicity for Tuktut Nogait. To take care of these special guests, Parks would provide a cook, food, camp chairs and dining tents. "Aw shucks," I wrote back. "I won't get to eat dehydrated meals I cook myself."

Moreover, as some of this park's most interesting places are quite far from the camp, and Parks Canada wanted to ensure that the media people would document those, a helicopter would be hired to shuttle us to those points of interest. "But I'll miss out on a hike!" I jested. Okay, twist my arm. I think I can live with this new type of adventure, even if it means the trip will be one day shorter than originally planned. Damn!

On August 3, 2015, four of us convened at the Parks Canada office in Inuvik, Northwest Territories, waiting for the all-clear to fly into the park. Our group was composed of Bruce Kirkby and Dave Quinn writing for *Canadian Geographic*, Jerri Thrasher from Paulatuk doing a review for the Inuvialuit Communications Society, and me, a park bagger. I found out that the issue Parks had had was not that they didn't have enough applicants to run the trip but that I was the only person to apply! No matter; with the three media people, I was going to get to Tuktut Nogait National Park.

Poor visibility had kept our Twin Otter flight grounded for most of the morning. After several hours of waiting for the all-clear we were bused to Shell Lake, where a float plane was being prepared for us. These planes are the workhorses of the Arctic – they are small but tough, and the pilots can handle anything. Fire-brigade-style, we handed our gear from person to person to stow in the back of the plane. Then we climbed in and strapped ourselves into the narrow, canvas-slung folding seats. I'd flown in Twin Otters before, but never in one on floats.

The co-pilot unmoored the plane and pushed it away from the dock, like a boat. He hopped from the pontoon in through the rear door, stepped over our gear and took his seat. I was amazed at how smooth the takeoff was, although I thought this might have been different on rough water. The loud droning and constant vibration of the propellers, along with the ear plugs, rendered communication with my fellow travellers impossible. Each of us privately contemplated the scenery below us.

Soaring over the Mackenzie Delta, I noted the infinite number of lakes, ponds and waterways, dark against the exposed beige rock, like liver spots on weathered skin. Thin clusters of scrabbly pine trees pockmarked the shoreline. From our vantage point, the hilltops looked devoid of vegetation. As we headed east, the trees on the low lands became sparser. We also noticed some dark clouds looming ahead of us.

Within 15 minutes we were told the weather had become too bad to continue, so we had to return to Inuvik, where the sun was still shining. There we waited again in the park office for a new call from the pilot. A few hours later it came: we would try again. This time we flew farther, past the treeline. I should say past the "bush line" because there weren't even any bushes down there anymore – just exposed rock and muskeg as far as I could see. The undulating, almost featureless landscape was scarred by the deep canyons of a couple of rivers: the Anderson and the crazily meandering Horton.

Then I saw the hamlet of Paulatuk, lying sheltered within a crescent-shaped peninsula on the Amundsen Gulf. The town is a 265-soul pocket of humanity 400 kilometres northeast of Inuvik. There is no road to this town; the only way to get to Paulatuk is by plane or boat. We landed at low tide at a narrow beach of dark-coloured sand and disembarked using one of our camping coolers as a stepping stone. Several Inuvialuit, walking, cycling and on ATVs, came down to the beach to greet us.

I gave the seven pounds of oranges I had put in my pack (to fully use the maximum weight allowance for my checked-in bag) to an elder from the community. The seniors at their next community meeting would be happy for this gift, I was told. Fresh produce is so ridiculously expensive in these remote communities because everything must be flown in by these little planes. Hence I've made a habit of filling my pack with bruise-proof, shareable oranges whenever I fly to the Arctic – it's just a small gesture.

Unfortunately we didn't get our hour to tour the hamlet. No sooner had we arrived at the local Tuktut Nogait park office than we received the call via satellite phone: the threat of poor weather meant we would have to fly into the park immediately or else be stuck in Paulatuk for at least a day.

Our plane was refuelled and ready to go. The four of us piled in again and were joined by several Inuvialuit. They were our cook, Sadie Lester-Grover, cultural interpreter Muffa Kudlak and wildlife interpreter Ruben Green (aka the man with the gun). We had another smooth takeoff. This flight was less than 100 kilometres, but the threatening storm clouds forced our pilots to reduce altitude. We flew lower and lower. I had been staring at the ground, hoping to spot caribou, moose or bears on the open landscape. Only when I saw two white swans sitting on a pond did I realize how low we were flying. The bushes I thought I'd been staring at were just clumps of grass!

We landed on Cache Lake (Uyarsivik Lake) next to a brand-new emergency shelter, the only building in the park. A large cache of fuel barrels lay on a spill-proof tarp nearby. A few orange tents dotted the hillside, and a group of people were standing on the shore waiting to be shuttled back to civilization. These were the conference people: Parks Canada execs, reps of various levels of government, and Inuvialuit. I gawked at the size of the lake trout they were taking back with them – at least a metre long! Friendly greetings all around, but unloading our gear and loading theirs was all done in an atmosphere of urgency. The wind had picked up and it was already drizzling. Our plane took off with all the park personnel except Maya, who'd be our team leader; Cass; and Tracey Wolki, who's also from Paulatuk. Our small group was left standing alone on the shore. And then there was silence.

After a few moments of surreal solitude, the ten of us pulled ourselves together to set up camp. We hauled all the heavy gear and supplies up into the emergency shelter, out of the rain. I carried my pack to my assigned tent and "set up house": my sleeping bag and mat covered half the floor space, my backpack another quarter of it, leaving a small square for my boots and washing bowl (aka soup bowl). This was truly minimalist camping.

Time to explore the neighbourhood. Besides the other bright-orange tents around mine, there were two outhouse tents with fancy toilets (do your thing in a paper bag, seal the bag and put it into a small self-locking bag – everything portable and decomposable). And that was it. No roads, paths, trails or anything else that might suggest human presence.

Wearing a raincoat over my winter clothes, I walked up the small hill behind our camp and looked out over Cache Lake. The huge grey lake had many bays, each of which was so long that I couldn't see the far end. There was a large patch of ice on a hill on the far side of the lake. All the hilltops were composed of exposed bedrock, with just a few tenacious bits of greenery and lots of loose stones. Only odd-shaped rocky outcrops differentiated one hill from another.

On my own I started to wander but found that the treeless valleys and meadows were awash with rainwater that could not drain into the underlying permafrost. Hummocks created by tufts of grass and brightly coloured flowers provided squishy spots to step on as I walked around. I clambered up another small hill and looked out to the horizon. Turning around 360 degrees, I noted there was no difference in the landscape no matter where I looked.

As I sat down on a large, wet boulder, I contemplated the stark contrast between this barren landscape and my woodland sanctuaries down south. This land up here is bare, naked, without a coat of trees to hide and protect it. I can see its skin, its wrinkles and age spots, all of it. Here, the land and I are exposed. We are vulnerable.

The next day, we went on a hike to Many Caches, approximately five kilometres away as the crow flies. Parks manager Maya and Sadie the cook stayed behind to mind the camp. Cass carried the emergency supplies. I had a hard time walking over the hummocks, trying to keep my hiking boots dry, looking around me and taking photographs all at the same time. It had been drizzling when we started out at 11:30, but the sky cleared as the eight of us set out across the vast, austere Arctic tundra. It seemed as though we were wandering back in time – a small, lonely tribe of early humans trekking to our hunting grounds.

Somewhere in the middle of nowhere, we came upon two tall stone inukshuks. Ruben explained that these were ancient signposts, their age being suggested by the extent of the red lichen growing over the rocks. Unexpectedly, rather than follow an imaginary line from one inukshuk to the next, we passed between the two at a sharp angle. However, we had faith that Muffa knew where he was taking us, and we followed without question. We arrived at our destination a couple of hours later.

Many Caches was a hunting site, getting its name from the many food caches built into the rocky outcrops near the Hornaday River. The caches are very obvious, with their large, flat stone lids carefully resting beside distinct cavities in the rocks. Each cache was large enough for a caribou or two. There was one unopened cache when we visited the site. We wondered whether there was anything still inside, but respectfully left it untouched.

We took some time to inspect an odd rock formation nearby, obviously human-made, in a shape suggesting a kayak cradle. We also spotted a small tent ring – the people who hunted here must have been short. Perhaps these were the "Little People" of Inuvialuit legend?

Muffa then took us over to two ancient graves not far from the hunting site. Due to the permafrost, the graves are above ground: mounds of large stone slabs. A skull was visible between the fallen stones in one of the graves. After making a small, private tobacco offering, Muffa explained that even the Inuvialuit do not know who these people were or when they were here – the oral history is silent.

Just as those people before us might have done, we sat down in the shelter of some rocks to eat our lunch. I ate in silence, wondering who this specific individual buried here had been. Man or woman? Happy or sad? Hungry, tired or excited? Did they have aspirations other than basic survival, and if so, what dreams did they have? Had those dreams come true? Who *was* this person?! Archaeologists need to get here, so that these people might live again in our human memory.

Time for us to move on from this ancient site. I had found the rhythm of the land: my steps had become easy and I'd figured out how to walk over the muskeg. This was a good thing, too, because as we left Many

Caches, dark clouds were rising in the distance. Muffa, Bruce and Dave set a quick pace of five to six km/h to get us back to camp before the rain started. I kept up with them for about an hour and a half, but I lost sight of them after I'd stopped to take some photos of wildflowers. I looked back for Ruben, Jerri, Tracey and Cass, but couldn't see them either. I should have been scared all by myself without any guides or trail to follow, but surprisingly I wasn't.

I happily skipped along on my own, comfortable with the land. Eventually I arrived at the two lichen-covered inukshuks. Instinctively I passed between them at an angle opposite of that at which our group had passed through earlier. Half an hour later I noted the patch of ice on a faraway hillside – that was my landmark. I knew that's where camp was. I walked over a couple more hills, then down to the lake and followed the shoreline into camp. In the shelter I found the men lounging in plastic chairs, sipping the hot soup Sadie had made for us. The rest of our group arrived in camp about two hours later, having made many photo stops along the way.

Our meals were oddly luxurious in this untamed wilderness. For instance, we feasted on fillets of Arctic char, caribou burritos, caribou jerky with butter (this is addictive stuff!), fish salad sandwiches made with a 30-pound lake trout fresh from Cache Lake, smoked salmon sandwiches, Inuvialuit donuts and blueberry pancakes. One evening Ruben made his own bannock recipe: "man-nock" we dubbed the oddly shaped, deliciously hot bread that came out of the frying pan. Of course, we also dined on southern staples such as pasta with sauce, cold meat sandwiches, bacon and eggs on English muffins, and scrambled eggs. In addition, Parks Canada provided an endless supply of snacks: granola bars, chocolate, dried mangos and even crisp apples and juicy oranges. I think I gained some weight on this trip.

The wind direction had changed that evening: it was cold and from the north. The night became stormy and my tent felt as though it was going to blow away with me in it. I hoped I was heavy enough to keep from flight. The next morning I stumbled half asleep through a thick fog to the latrine. Clouds had obliterated the lake and the low hills around it. We weren't going hiking today – there'd be nothing to see, not even those traditional landmarks I'd learned to rely on. After breakfast I snuggled back in my sleeping bag and caught up on my travel journal entries in my warm tent.

Fortunately, that strong wind blew the clouds away late in the afternoon, so we were able to go and explore the other side of Cache Lake. We stopped in a soggy meadow to inspect some interesting plants. Sadie plucked a few leaves and dug up some roots. Country food, she described them, as she offered samples for us to taste. Very interesting: there was sustenance to be found in this seemingly desolate land. However, even with this instruction I still didn't think I'd be able to survive on my own.

We climbed up onto the bedrock hills to examine various erratic boulders perched on top. We explored the rocky outcrops, imagining how ancient peoples might have used these resources. Maybe like us, they had huddled under one of those outcrops, out of the frigid wind, to eat lunch.

Then we hiked up to the highest point overlooking the lake. There at the pinnacle we found a semicircle of six-foot-long boulders standing on end, one next to another. This looked man-made. Ruben nodded, placing his gun between two of the rocks. "Would have been used as a hunting blind" he stated, obviously imagining snow geese flying by. We stood behind the boulders for a while, out of the wind, admiring the infinite vista before us. Slowly, with new appreciation of the land, we walked back to our camp.

We woke up on Wednesday to very sunny weather. The air in my tent was too hot and stale to stay inside and sleep. Even though mosquitos were swarming outside the zippered door, I had to take advantage of the awesome weather. More fortuitously, this was the day Parks Canada was to bring in the helicopter. With the helicopter came a couple more Parks personnel, including one from Ottawa who wanted to see how their venture into outfitting wilderness trips was coming along. I hope he was pleased, because this seemed like the only way a park bagger like me could ever get to a remote national park like this.

Four at a time we were shuttled to La Roncière Falls on the Hornaday River – I was privileged with being on the first flight. The river flows northward, rushing almost 200 kilometres from the inland plains to the Arctic Ocean. Along the way, the swift-running river had eroded the land into steep, narrow valleys meandering around impenetrable bedrock before broadening out into the sea. Our pilot flew us southbound, upriver to the renowned waterfalls. I wanted to capture everything in photographs, but had to remind myself not to witness the world only through a viewfinder. I forced myself to put down the camera and look around, to absorb the entire experience.

The land is relatively flat, with low, rolling hills all lined up in the same direction like swells on the ocean. The Hornaday River gorge is an anomaly in the monotonous, undulating landscape. The canyons are twisted, sometimes almost turning back on themselves. The silver running river fills the canyons from wall to wall. There are long stretches of straightaways between bends in the river. We saw hoodoos and giant boulders in the river sides and huge white rapids everywhere. And then we saw the falls, 23 metres deep. We hovered for a while over the mist rising off the falling water, before landing on a large flat rock two-thirds of the way up the cliff. A few more shuttles brought our entire group together onto the football-field-sized rock.

Each of us looked upon La Roncière Falls with awe: there was so much water tumbling, like a narrower version of Niagara Falls. We began our day by taking photographs, from every conceivable angle. "Go out farther, to the edge of the cliff," we taunted each other while trying to get the perfect shot. I hopped over a broad, deep gap onto a free-standing narrow tower of rock at the edge of the precipice. Feeling too uncomfortable to stand there, I sat down for the photograph. But when I stood up to return to the "mainland," my knees went weak. Fear threatened to immobilize me. I had to dig deep into myself to take control of my thoughts so I could turn around and jump over the 14-metre-deep crevasse. It took me a couple of minutes, but I managed to get back to solid ground. "Your turn," I nervously called to Bruce, my photographer!

After having our fill of photographing the falls, we settled down to actually enjoy the afternoon. We ate our fish salad lunches while lounging on the sun-warmed rocks. We explored the area, clambering over, under and around the house-sized boulders that had fallen from the cliffs above us. I marvelled at the small, brick-sized stacks of slate that seemed to hold up the monstrous rocks above. I snuck into the shallow caves under the cliffs, getting dripped on from water seeping through the melting land. Eventually I was comfortable enough to stroll out onto a very long rock overhanging the top of the falls, where I sat down cross-legged and meditated on existence. Too soon, it was 5:30 and we had to return to camp. The 15-minute flights felt too quick, an anti-climax to this awesome day.

However, the day had more "awesomeness" in store for me. That evening, at around 11 p.m. under a sunny sky, Jerri and I carried the canoe down from the emergency shelter to the lake – yes, someone before us had flown a canoe into the park and left it at Cache Lake. Neither Jerri nor I had known the paddling abilities of the other, but we were pleasantly surprised to discover we were both accomplished canoeists. The water was perfectly calm as we navigated around our end of Cache Lake. The lake was so clear we could see those huge trout swimming below us. We explored the lakeside and noted the profusion of wildflowers growing in the meadows where creeks emptied into the lake. As the sun set, the wind picked up. We had to work hard, paddling against a strong current to get across the lake. We arrived back at camp elated and thrilled to have had the opportunity to paddle.

I decided I needed to end this amazing day on this high note – there couldn't possibly be any more good stuff that could be crammed into a single day. The comfort of my sleeping bag was just the ticket.

The next day, Thursday, we were supposed to leave the park. The sun was shining in a bright blue sky and I was sad my adventure was coming to an end. However, at 9 a.m. we heard over the satellite phone that a thick fog had blanketed Paulatuk. The plane couldn't take the locals home, so we had to wait. The hourly phone checks did not bring any change in the news. By 2 p.m. our flight was cancelled and I got my sixth day in the park after all.

Six of us went for a hike around our side of the lake. Bruce, Dave and Ruben with the gun were far ahead of the women. Jerri, Cass and I were happily photographing flowers and caribou skulls. In the lee of a hillside, where the sun had warmed the rocks, I decided it was time for a swim. Since arriving in the park, I'd done no more than sponge bath my private parts. A dip would wash off the sweat and grime of camping, I reasoned. So I stripped down and tentatively stepped thigh deep onto the slippery pebbles in the lake. It was cold, but my toes weren't turning blue – a good sign, I thought. Within a couple of minutes I dove in, carefully keeping my hair dry. Okay, yes, it was cold. I only got a couple of breast strokes done before I figured that was enough for me. The air on the pebble beach was relatively warm and it dried me as I pulled on my thermal long underwear. Jerri and Cass had waited for me to get dressed, and then we hurried to catch up with the guys, who'd been waiting on the far side of the large bay.

The hiking through the meadow was tough; the terrain was flooded and there were no hummocks to step on. I was worried the water would get too deep and come in over the tops of my waterproof boots. Jerri was weary of the hard slog, and Cass had a leaky rubber boot. The three of us decided to turn back; the guys could continue on their own. Just as our group was splitting up, we heard the thumping of a helicopter. In a few minutes it flew over us towards our camp, then came back and landed next to us. How very, very odd, I thought. We're out here in the middle of nowhere and a helicopter comes to us out of the blue, literally! Turns out these were survey geologists working in the park who were wanting to camp at our site after we'd moved out. They were checking if we had left the previous day as planned. Obviously not. We couldn't leave for the same reason they couldn't do their research on the Arctic shores of the park: too much coastal fog. The helicopter flew off again with the scientists, leaving us in silence.

Not 15 minutes later, on a photo stop, Jerri, Cass and I looked back to see a male caribou with massive antlers, galloping away from the guys! Through binoculars we watched the buck, a member of the dwindling Bluenose caribou herd. The beast ran up the far hillside, turned around and ambled back down, to what looked like just a few metres from the guys, then continued past them and up another hillside. We must have stood there for 20 minutes just watching. We were envious of the great photo opportunity the guys were having – we were sure they could have taken pictures of the buck's nose hairs, they were that close. Then we thought of Ruben with his gun – he'd surely be thinking of what a great dinner that caribou would make. As we later learned, the animal was farther away from the guys than it had looked from our vantage point. They did get some awesome pics with their 800mm lens, but no one was eating caribou that night.

The next day started out the same as the previous one: great weather in the park but reported fog in Paulatuk. We had learned that the coastal fog normally lifted in the afternoons, so we optimistically started packing up. By 2 p.m. we received confirmation that our plane had left the town of Norman Wells to collect us. Just as we finished striking camp, the plane landed on our lake. We loaded the gear in. Speeches, sad farewells, promises to stay in touch, damp eyes and hugs all around. Jerri, Maya, Muffa, Ruben, Sadie and Tracey were going first, to be flown home to Paulatuk.

The remaining four of us – Bruce, Dave, Cass and I – sat in camp chairs lined up along the lake, as though on the veranda of a posh northern resort. We were aware, however, that we were all alone with only emergency provisions. Would the plane be able to come back for us, or would we be abandoned for another day? An hour later the Twin Otter was back to collect us. On our flight back to Inuvik, we silently stared out the windows, down at the park, at the land. It was sad to be leaving this amazing country, but it was time. Winter was coming.

Six days is a long time to go without washing, and I think we were all quite ripe by the end of our trip. That was okay in the wilderness where everyone else smelled the same, but it was not appropriate in town. So the first thing I did upon entering my hotel room in Inuvik was to take a long hot shower and wash my hair. Bruce, Dave and I went out for dinner that evening and shared our impressions of our trip together. The Arctic wilderness had captivated us!

And just like that, after years of wondering how I might possibly get to see this park, I'd been there. I'm still amazed how seemingly impossible opportunities simply appear – I just need to be patient, vigilant and flexible, and jump on them when they come. And the parks are mine.

7
Nááts'įhch'oh Reserve

THE MACKENZIE MOUNTAINS
QUICKSAND, ANTS AND LOST LAKES

In 2009 the preserved lands of Nahanni National Park in the Northwest Territories were expanded to the northwest to include the Moose Ponds at the Yukon border. The additional protected land contains the powerful and sacred mountains, lakes and rivers of the Sahtu Dene and Metis peoples. Having its own special management agreement with the local peoples, the area was officially designated in 2014 as Nááts'įhch'oh National Park Reserve. The name of the park refers to the porcupine-quill shape of the summit of Nááts'įhch'oh Mountain.

I could kick myself, twice, for not having paddled the South Nahanni River from the Moose Ponds in 1991. Back then I had greatly underestimated my whitewater canoeing skills and therefore shied away from the technical northern section of the river. But after having paddled the river within the Nahanni National Park Reserve, I knew I could have had fun in the Moose Ponds as well. Secondly, now that the Moose Ponds are part of a new national park, I had to go back to the area to check the new park off my bucket list. All things considered, though, I was actually quite happy to go back, because the area is so beautiful.

My visit to Nááts'įhch'oh in 2018 was not for a thrilling whitewater canoe trip, however. Instead I flew to Backbone Lake to do some preliminary exploration on foot from a base camp. Joining me were my friends Sue and Paul, with whom I'd explored Qausuittuq National Park a couple of years earlier. Black Feather Adventure Company was our outfitter and provided Gail as our guide. Paul, Sue and I had all travelled with Gail before. Parks Canada sent two staff members with us: Joanne, who is Sahtu Dene; and Katelyn, who is Metis. As Sue, Paul and I would be the first visitors to this part of the park – the guinea-pig group – Joanne and Katelyn were tasked with recording what was of interest to us and tracking our explorations. Their notes were to be used for suggestions to future visitors.

Early in July our little group flew 1500 kilometres northwest from Edmonton to Norman Wells, a secluded town of about 800 people, situated on the Mackenzie River in the Northwest Territories. With just a winter road, the only way to get to Norman Wells in the summer is by plane or boat. The town, originally established to provide oil during the Second World War, is now the regional centre for the Sahtu and for local tourism. Sue, Paul and I took some time to visit the local museum to learn more about the area.

The little museum building is crammed with information and paraphernalia relating primarily to the Canol (Canadian Oil) road and pipeline that was built and promptly abandoned in the early 1940s. We were impressed by the stoicism of the people who had put up with the extreme cold; dense, buggy forests; steep mountains; hard labour and isolation in order to build the oil facilities. In contrast, now the town boasts several fishing, hunting and boating outfitters that provide comfortable wilderness experiences to well-to-do tourists. And of course, hardy backpackers can hike the 372 kilometres of the newly designated Canol Road National Historic Trail.

We stowed our suitcases, with a set of clean clothes, in one of Black Feather's pretty log buildings overlooking the wide Mackenzie River, and got ready to head into the park 300 kilometres away. Gail had already sorted and arranged our food and equipment into large waterproof barrel packs and duffle bags for our nine-day trip. We wondered what delights – fresh foods? – were in the huge cooler she had us carry to the dock. Floating on the river was the usual Twin Otter plane, waiting for us to load up. In addition to the camping gear, we stuffed two red whitewater canoes into the small plane. Our 872 pounds of supplies left us no space to stand or walk in the Twin Otter. To board, we had to climb one at a time over the six single fold-down seats along the side wall.

I downed a quick-dissolving motion sickness tablet and stuffed spongy plugs into my ears. The co-pilot untied the plane from the dock and hopped into the overcrowded cabin, latching the door shut behind him. He clambered over our gear to the cockpit, and the pilot revved the propellers. The plane motored away from the shore and almost instantly we were in the air.

The Twin Otter vibrated and rumbled as we flew low across the broad, green Mackenzie valley. We gained altitude to fly over the rocky, snow-peaked mountains that rise like a wall at the western edge of the flatlands. The turbulence at higher altitude caused the little plane to sway and drop through air pockets. Over and over again I caught my breath on the abrupt uplifts and held my stomach on the gut-wrenching falls, all the while praying that the anti-nausea pill would be effective! Seeking a flight path with less turbulence, our pilots took us lower, flying between and around the mountaintops but that meant more banking and pitching. Although I'd hoped to watch the ground not too far below for animals, I soon couldn't handle the motion. I had to secure my constitution by staring straight out between the mountains towards the farthest peaks.

What a relief, after an hour of agony, to finally see Backbone Lake! Within minutes our pilots had expertly landed us on the calm water and motored to the northeastern shore. One by one we fell out the back door onto a pontoon of the little plane and hopped to the pebbly beach. For several moments I simply stood there collecting myself.

As I began to feel grounded again, I looked up and noticed that everyone else, including our pilots, were also standing around motionless, settling themselves after the rough flight. Everyone had become somewhat nauseated. Without the drone of the engines, we could finally speak to one another, so I asked our pilot how he manages motion sickness. His response was that he takes the controls back from the co-pilot – drivers never get sick because they are in control. Good to know!

Now that we'd settled, we had work to do, starting with unloading our gear so the plane could return to Norman Wells. Then we waved goodbye as the Twin Otter disappeared behind the mountains at the end of the lake, and we were left alone in an overwhelming silence. Bewildered by the sudden quiet, we gazed at the world into which we'd just been deposited.

Backbone Lake is situated near the edge of the Black Wolf Creek valley. A steep mountain pass closes off the other end of the lake. On our old maps the lake was labelled "Grizzly Bear Lake," but the Sahtu Dene elders were concerned that so honouring the bears might attract them to the area. Consequently, as Katelyn explained, the name has been formally changed to "Backbone Lake." The new name recognizes the way the lake ties together the rivers, valleys and mountains around it. From her pocket, Joanne took a small jar of mixed tobacco and tea leaves, and let us each take a pinch of the hallowed gift. We followed her lead in thanking the spirits of Nááts'įhch'oh for allowing our visit and granting us safety. Some of us sprinkled the offering into the lake. I let the wind catch my offering, to be distributed wherever the spirits would like. I sensed that we would have resplendent adventures in this park.

Black Wolf Creek valley, at the north end of the lake, is lush green, dense with 2-metre-tall willow and alder shrubs. The far reaches of the emerald green vale are polka-dotted with dark-green spruce trees. The meadows reach right up the mountainsides to where the slopes became steep rocky cliffs. The mountaintops, including the one across the lake from our camp, still had patches of snow on them from the previous winter. The other end of the oval lake was sealed off by several steep mountains. With the sun at just the right angle, we could see the tiny white reflections of three weather research boxes way up on the mountainsides

We set up camp near the bank of an estuary; the unnamed creek we dubbed "Kitchen Creek" because its swift current became our source of drinking water. The main channel of Kitchen Creek ran clear and cold in its gravel bed. Many dry creek channels, like gravel paths, braided around the main waterway. Purple and white fringed vetch, yellow fleabane and a few fuchsia blossoms of broad-leaved willow herb grew along the banks.

Working together we set up our large kitchen teepee near Kitchen Creek. We created a tripod out of three canoe paddles, from which to hang our gravity-drip water filter: water poured into the top of a bag flows down through a filter at the bottom, then through a hose with an on/off valve and into a pot or water bottle. We all agreed that this water purification process was much more efficient than pump style filters.

That tripod doubled as a boundary line beyond which we didn't walk, because down near where Kitchen Creek enters Backbone Lake was a pair of plovers with two tiny chicks in a rocky depression of a nest. Those shorebirds were being harassed by a pair of gulls whose own relatively huge hungry chicks waited on the other side of the creek. On our second morning in camp we noticed there was only one fluffy plover chick left. A day later Paul watched as one of the gulls nabbed the second plover chick and fed it to its own offspring. Sad, we agreed, but that's now nature works.

Paul and Sue shared a three-person tent, as did Joanne and Katelyn. Gail had her own two-place tent. They had pitched their tents on the gravel beach that made up the lakeshore. I was leery of the powerful winds I knew could arise in these northern lands, so I set up my two-person tent on a small rise behind a stand of alders set back a bit from the lake.

Near our tents on "our" beach was a pair of Parks Canada's red resin Muskoka chairs. We noticed that on calm mornings, these perches were perfect for enjoying the lake as it mirrored the surrounding mountains.

There were trails leading off in several directions from our base camp. By the fresh scat and prints on those trails, we quickly realized they were moose and grizzly bear paths, not human. We'd have to be on our guard.

The following day, we set out to explore a bit farther afield. Our first hike was to a waterfall off a small unnamed creek near where the mountains closed off the southeast end of the lake. Joanne and the elders of her village had visited the waterfall earlier in the summer. Wanting to show off this feature of the park, Joanne led Gail, Sue and Paul tramping along the lakeshore trails. When they came to a swift metre-wide creek flowing into the lake, they followed it upstream, bushwhacking their way towards the waterfall.

I'd awoken that morning with a debilitating migraine and had taken medication that knocked me out. Katelyn graciously stayed behind with me. Two hours later I'd recovered enough to join the others. To catch up to our friends, Katelyn and I paddled one of the canoes to the waterfall creek. As we travelled down the lake we noticed that the snowy mountain on the other side of the lake actually had two peaks. Against the bright blue sky, the sun reflecting off both snowy summits made for a pretty sight.

Paddling close along the shoreline, Katelyn and I scanned the mountain on our camp's side of the lake, watching for the rest of our team. Through binoculars, we spotted them sitting on the bank of a rocky creek far above. We beached our canoe and secured it to an alder shrub at the mouth of the creek. Katelyn radioed our friends to let them know where we were. They in turn spotted us. We watched each other through binoculars and waved. They beckoned us up, pointing out the shrub-overgrown route of the creek.

By some inexplicable folly, instead of following the long arc of the creek towards our team, Katelyn and I decided to bushwhack straight up the steep slope, through dense alder shrubs more than a metre tall. We laughed at the insanity of forcing our way around, under and often on top of the branches, until finally we fell out of the bushes right into the little clearing where lunch was being served.

After consuming our fill of dry bread with cheese and hard salami, and pump-filtering more drinking water from the creek, our reunited group set out to find that waterfall. We hiked single-file along the narrowing rocky waterway, hemmed in by the cliff edge of the mountain. Each of us chose our own stepping stones through the gorge.

As it turned out, the waterfall was just five minutes upstream of our lunch stop, but hidden in the far side of a steep bluff. At the end of the short chasm, a long, narrow ribbon of silver fell straight down from a gully in the mountaintop. Dense shrubs muffled any sound the water might have been making as it struck the base of the cliff. We lingered, delighting in the light reflecting off the clear, cold water.

Heading back to camp, Joanne, Katelyn and Sue paddled the canoe, while Gail, Paul and I hiked overland. Just to see something different, rather than walk along the rocky lakeshore, we bushwhacked (because I love it so much – not) through the lowlands behind the mountain. In that valley we quickly lost sight of Backbone Lake to our northwest. We followed overgrown moose trails that led us into wet bogs.

We edged our way around those grassy wet patches and found more animal trails to follow. Amazingly, I found a fallen land-claims post, metal ID tags still attached. Katelyn explained that this was a leftover from long-ago prospectors searching for whatever riches they might find: silver, gold or even tungsten.

As we hiked, Gail kept track of our route on her map. I kept an eye on the mountaintops beyond where Backbone Lake should be: when the twin peaks lined up, we'd be directly across from our camp. Sure enough, at the point where we could no longer see the second peak, we came upon a stream flowing towards the lake – Kitchen Creek. We rock-hopped along that, right into camp.

That evening, Joanne surprised us with a fresh moose hip-joint she'd stashed in the cooler chest. Together, following Joanne's guidance, we trimmed the sinew off of the dark-red meat. The resulting lean moose-meat stew, flavoured with caramelized onions, was delicious with the fresh bannock bread Joanne had baked! The following day she boiled up the bone for her own traditional meals, which she preferred over our Western-style camp meals.

Moose are very important to the Indigenous Peoples of the area. Joanne showed us a very detailed 60-centimetre-long model of a traditional moosehide boat she'd brought with her on our trip. A Sahtu Dene Chief had asked her to show it to us and explain how people had made these types of disposable boats to return to their villages after major hunting trips. In my typical Western way of thinking, I was concerned about the safety of this fragile-looking model Joanne had brought into the wilderness in a cardboard box. However, both the Chief and Joanne were obviously comfortable with the risks of transporting delicate objects.

Our second hike was a long one: five kilometres, as the crow flies, to a natural hot spring. But there were no crows in these mountains, and ours was a long, roundabout route. We started this journey with an easy 10-minute paddle to an impasse at the far southwest end of the lake. From there we clambered over a high mountain pass on a well-used animal migration route braided with moose trails. The trail was primarily composed of loose rocks and was heavily overgrown with shrubs. We had to grab on to boulders and branches to pull ourselves up the steep slope. From the short plateau at the top, we looked back down the length of Backbone Lake. Our camp was just a speck in the immense wilderness. At the bottom of the other side of the pass, sparkling water cascaded over a rocky creekbed towards our destination and beyond to the Broken Skull River.

We discovered that the creek sprang from underneath the pass. Backbone Lake flows out, filters through the ground and emerges into a milky, turquoise-coloured pool on the other side of the pass. The resulting creek splashes through a very picturesque gorge bordered by stands of spruce trees stretching up the steep slopes of grey stone mountains. We followed along the creek, rock-hopping where we could. Occasionally we had to climb up the steep banks, around ancient rockslides.

Joanne carefully guided us up the rocks around the landslides, advising us that the mud was like quicksand. Unfortunately Gail, at the rear of our group, hadn't heard the warning and walked right into what looked like an easy way up the slope. Down she sank. The more she struggled, the deeper the mud sucked her down. As Paul and I were on a boulder just uphill of Gail, within reaching distance, we knelt down and grabbed her arms. With hand-to-wrist sailor's grips we tugged and pulled. She'd already sunk thigh-deep before finally getting a knee out onto our rock and eventually wrenching her other leg out. Gail stood up on our boulder, surprised that she hadn't lost her boots, and thanked us. While we wondered how deep the quicksand went, we decided not to test it because it could be dangerous without the appropriate equipment – and we were far from help. Back down at the creek, Gail washed off the tons of clay that had clung to her boots and pant legs.

Temporarily changing out of our hiking boots, we forded the rushing creek at a wider point that we hoped wouldn't be too deep. Working in groups of three, we supported each other as we gingerly stepped down into hidden holes and onto rocks under the rushing white current. The cold water instantly numbed our skin, but we felt refreshed when stepping out onto the sun-warmed rocks on the other side.

Around the next bend in the creek we got our first glimpse of Sadéé

Shuh – Sunlight Mountain – the pillar-like peak marking the location of the hot spring. After three hours of trekking, we finally arrived at an ancient tufa mound. These continuously accumulating mounds are made of carbonate minerals brought to the surface from deep underground by the hot spring. Steamy water trickled over the hard, whitish crust of the mound and down to the creek. We climbed up the mineral hill to the first hot pool. The surface of the small spring was completely covered with a dense layer of brilliant green and tan algae. Fuchsia flowers blossomed around the edge of the pool and the sun reflected off of Sadéé Shuh in the background. I just had to photograph the scene.

Just as I was crouching to get the right perspective for my shot, Joanne casually commented that there seemed to be a lot of ants around. Too late: I was already down, lying on an ant nest! Instantly I was covered with them! "Help!" I shouted as I jumped up, tearing off my camera, hat and jacket. Paul and Sue helped brush the ants off me. While the ants didn't bite, it was a horribly creepy feeling. Even after everyone was sure I was ant-free, I was still itching and scratching. And I hadn't gotten the photograph I wanted, either.

Another, larger pool farther uphill was mostly free of the unusual algae, and it had an inviting sandy slope running down into it. Still itching, I was one of the first to get into that hot spring. Wearing just my bra and panties, and neoprene booties, I eased myself into the thermal water. It was so hot that I couldn't get my feet down without boiling them. I had to stay floating at the very surface of the pool, and even that was almost too hot. Gail had gotten into the natural spa ahead of me. Joanne and Katelyn tried out the waters after me. Paul and Sue sat smartly on the bank, dangling their feet into the scalding pool. None of us could stay in the water for more than a few minutes.

Rather than being rich in smelly sulphur like many hot springs, this water has unusually high levels of strontium. Strontium is the chemical that makes fireworks deep red, hinders x-rays in television screens, and, oddly, is used in toothpaste for sensitive teeth. It also effectively removed all traces, real or imagined, of the ants on my skin.

A few hours later we were paddling back across Backbone Lake. Sue and I were the princesses, each sitting in the middle of our respective canoes. The wind had picked up considerably during the day, and our four paddlers had to work hard to control the boats. I looked out towards our camp. 1, 2, 3. 1, 2, 3. I counted the tents over and over again. 1, 2, 3, and …? There ought to be four tents. Where's the fourth tent?! And I couldn't see the kitchen teepee either! We arrived at our camp to find the kitchen strewn all over the estuary and the fourth tent snagged on a bush far inland. The pegs and rocks we'd used to anchor everything had been no match for the north winds. Although my tent was still standing, I supressed my bit of smugness and diligently helped gather up the scattered belongings and reset our kitchen. We were all relieved to find that no animals had taken advantage of the opportunity to raid our wrecked camp.

That night, the strong winds brought rain into our valley. We spent the following morning sitting in the kitchen teepee learning from Joanne how to make traditional porcupine quill and bead earrings. I discovered that beading is a skill that requires considerable practice – my creations that morning were definitely amateurish.

As several long days wore on, the rain eventually eased. On a couple of light drizzle days, we explored nearby Black Wolf Creek, walking along the dry gravel bed or the rocks on the edge of the creek when we could. Where there was no bank, and where the lowland was too swampy, we were forced up onto the higher shoulder plains, bushwhacking through dense alders and willows. Where the shrubs became impassable, we hiked still higher up, along the scree edge of the mountain slopes.

Downstream we found hoodoos, one with a huge rock balanced precariously atop the tall spire that had been eroded out of the mountainside. We came across a couple of possible campsites on the plateaus above the creek. Katelyn took careful notes for future use.

Upstream, hiking along the high scree edge, we saw another waterfall feeding from the mountains on the other side Black Wolf Creek. Still farther upstream we found a split in the creek, the streams rushing down from narrow canyons. Katelyn, Gail and I each documented our exploratory trek.

As we became familiar with the terrain, we got more ambitious with our explorations. Our last big hike was to another lake we'd noted on the topographical map. The map showed this little unnamed lake as being on a higher plateau due north of our camp, but there were no obvious routes around a mountain to get to it. Katelyn and Joanne were unaware of anyone ever having gone there, though they were sure that hunters would have been familiar with the area. So on a bright sunny morning, we set out to find that lake, again by first paddling across Backbone Lake in order to save time hiking along the narrow gravel beach around the north end of Backbone.

We tied up the canoes near the collapsed floorboard timbers of an old hunting camp and started our trek along a rocky creek under a steep, arched bluff. That creek veered off to the west, so we continued by following northbound moose trails until they too headed off in the wrong direction. We took turns in the lead, slowly bashing back the bushes as we went. The last person always had it the easiest, as they could follow the path cleared by those ahead. Often, though, the last person would become impatient at the slow progress and try to shortcut by bushwhacking their own route. The group dynamics were interesting.

At one point I led the group along what, based on the pile of fresh scat we carefully stepped over, turned out to be a grizzly bear trail. We bushwhacked over to another trail, with a deluded idea that a few shrubs would protect us from a grizzly. I patted my pocket to ensure that my bear spray was still there; I think everyone else did the same.

After a couple of hours of this crazy trekking, we took a lunch break in an open, flowered meadow. The sun was warm, and with mosquito nets for protection we lay back comfortably for a nap. But we soon grew restless. Checking the GPS, we saw we were only half a kilometre from the little lake. Onwards, we decided. We'd come too far to turn back without having made our destination. We skipped over another rocky stream and climbed up another steep cliff to find ourselves on a high grassy plateau. The lake was just a short walk away.

After all our hard work, our arrival at the little lake was sort of anti-climactic. The lake, more of a quaint pond, was situated in the middle of an almost manicured, park-like field. Only the park benches and Sunday strollers were missing. The pond had a very small, sandy beach that Katelyn made the best of. She stripped down to her underwear and took a dip in this obvious swimming hole. After a few strokes she hurried out of the cold water. Oddly, I wasn't in the mood for a cold swim. There was a cool breeze and I was tired. And I was leery of having to hike back to camp with wet hair.

From the edge of the plateau we could see a series of small meadows (swampy land no doubt) all the way down to a stream leading into Backbone Lake. We followed around the dry perimeters of those wet fields and then along the boulders in the stream. We noted some very impressive seashell fossils and a fossilized chunk of coral along the way. Yes, this route was much easier than the bushy way we'd scrambled up to the little lake. We'd spent four hours getting there and just two hours coming back down. Katelyn tracked it all on her GPS, for a possible future trail.

When we finally arrived back in camp, each of us was exhausted, hot and sweaty. Everyone went for a swim in Backbone Lake. The frigid temperature of the water shortened our swim, but the joy was achieved upon exiting the water, refreshed, into the relatively warm air. I had managed to keep my hair mostly dry. Only the attack of the mosquitos hastened my retreat into my tent, where I changed into dry, protective clothing.

And all too soon, our nine-day adventure was over.

We packed up all our gear – a bit lighter for all the food we'd eaten – and piled the bags and barrels on the beach. The last thing to be dismantled was the kitchen teepee, which we dropped down only when we heard the drone of the plane – the confirmation that we were actually leaving Náàts'įhch'oh. The Twin Otter was right on schedule. We left a last tobacco/tea offering of thanks in the lake. As we sat in the plane circling up over Backbone Lake, I looked back at our campsite. I was sad to leave, yet content and grateful to have had the opportunity to visit this beautiful yet powerful place.

Our flight back to Norman Wells was much, much more stable than the flight out. The mood was sombre as we stared out the windows, watching the mountains slip away from us.

8
Nahanni Reserve

THE MACKENZIE MOUNTAINS
CANOEING BIG WHITEWATER

I had done many week-long canoe trips with friends and with clubs I'd belonged to, but those were all on flat water in southern Ontario and Quebec. Then, sometime in the 1980s, I decided I should learn how to paddle whitewater, the idea being that I would no longer need to portage every little ripple on a river trip. Although my Girl Guide warnings that "only fools shoot the rapids" lurked in the back of my mind, I gave it a go.

True to my risk-averse nature, however, I started on this adventure by taking a course in whitewater paddling with Harbourfront Canoe and Kayak Centre. I arrived at the school's base on Lake Ontario early on a cold March morning. Five other students were already there, all men. I worried: no one told me I would need major strength to do this. Apprehensively I climbed into the van with the men, and our instructor drove us to the Humber River in the heart of Toronto. The other students confessed that they too were anxious about this course, boating on moving water on a day when the air temperature was just 5°C. We arrived at the river and found it was fast-moving but still ice-choked. This did not look promising.

Bravely I donned my pink and purple wetsuit, my fuchsia-coloured spray jacket, neoprene booties, PFD and helmet, and stepped into my assigned canoe. As soon as I knelt into the stern position, my fears subsided. I was at home in a canoe. I knew I could do this.

To my surprise, I excelled at whitewater canoeing, largely because, not having the strength to bull my way through, I had to pay attention and apply the skills that were being taught. In fact, I got hooked on the adrenalin rush of the sport. This was fun!

Each year for three years, I took whitewater canoeing courses, steadily advancing to more and more challenging rivers. Eventually I earned my Ontario Recreational Canoeing Association moving-water certification, allowing me to lead whitewater canoe trips.

So with all this training and experience, I felt I was ready for a true northern challenge. I wanted to paddle the fabled Nahanni River. Still, with just three years of moving-water experience, I shied away from the "rock garden" in the "Moose Ponds" at the headwaters of the river, just outside Nahanni National Park. I opted instead for a safer 12-day trip from "Rabbit Kettle" south to the end of the Nahanni at the Liard River. This was to be my first big whitewater wilderness trip!

At the end of July 1991 I flew to Yellowknife, the capital of the Northwest Territories, where I met the rest of my group: Russ and Gene, two retired gentlemen travelling together, and our young Black Feather guide, Carolyn. From Yellowknife we took a flight on an old DC3 some 500 kilometres west to Fort Simpson. The village, with a population of about 1,100, is situated where the northeast-flowing Liard River merges into the Mackenzie to continue north to the Beaufort Sea. Thousands of hectares of dense boreal forest and an infinite number of lakes surround these rivers. There are few highways, and those that exist are mostly dirt roads or winter-only ice roads.

Reports of poor visibility on the Nahanni delayed the last leg of our flight. As we were stuck in Fort Simpson for the night, we pitched our four tents alongside the charter-flights runway. We ate a camp dinner in the shelter of an old airplane hangar. We were making do with the few resources available to us. The next morning we were awakened by the first small plane to land on "our" runway, its wings seeming to pass right over our tents. Camping on an airfield was a novel experience.

Shortly after breakfast we received the news that the weather in the park had cleared sufficiently for our flight to be attempted. Everything, including three two-person canoes, was stuffed into a Twin Otter propeller plane. The cabin was so small and so full of equipment that there was no aisle to walk down. To get to our seats we had climb one at a time over the four canvas-slung seats that were snapped to the floor along one side of the plane. This was a tight fit. The open cockpit doorway (there was no door) allowed us to see past our pilots and the flight instruments and out the front windows. Up until 1991, I'd never been in such a small plane before, and this experience added to my excitement!

At 9 a.m. the two propellers started up, the plane sped down the runway and we were airborne. We flew northwest, over what looked like a vast swampy wilderness. Then we approached the first range of mountains – barren topped with deep green valleys in between. Although it started to rain, we flew on. We flew over another, wider rugged range. These mountains were vertically layered, treeless, massive rocks with razor-sharp crests. We passed over a river canyon that looked only about 50 feet wide but 1,000 feet deep, like a crack in the earth. On the other side of that crevasse was another set of mountains, but these looked as though their tops had been lopped off. Their plateaued summits were covered with vegetation. Dense forests filled the valleys far below.

And then we saw it: the Nahanni, river of the Naha Dene people, a UNESCO World Heritage Site. Our pilots took us down into the valley, below the mountaintops to give us a better view of what we were going to be paddling. We flew over about two days' worth of canoeing along the winding brown river. The river was fast moving, its banks overflowing with flood waters from the recent rains. I noted the oxbow lakes at each twist of the river – they were just like I had learned about in my high school geography classes.

There was no rain in the broad valley when we made our descent and landed on the narrow gravel bank of the Nahanni. We unloaded everything through the back door of the plane, passing bags and barrels, fire-brigade style, from person to person to the edge of the forest. Then the Twin Otter gave birth to three identical canoes – all healthy and safe.

With everything unloaded, the plane could be turned around. To do this, the pilots had to back it down into the river, wheels in the water, because the beach was too narrow. The two propellers revved and the plane took off up over the river valley, circled back above us and flew off out of sight. And then there was silence. The four of us were alone – completely alone. This was it. We'd have to fend for ourselves and make it to our rendezvous point at the end of the river, in 12 days.

We trimmed two of the canoes, ensuring that all our belongings were evenly distributed, and strapped rain covers over the lot. We left the third canoe overturned under the bushes for another group arriving a couple of days later. As the rain started again, there was nothing left to do but to start paddling.

The men were strong paddlers with years of canoeing under their belts, but neither of them had any moving-water experience. So Carolyn paired up with Russ, and I with Gene, to provide some white-water knowledge in each canoe. I got the impression that the men weren't too happy about being outclassed by two women, though they seemed to rationalize the situation by taking the position that they would be taking care of "the girls."

We were warm and dry under the spray covers of the canoes, wearing our spray jackets over cozy fleeces as we paddled downstream. We didn't actually paddle much; mostly we just steered. The current was so strong that we floated at a very quick pace.

The fast-flowing water had been cutting away at the riverbanks, bringing down many trees along the way. We watched a large chunk of sod fall almost two metres into the river. There was a huge boom as the earth hit the water. Riverbank dust billowed up like smoke until the rain dampened it down and the site looked like nothing special had happened. We took this as a warning to stay well clear of undercut banks.

The river zigzagged from one side of the broad valley to the other, often bending back on itself so that it seemed to be flowing eastward, then westward, more than southward. Often just a few metres of land separated the eastbound and westbound stretches. As a result, the speed at which we were floating along the fast-flowing river didn't move us far down the valley. We were often tempted to just get out and portage across the narrow bits of land to the next stretch of river. However, we weren't in any hurry, and portaging our heavy load wasn't appealing or seemingly worthwhile. So we continued to drift, albeit quickly, from one side of the valley to the other and back again, over and over, all day long.

On the left side of the valley, low rain clouds obscured the tops of the mountains. On the right side we could see ice hanging from the peaks. Half-frozen waterfalls and silvery laced runnels disappeared into the thick pine forests that lined the Nahanni valley.

The river, the forests, the valley, the mountains – everything was excessively massive. I felt like a speck on the face of the earth, just floating along wherever the current took me. I contemplated how insignificant I was in this huge, magnificent landscape. My presence seemed irrelevant.

Some 40 kilometres downstream, we stopped to set up our first night's camp on the delta of Hell Roaring Creek. I just love the descriptive place names we use all over this country; this particular creek had more voice than water in its very deep channel. Even the smallest sounds were amplified by the echoes in the canyons and mountains.

The trickle of a single loose rock far above us announced the passing of Dall sheep. They were bright white against the rain-darkened rocky cliffs. Fortunately these animals don't need much camouflage in the summer because few predators would dare to stalk them on the impossibly narrow ledges where they grazed on grasses clinging to the cliff faces.

The four of us quickly established a camp routine, thereby imposing some sense of civilization on the wilderness. This small gesture gave us a feeling of community and belonging and made us more comfortable. We weren't completely lost and exposed to the forces of nature. This was our fundamental human nature revealing itself. Then again, all creatures do this – it's how every being survives.

We set up our tents. The men collected and chopped driftwood for a fire. The women cooked meals. The men washed up. The garbage was burned and everything was stashed away each night. We kept our food in large, thick-plastic barrel packs – not really bear proof, but the odours were at least contained so as not to attract the animals in the first place. We used two of the barrels to prop up an overturned canoe which we used as a table. All cooking and baking was done in a large metal firebox so as not to scorch the earth.

Breakfasts consisted of bacon and eggs, omelettes, pancakes or porridge – and always lots of fresh-brewed coffee. The waft of bacon and coffee was intoxicating in the cool, clear air. Lunches were composed of soups and sandwiches. Stews, spaghetti, stir fries, pizza, baked biscuits and yeast-raised breads made up our dinners. Due to our lack of refrigeration, cured meats and legumes replaced fresh meats after the first few days. The fresh air and exercise whetted our appetites, and we ate well!

Although the evenings were very cold, my winter sleeping bag was toasty warm and comfortable. I lay awake in my tent that first night, writing up my adventures and impressions of the day in my travel journal. We were so far north that even at 3 a.m. I could read and write without needing artificial light. This was my first experience with nearly 24 hours of daylight, but sheer exhaustion kept me from monitoring if it ever did get dark at night. I slept well.

On our second day on the river, it was still drizzling. As there would be no difference in comfort whether we sat around in a wet camp or in a canoe, we decided to continue downstream. We packed everything up wet. We paddled, or drifted, about 90 kilometres that day. The river continued its zigzagging course from one side of the valley to the other, right to the base of the steep mountains. We floated past more Dall sheep on the cliffs, far above the treeline. A beaver swam towards us, slapped its tail, and then dove underwater never to be seen by us again.

We deftly steered around gravel bars and small islands. Occasionally, while we were preoccupied with the scenery, one or the other canoe would become grounded in a shallow rock garden. To avoid stepping out and getting our boots wet, we'd prod and push with our paddles to free our boats and continue our southward journey. So far, this trip had proved to be very laid-back and lazy – not bad for a vacation.

At 3:30 the sun peeked out and we stopped for lunch on a little island in the middle of the river. The island was covered with low shrubs, berry bushes and wildflowers. Amidst the brush we found a camp of four people. How odd that we should bump into other people in this vast wilderness. Then again, where else but on a river route would one expect to meet someone? We shared our lunches and stories and dried off at their fire. The rain started again, this time pouring down – it was time for us to move on. Two hours later we drifted into the campsite above "the Sluice Box" and Virginia Falls.

The Sluice Box is a canyon that compresses the broad, fast-flowing river into an insane rapid with waves curling up at least six metres high. Monstrous boulders break up the waves and the canyon walls deflect them in all directions. The thunder was tremendous. There wasn't a square centimetre of calm water in the channel. The Sluice Box can't be paddled and there is no way out other than over the falls.

We took out at the official campground landing, well north of the Sluice Box. The campsite is far enough upstream, and nestled deep enough in the forest, that the noise and vibration of the river are damped. In fact, I was surprised at how domesticated the Virginia Falls campsite was: boardwalks to protect the soil from erosion, tent sites, fire pits, latrines and even a helicopter pad! A float plane arrived while we were setting up camp, bringing day tourists and park wardens. After officially checking into the park with the wardens, we hiked over to the edge of the Sluice Box and the top of Virginia Falls.

Virginia Falls is 92 metres high (almost twice as high as Niagara), and is 260 metres wide. Here the Nahanni River falls out of the Sluice Box and down around Mason's Rock, a massive towering boulder named for the famous canoeist Bill Mason. The power, noise and spray were overwhelming! The earth itself trembled. My knees were weak as I climbed to the top edge of the rocky canyon wall to gaze at the sight. Even as the full extent of the falls is not visible from the top, I was simply humbled. It is too big, too powerful. Or was it that I was too small, too meek, by comparison. I was happy to be able to walk away with still some sense of self.

On our second day at the falls we went hiking. Our objective was the view from the 915-metre-high Sunblood Mountain. But since Sunblood is on the other side of the river, we had to cautiously paddle well north of the Sluice Box and ferry our canoes across the Nahanni. From the riverbank our trek commenced with a squishy slog through the marshy valley, then up through the forested slope of the mountain.

As we climbed higher, the trees gave way to open scree, a steep slope of small, flat, loose rocks. We followed sheep trails along the scree, where the rocks had become compacted and more stable, switchbacking up the sunlit mountainside. I stopped often to catch my breath, admitting I'm a poor climber. Then we followed along the sparsely forested crest of the mountain. The temperature dropped as we gained altitude. Finally, after 3½ hours, we emerged from the forest onto the barren, rocky plateau.

What a view! We could see all the way up the Nahanni valley to where we had started paddling, and far down the valley to where the river disappeared into narrow canyons. The forest stretched out all around us, right to the curve of the horizon. On that mountaintop, with the world laid out before us, we sat down for a picnic. A couple of ground squirrels joined us. Eventually, each of us got up and added a stone to the cairn that marks all successful climbs. Since standing exposed us to the chilly wind, we hastened our retreat to the shelter of the forest below us. Our descent and return to our comfortable camp was much quicker than the ascent had been.

The official portage to get around the Sluice Box and Virginia Falls starts downstream of the campsite, very close to the rapids. Too close, it seemed. After two nights at the campground, Carolyn and I together nervously paddled each of our two canoes from the campsite to the portage point. The men tentatively watched us from the riverside trail. We made it. The daunting paddle had significantly cut the distance we would have to portage our heavy load.

Our next challenge was the actual portage around the rapids and falls. We had a lot of gear and I couldn't lift any of the barrel packs – they were so heavy. Always helpful, Gene picked up a hefty barrel and strapped it onto my back. As the top of the barrel was flat, another bag was loaded on top, with a tumpline across my forehead to keep the load from falling. Oh, and as my hands were empty, "Here, take these paddles with you while you're at it." I slowly made my way along the boardwalk to the narrow, steep descent next to the falls. The path was less than 60 centimetres wide, hugging the solid rock wall, switchbacking through the spray from the falls. It occurred to me that if I slipped,

I'd be dead before I hit the bottom because the top edge of the barrel was just at the right height to instantly break my neck – lovely thought! Finally on the gravel beach at the base of the falls, I dropped the paddles and let the barrel and pack slip off my back. I felt like I had jumped a few inches off the ground as my back decompressed. After taking a moment to recover, I climbed back up the portage, stopping in a corner to let other overloaded portagers descend past me. I hauled my second load of packs, relieved that others were handling our heavy whitewater canoes.

With all our gear, and ourselves, safely at the base of the waterfall, we had time to look up and appreciate where we were. Virginia Falls is massive, Mason's Rock is massive, Sunblood Mountain is massive, the canyon walls are massive, the noise is massive. Dwarfed and overwhelmed, we stepped closer to one another and together found the strength to carry on.

A rainbow arched over the river, and just in front of us was a nice large eddy where the water seemed to stand still. Beyond the eddy, in the middle of the river, was a large pool of relatively slow-moving water that slid into Fourth Canyon, also known as Five Mile Canyon because it is about five miles long. This yellow and orange canyon is almost 1200 metres deep – awesome.

We loaded up our canoes and ferried out into the centre of the river, then aimed downstream. However, the canyon is not a straight cut; there are numerous tight corners and the rushing water slams off the walls at each turn.

The waves pushed our canoes into the opposing walls, while 1.5-metre-high standing waves washed over us. Since I was in the bow of my boat, I took the brunt of the deluge. One of my contact lenses got slapped out of place, but I couldn't take my hands off my paddle to do anything about it. Frantically I wielded my paddle, pulling the canoe forward, oftentimes drawing only air between waves. Gene, I discovered, was afraid of leaning our canoe so that it could be guided safely through the currents. As a result, we ended up ricocheting from wall to wall. We did a 360° spin, and despite our spray-covers we took on a lot of water. Amazingly, we managed to remain upright.

We limped out of the canyon barely able to stay afloat, and I finally pushed my contact lens back into place. "Let's stop at that eddy over there," Gene suggested, pointing to where the river sped along the straight riverbank and there was no eddy. "How about behind that boulder over there," I countered, and the other canoe escorted us into the safety of the eddy behind that boulder. There Gene and I bailed litres of water out of our canoe. I was so thankful that everything in our canoe, including me, had been waterproofed.

By late afternoon we had settled into a campsite and eaten lunch. The insanity of our voyage through First Canyon was quickly forgotten. As we sat on driftwood overlooking the relatively calm though still fast-moving river, a caribou with a calf wandered by. The sun set behind Sunblood Mountain and the temperature dropped. Snug again in my tent, I reflected on how little time I really had had to enjoy the beauty of the coloured canyon walls. I had been too busy trying to navigate the whitewater to gaze at the splendour.

Sometime in the middle of the night, which was still light, Carolyn started hollering, "Get out of here, you bear!" We all jumped out of our tents to see a black bear in our kitchen area. We clustered together making ourselves look more like one bigger being, waving our arms in the air, clapping and yelling. The bear wasn't interested in us. Eventually Carolyn set off a bear banger with a flash in the air and an explosion so loud that it echoed off the mountains and must have scared everything for kilometres around. The bear was gone. A lone curious golden eagle circled above us.

Due to high water, we had to portage around Figure 8 rapids. By the time we arrived in Third Canyon, we were enjoying the ride, craning our necks to look up at the cliffs around us. I theorized that the profile of European cathedrals, with their many elaborately decorated spires and protrusions, were probably inspired by natural walls such as these. Indeed, a momentous boulder at the side of the river is called Pulpit Rock. And above Pulpit Rock, with some imagination, one can see the preacher. We took some time to climb up behind the Pulpit. From that vantage point, our canoes looked like toy boats down by the river. Yet still the cliffs towered over us, beyond our reach.

Through the next few days, we paddled on, over rollercoasters of standing waves, around whirlpools and through the big waves in Second Canyon. The strong current carried us forward, and as we entered Deadmen Valley the river became broad and shallow. The sun beat down on the rocks, creating an oven-like effect. We made a stop at an old warden cabin to leave entries in the logbook and hang up a tiny paddle I'd carved out of driftwood, to represent our group. The "paddle cabin" is full of such mementoes with the names of previous groups that have come down the river.

We went for a long hike up Dry Canyon Creek. Massive rocks cluttered the canyon; Gene literally pulled me up onto some of those where I couldn't reach the next foothold. Farther up the canyon we finally found some small streams and some very cold pools of water – too cold for bathing, we lamented. Eventually we came to a dead end: a very deep crevasse beyond which a crescent of towering grey stone cliffs marked the end of our route. Sheep stood at the top, bleating down at us. Somewhere in that canyon I lost my watch. Without a watch, and in continuous daylight, I no longer had any idea of time. That was okay; clocks don't matter on the river. We were living on nature's time.

One day, before the others had risen, as I was stepping back into my tent after having used the "facilities," I stopped to watch a black bear amble by the other side of my small tent. In my mind I spoke to it. I said, "I won't make any noise or bother you if you will just keep on going." And it did; the bear disappeared into the bush. After it was gone I woke up the rest of the crew and we checked our campsite. All was in order, although the bear had left his calling card: a huge pile of dung right next to our canoe-table. I went back to bed noting the pleasant delusion of safety my thin nylon tent created.

For days we paddled silently. We passed more caribou. We watched moose swim across the strong current. Eagles flew above us. We were traversing through a foreign land.

I had a lot of time to contemplate life and my own reason for being. At one point I compared myself to an ant on a sidewalk. If I got squashed, if something happened to me out here, in the grand scheme of things, no one would even notice. The world would continue on. I was losing my sense of self.

Fortunately, the next bout of whitewater forced me to pay attention again and concentrate on my own survival. After first scouting out George's Riffle, we had fun paddling over the extra-large standing waves. Then First Canyon presented us with kilometres of twisty rough waves rebounding off the canyon walls. A strong headwind offset the pace at which the water pushed us forward. Always those cliff walls towered over us. Lafferty's Riffle was a washout due to the high water.

Exhilarated, we exited the canyons and floated out into a broad, flat river valley. A strong wind whipped sand up from the shallow banks. A sandstorm of many small twisters spun around us. We had to squint and keep our mouths shut to avoid ingesting the dirt.

Kraus Hot Springs was a wonderful treat, despite smelling of sulphur. Visitors before us had piled up large pebbles forming two big tubs to contain the 35°c water that springs up from the ground. This was the first time in 10 days that I'd purposely immersed myself in water. Naturally, we wouldn't use soap in this natural bathtub, so as not to pollute the water. But still, this felt better than any of the sponge baths I'd been giving myself the last few days.

We had set up our camp on the grassy lawn between the hot springs and a warden cabin. As everyone paddling the Nahanni stops at Kraus, there wasn't any driftwood to be found in the vicinity. The men had to walk far downstream to look for firewood.

In the meantime I wandered around to the back side of the locked cabin and found several downed trees and a large bowsaw chained to one of two sawhorses. Obviously these were supplies left here to be used, else the saw would have been locked up inside the cabin. I struggled to haul one of the trees onto the sawhorses, and then I easily cut it up into short logs. As I was bringing my second armful of logs back to our kitchen area, the men were coming back with a few pieces of driftwood. Surprised, they asked where I'd gotten the wood and I told them what I'd found. Astonished, they dumbly asked: "And the logs were already cut up for you?" "Yes," I answered, "the beaver cut them for me." The tension between the two old-fashioned men and the two strong young women was coming to a head.

That night, Carolyn decided it was time the men helped cook. She told them to follow the directions on the package she gave them: cheesecake. After about half an hour, they returned from the side of the river, tail between legs, and asked for help. Something was wrong. They had followed the directions but still had only a pie pan full of powder. Carolyn needed only a moment to figure out what had happened: instead of a cup of milk, they'd added a cup of powdered milk. Okay, they can't cook, not even a no-cook, chill-set cake.

I was becoming wistful. With only two days left on the river, I wrote in my journal: "I want to continue paddling; paddle for the rest of my life! There are these wonderful hours in which my mind goes blank – I don't think of anything at all when I'm paddling. What a wonderful feeling! I guess that's what a vacation is supposed to be. It's felt like I've been on this river forever, and I'll continue to be on it forever. Bliss."

Those last two days of paddling continued to be fascinating. The landscape flattened out and the river braided around innumerable gravel bars – The Splits.

We passed by the last low ridge of mountains. The trees were arranged like soldiers charging over the hills. Many trees had fallen off the edge, as if slain in battle at the riverbank. Long narrow pines leaned over the river, straining across the water, as if reaching out to us for help. As tempting as it was to reach back to touch them, we knew these were dangerous spectres whose only interest was to drown us with them. Ours was just to bear witness to their fate as we passed by. We steered clear of their threats.

We paddled past the aptly named Twisted Mountain and checked out of the park in the hamlet of Nahanni Butte. We were not done paddling, however. We were about to meet the extremely silty Liard River. To ensure we had enough drinking water, Carolyn had us fill a barrel with relatively less silty water while we were still on the Nahanni. Then, almost without noticing it, we had drifted into the Liard.

We paddled downstream towards Fort Simpson and the Mackenzie River.

Along the way we stopped to rescue a fisherman whose motorboat had grounded on a sandbar. We were initially surprised to see another person in this vast wilderness, let alone someone occupied in industrious activity. But curious things do occur in this northern land: our two human-powered boats were going to the rescue of that engine-powered vessel. Using our paddles, we dug a channel through the sand. Then, with ropes tied from our canoes to the fishing boat, we paddled hard and towed the stranded vessel to freedom. With a wave "thank-you and so long" the fisherman was gone, upstream towards his camp.

Our last campsite was on the Liard River, at Swan Point, a mosquito-infested ridge. This was the first time we all went to bed early, just to get away from the bugs. We packed up quickly the next day and hurried our escape from the swarms of bloodsuckers.

We canoed along the Liard to Blackstone Territorial Park, where we made our first stop back in civilization. We took some time to visit the park museum's display of Dene traditional work. From there we paddled on to the Lindberg Landing homestead.

This isolated, mostly self-sufficient farm was where I got my first hot shower in 12 days. I wanted to linger in the soothing warmth, but knew there was only a limited supply of hot water, and others who also needed to shower. After we were cleaned up and presentable, wearing the cleanest of our dirty clothes, dinner was served to us. Our first non-vegetarian dinners: barbecued moose burgers! And a fresh green salad! And a fully loaded baked potato! Camp food goes down well when you're in the bush, but nothing beats fresh food for taste. That night I fell into a real bed for a good sleep in a solid, wooden, bug-free cottage.

After approximately 460 kilometres, we were off the river and the paddling was over. I was in civilization again.

The next morning, we noshed on a hearty breakfast of bacon and eggs. Then we loaded our gear into an old van, strapped our canoes on top and were driven 150 kilometres down a dirt road (aka the Mackenzie Highway) to Fort Simpson. The drive was uneventful. I wasn't used to being cared for. I just stared out the window at the monotonous landscape of trees and swamps.

Back in Fort Simpson, waiting for our flights to take us home, I sat myself on the ground, leaned back against the airport hangar doors and cried. I'd converted to life in the wilderness, but was being thrown back into my real life in the big city.

9
Wood Buffalo

THE NORTHERN BOREAL PLAINS
CLOSE ENCOUNTERS
WITH BISON AND BEARS

Wood Buffalo is Canada's largest national park, about the size of Denmark or half the size of South Carolina, extending across northern Alberta and into the Northwest Territories. The nearest access to the park is Fort Smith, a town of 2,500 people on the Slave River, just north of the Alberta boundary. Fort Smith is a typical rural community, with low-profile buildings on spacious plots of neatly mown lawns and large parking lots. When I visited in July of 2018, it seemed like everyone drove a pickup truck.

Avoiding a lonely 750-kilometre drive from Yellowknife, I flew into Fort Smith in a small 19-passenger plane. After checking into a two-storey hotel, the largest in town, I walked across the street to Wood Buffalo National Park's visitor centre. I needed to purchase a permit to set up my little tent in the park's Pine Lake campground.

At the visitor centre I discovered that the park had two new log cabins for rent, but with no electricity or running water, so those didn't seem to offer many benefits over my tent. However, when the visitor experience personnel explained that the cabins had screened-in porches, I started to change my mind, having spent the previous three weeks camping in other mosquito-ridden Arctic parks. So, although a two-bedroom cabin seemed a bit large for a single person, I rented one of the cabins without hesitation. The mosquitos were so bad in Fort Smith that I would have rented just a screened porch.

There were no car rental agencies in Fort Smith, but I was of course able to rent a pickup truck. So the following day I loaded my backpack and fresh groceries into the huge truckbed, climbed into the cab and drove to my cabin with the screened-in porch in Wood Buffalo National Park.

The two-lane Pine Lake road, though lined with broad strips of manicured grass, was hemmed in by a wall of trees that created a canyon-like effect. My view was narrowed to the ribbon of road that stretched out before me to the horizon. The rolling landscape of the endless forest meant that radio, cell phone and internet access were lost within the first half-hour of the 90-minute drive. I hoped I hadn't forgotten anything, because I wasn't going to be able to call for help. There'd be no "30-minutes or it's free" deliveries to this park.

As if to validate the name of the park, just after the "Wood Buffalo" sign I had to stop for a small herd of American buffalo – bison – crossing the highway. There were bulls, cows and even a few nursing calves in the group. Some of the animals looked over their shoulders at me as they passed. Some paused on the road, as if to let me know that this was their territory. I of course put the truck into park, rolled down my window and photographed them. When all the bison finally got to the other side of the road, I continued my journey, smiling broadly. Yes, I'd made it into another national park!

I found my cabin to be rustically furnished, including two red Muskoka chairs on the porch. Those became my primary living space. I would sit there reading a novel, writing in my travel journal, eating my meals, sipping wine and watching the 10 p.m. sunsets, all safe from the swarms of mosquitos on the other side of the screen.

My cabin sat atop a slight hill overlooking beautiful Pine Lake. The lake is actually a natural merger of three water-filled karst sinkholes of a type commonly found in this, the most northerly extent of Canada's boreal forest. Spruce, pine, fir, aspen and poplar trees surround the five-mile-long lake in a collage of lush greens. The lake beckoned.

I left a note in my cabin stating where I was going, grabbed my camera and day pack and walked down across the ragged lawn to Parks Canada's canoe shed. The cabin rental included the use of a canoe, so I had the combination key to get into the locked outbuilding. I grabbed some safety gear and a couple of paddles and hauled a blue two-person canoe down to the boat launch. Though my load wasn't heavy, the portage was awkward for a single person. Fortunately it wasn't too far. Once in the canoe, floating on the calm lake, I felt at home. Kneeling in the centre of my canoe, leaning a bit to my paddling side to improve the tracking, I deftly paddled my way around the perimeter of the lake.

The lake was so peaceful. The sun warmed a gentle breeze. The shadows of a few wispy clouds passed across me and the still water. Silently I paddled through stands of lake grasses and flowering arrowheads. I glided past the quiet First Nations lands at the north end of the lake. A pair of loons called to me in their classic haunting way. I rounded the bay and headed south. Vacationers were reposing on cottage decks tucked in amongst the shoreline trees south of my cabin. They waved as I passed. There were children building castles on a sandy beach who didn't seem to mind the cloud of mosquitos they were sitting in. I suspect their parents had coated them with bug repellent. The park campground at the south end of the lake was tranquil. Contented, I quietly paddled back to my dock and locked away the paddling gear.

I looked back at the lake and saw that a pair of brown sandhill cranes had landed at the dock. Of course I stopped to photograph these metretall birds. At the sound of my camera clicking they nimbly spread their two-metre wings and flew off again, disappearing beyond the far end of the lake.

As I sat in my screened porch recording my day's worth of explorations, I was distracted by a dark shadow approaching my cabin. I put down my pen, grabbed my camera and silently stepped out the screen door. There was a black bear ambling down the dirt track directly towards me. I snapped lots of photos, yet the bear didn't seem to realize I was there. I looked down for a moment to adjust my camera settings and when I looked up again the bear was just five metres in front of me! And it still hadn't noticed me standing there. It continued its advance. In a hushed tone I calmly spoke to it: "Hey, bear, you might want to look up and notice me here?" The bear finally looked up and either didn't really care about my presence or didn't relish an encounter. Whatever its motive was, the bear simply turned and walked off into the bush behind my cabin.

Comfortably reseated in one of my Muskoka chairs, I mulled over this encounter. I'd just stood before a wild black bear with only a useless screen door to back away into. Fair enough, the solid cabin door had been just three steps behind me, and my can of bear spray had been in its usual place in my pants pocket. But how quickly could I have reacted if I'd had to? The net result, I shrugged, was that I'd behaved appropriately and no damage had been done. Plus, I had a great story to add to my travel journal!

The following day I set out to explore the park on foot. Despite the very hot weather, I dressed in a long-sleeved camp shirt and long pants. I wore a bug net over my sun hat. I slathered bug dope on the backs of my hands, my only remaining exposed skin. I carried a picnic lunch, drinking water, snacks and first aid kit in my day pack. I tucked my bear spray into my pocket. Again I left a note in my cabin documenting my plans. As I was going to be hiking alone in a forest with no cell phone or internet access, I had to take these precautions.

I parked at the deserted Salt River day use area and walked by a few desolate picnic tables to the river. Peering down from the cliff, I smiled at how the tall, windswept yellow wildflowers softened the appearance of the deep, rough river banks.

Nearby I found the head of the seven-kilometre Salt Pan Lake Trail and commenced my hike along that north loop. The wooded trail starts on a rocky escarpment. An information board explained that the cliff contains gypsum karst crevasses that provide wintering homes for red-sided garter snakes. On that hot summer day I visited, though, nothing slithered across my path.

Once off the rocks, the trail widened and flattened out, making for easy walking. The way was edged with red mushrooms, orchids, purple asters and other wildflowers. Bees and butterflies fluttered about. I was entranced by the stands of aspen. The sunlight accentuated their long, thin, white trunks against the dark green of the deeper forest. Farther along, the trail wound through a burnt section of aspen forest. There, instead of bright white poles, stands of sombre black poles dominated the picture.

At Salt Pan Lake I stepped off the trail for a closer look. The lake is aptly named, as its water is naturally salty, seeping up from the remains of a long-lost inland sea. The shoreline is edged with a white, salty crust because of the water evaporating from the warm shallows. A red squirrel chattered at me from a spruce branch above my head, trying to encourage me to move on. So I did.

It wasn't long before I arrived at an unpaved parking lot at the other end of the trail. A single car was parked there. As there were no benches, logs or rocks to sit on, I sat on the ground at the edge of the forest and ate my lunch. I took my time. Eventually I leaned back against a tree to enjoy the sun and let the heat dry my sweat-soaked shirt. I must have fallen asleep because with a sudden jolt I found myself lying fully prostrate on the ground. Good thing no one had driven into the lot while I'd slept, or they might have thought I was dead, or worse, they might have run over me.

I got up and started hiking along the 8.5-kilometre Benchmark Creek Trail, the south loop, back to my car. At Grosbeak Lake I came upon a couple with two dogs hiking towards me. They'd found that the other end of this trail was closed for maintenance, so they were on their way back to their car, the one I'd seen in the parking lot. I accompanied them back out of the forest, and we shared our stories of our park experiences. I was grateful when they offered to drive me back to my car parked at the trailhead.

Since my cabin had no shower or tub, I went for a cleansing swim in the lake after each day's explorations. The mosquitos always hastened my entry into the cool water, and kept me in there probably longer than I really wanted. By the time I'd finished swimming the 200 metres to the reedy shallows on the other side of the lake and back again, I'd be chilled. Eventually the cold would drive me out of the lake, and the attacking mosquitos would force me back to the safety of my porch.

The following day, I set out to hike the Lakeside Trail for 1.5 kilometres from the campground to the head of the Lane Lake Trail, and then up that for 6.5-kilometres and back again. I didn't get far.

I'd stopped to take a photograph of a small sinkhole lake beside the Lane Lake Trail, but because a few pine trees obscured my shot I took a couple of steps off the footpath. As my camera shutter went click, a branch snapped a couple of metres to my right. I looked up and peered around a clump of aspen trees. A very large bison was peering back at me! The animal must have been lying on the ground so that I hadn't noticed it before. It was now standing almost beside me. Gingerly I started retreating. But before I got to the trail, the monster, 20 times bigger and heavier than me, turned and went rampaging through the forest away from me, frantically breaking every branch and tree that stood in its way. My heart was racing in alarm even though I was standing still, frozen with fear.

When the clamour finally stopped, I tentatively stepped back onto the trail and took a few minutes to compose myself. I reminded myself that bison, also known as American buffalo, are what Wood Buffalo National Park was designed to protect. It was not really surprising that I'd come across one of them in the forest. Once settled enough to continue my hike, I proceeded more cautiously. A few metres farther on I heard more branches breaking. There were cracks on both sides of the path. Through the trees I discerned the dark shadows of several more buffalo. The whole herd was in the forest ahead of me! This time it was me that turned around, but I withdrew quietly. Hastily I walked the three kilometres back to the safety of my car.

The drive back to my cabin was unusually uneventful. Every other time I'd driven along that road I'd had to stop and wait for bison to get out of the way. That afternoon, there weren't any blocking the road, and I well knew where they were: in the forest blocking the trail. However, later that evening, as I sat on my porch eating dinner, I ascertained that my supposition wasn't quite correct. A lone bison wandered by my cabin. It stopped to roll in a sandy depression and then disappeared down the laneway, leaving a cloud of dust behind him. There's always someone that has to be different.

On my last day in the park I took advantage of Parks's guided visits to the Salt Plains. Starting at the viewpoint at the top of an escarpment, four of us, including two guides, surveyed the grassy plains that stretch out to the horizon. In the foreground flowed the meandering Salt Creek, with huge white pelicans bobbing on the current. Then there were small clusters of pine trees and expanses of green shrubs, colourful wildflowers and maroon samphire plants growing amongst a myriad of small ponds and creeks. In the far distance, where the specifics of the landscape blur, broad brush strokes of white colour the land. Those are the pans of salt left over from the ancient inland sea.

Our little group climbed down the steep 350-metre cliffside trail to the plain. Under the shadow of the escarpment the land was crystalline white. Salt. Taking advantage of this natural exfoliant, I walked barefoot on the warm, damp salt pan. I left my footprints next to those of a bear and a wolf who'd crossed the plain before me. Though I hadn't seen the animals, I was quite certain they hadn't come for the spa value. More likely they'd simply savoured this giant salt lick.

Parks staff took us to where a small creek bubbles up from the ground and distributes its saline solution over the plain. I dipped my finger into the liquid and had a lick. Yup, I concurred with the experts that this water is much saltier than any ocean. Evaporation had concentrated the salt remaining in the leftovers from the now underground sea.

The hike up the cliff wasn't as bad as I'd expected. I walked slowly but continuously along the switchbacks, chatting with the other tourists on the trip. We were surprised at how quickly we'd arrived back up at the lookout. We still had plenty of time to explore, this time with a scope.

Somewhere about a third of the way to the horizon, in a clump of green weeds, we spotted four large birds. Through a powerful scope supplied by the park staff, we could barely discern two 1.5-metre-tall white adults and their two nearly fully grown young. By their shape and stance we knew what they were: whooping cranes! I was so excited for this rare sighting. With just over 800 individual birds left, whooping cranes are a seriously endangered species. Due to hunting and habitat loss, their numbers had been down to fewer than 25 in the early 1940s. In the '90s my friend and fellow Explorers Club member William Lishman (*Father Goose*, 1995) had used his ultralight planes to help teach captivity-raised whooping cranes to find their migratory route. I felt sorry I couldn't tell Bill that I'd met some of the descendants of "his cranes" – he passed away just a few months before my trip to Wood Buffalo National Park.

In 1983 Wood Buffalo was designated a World Heritage Site by UNESCO because it contains the natural habitat of the last wild whooping cranes and one of the largest free-roaming herds of wood bison, as well as several other unique features. Despite the immense size of this park and the efforts to protect what's within its boundaries, its environment is threatened by reduced water levels and increased pollution. As I experienced and learned about the park, I became acutely aware of the importance of recording what it was like during my visit. The park is changing, and its plants and animals will, for better or worse, adjust to their changing environment.

10
Thaidene Nëné Reserve

THE ADVENTURE CONTINUES

In 2019, a few weeks after I finished my personal mission to visit all the national parks, Parks Canada announced the opening of Thaidene Nëné National Park Reserve. Yes, I thought, the adventure continues! Not that I can't go back and revisit the other parks (which is always a pleasure), but it's fun to see and learn new things.

I started my exploration of this new park by researching and reading up on everything I could find about Thaidene Nëné. But there wasn't much beyond a brief description on Parks's website, a few news releases and some academic articles. I followed those scant notes, interviewing scholarly researchers and people living near the new park to see where their knowledge would take me.

Thaidene Nëné is located on the east arm of Great Slave Lake in the Northwest Territories. The reserve's more than 14,000 square kilometres of wilderness is the traditional home of the Łutsël K'é Dene, who have lived, hunted and fished there since the beginning of time. During the last 50 years, a relative microsecond in all that history, the Łutsël K'é Dene worked with Parks Canada and the NWT government to find a way to protect their land. Eventually, the proposal of a much-needed hydroelectric dam, which would have flooded a vast area, seems to have intensified the need to come to an agreement. Thaidene Nëné National Park Reserve was finally created, showcasing another aspect of our country.

Being managed jointly by the Indigenous community and Parks Canada, the park is labelled a "park reserve." In 2020 the Łutsël K'é Dene were recognized by the United Nations for their work in establishing the Thaidene Nëné ("Land of the Ancestors") Indigenous Protected Area, which includes the new national park.

Like so many of the lands protected by the Canadian parks system, Thaidene Nëné has no road access. The only ways to get there are by air or by a very long boat ride from Yellowknife. In the winter people can get to the park by snowmobile from the nearest community, Łutsël K'é (Place of Cisco Fish), which itself has no road access. So how do I get there, and what will I do when I arrive?

My research led me to a high-end fly-in fishing camp, Frontier Lodge, right on the edge of the park. I'm no fisherwoman, but I could see myself based in a cozy-warm cabin, exploring the park in a series of day trips. Frontier's fishing packages include daily guided boat excursions, so I'd have a motorboat at my disposal. If I went in August and the weather was good, I might even be able to spend a few nights sleeping in the park – on thick carpets of lichen, under the northern lights! I hoped too to see some of the moose and bears that roam the area, the beavers whose pelts had attracted Europeans to North America, and the caribou that have always sustained the Dene. Oh, and I definitely wanted to take a boat into town one day, to meet the people. I could learn so much more from them, about their history and their relationship with the land.

Wow, I thought. This would be a very different experience for me. I wouldn't have to organize and prepare my access to the park, shelter, food, protection from animals, and, and, and…. The potential advantages of staying in a resort were outweighing the costs.

The manager of Frontier Lodge was especially excited about my ideas because the lodge is now owned by the community. They were eager to show off their beautiful land and share their knowledge. And they promised the fishing is so good that they'd make an angler out of me yet!

I wasn't so sure about the fishing part, but if someone were to catch a nice trout (my favourite type of fish), I'd be more than happy to gut, clean, cook and eat it. I'd be sharing some of it, too, since I'd heard their lake trout can weigh up to 27 kilos! That's a lot of yum.

My friend John Borley, who's explored a few of Canada's remote national parks with me, was eager to join me on this trip as well. However, John's primary reason for wanting to go to Thaidene Nëné was that, as a fisherman, he really wanted the fly-in fishing experience. So in January 2020 we enthusiastically sent in our deposits to make our reservations for the last week of August.

And then the Covid-19 pandemic broke out.

The Northwest Territories closed its boundaries to all but residents and essential service providers, and our planned escapade became a coronavirus casualty. In the grand scheme of things, John and I were happy to be safe and healthy, although saddened for being stuck at home. Optimistically, we rebooked our adventure to 2021. We have something to look forward to!

THE WESTERN MOUNTAINS

11
Gwaii Haanas Reserve

KAYAKING TO TOTEM POLES

The summer of 2017 was an extraordinarily hot and dry one in British Columbia. As a result, a record number of wildfires were devastating the forests. On Haida Gwaii ("place of the Haida," formerly known as the Queen Charlotte Islands), I think we found the only rain in the province that season. It rained every day of the week-long kayaking trip Martin and I did in Gwaii Haanas National Park Reserve. This Pacific rainforest was living up to its reputation, if not to the sunny-skied photos in the tourist brochures.

We joined a group of eight others in the community of Sandspit on Haida Gwaii, 750 kilometres northwest of Vancouver. It was raining when our small jet landed and as we pushed an airport trolley laden with our luggage down the road to our bed and breakfast. The next morning, the skies were still heavily overcast and the dense forest around the town was dripping. The ground was awash with puddles. Moresby Explorers collected us with their old van and drove us down a very long, winding, muddy road through the mountains to a rough camp and boat launch. I was grateful for the motion-sickness pills I'd swallowed before the drive. During the two-hour trip, mostly along unpaved, bumpy logging roads, we got our first impressions of these islands: besides the massive logging machinery, there were bald eagles and deer, and even a black bear with two cubs in the woodland of cedar, pine and western hemlock. There was a slight drizzle in the cool air when we arrived at Moresby Camp.

Over thick fleece jackets we donned the heavyweight raincoats and PFDS Moresby offered us for the next part of our journey. We climbed into a large inflatable motorboat for a 2½-hour journey to the southern islands. For most of the way on the water I kept my face down to avoid the freezing sting of the oncoming rain and ocean spray. The roar of the engine and the boat crashing through the choppy ocean waves rendered conversation impossible. Periodically I would peer over the boat's gunwales to see where we were, but it was impossible to discern the landscape because of the low, dark clouds. Finally we slowed down, almost to a coasting pace. We were carefully making our way through Burnaby Strait between Moresby and Burnaby islands. We'd arrived in Gwaii Haanas – the "islands of wonder."

The boat dropped us off in Bag Bay, where our guides Jess and Alyssa of Tofino Expeditions were waiting for us. We unloaded our gear and food bags on the narrow, sandy beach and transferred our raincoats to a tour group who'd just finished paddling in the park. They in turn left us their kayaks and camping equipment. As the motorboat sped off back to Moresby camp, I looked around our secluded little bay.

I stepped through a gap in the dripping grey mosses that draped from the tall seaside trees. Behind those heavy, sodden curtains, the sky was blotted out by a ceiling of dark-green conifers. Rain dripped down through unseen cracks and was being sopped up by a thick apple-green moss which carpeted the forest floor. This verdant, soggy ground cover undulated over giant fallen trees and massive boulders, between huge ferns and down to a tiny stream which slowly drained towards the sea.

In this Tolkienesque setting, Martin and I chose a tent on a very tiny bit of flat area hemmed in by a couple of huge hemlocks rotting on the ground. I lay down inside the tent to test its levelness, and when I sat up again I noticed a big fat yellow thing just inside the door. It was a 20-centimetre-long banana slug. Not having anything handy with which to scoop it up, I gingerly picked it up between my thumb and forefinger. Ugh, it was soft and squishy! Hastily I flung the creature out the door. Yuck, my fingers were covered with slug slime! I wiped my hands on the damp moss outside and then dried them on my pant legs.

We got to do our first kayaking that afternoon after the drizzle subsided. Besides confirming everyone's paddling abilities, this short trip included an important stop at a small creek that cascaded into the end of the bay. This creek would be the source of a day's worth of fresh water. Carefully we filled the bladder containers which would always be transported at our feet in the kayak cockpits. We purified this drinking water one litre at a time, using hi-tech UV wands, as we transferred the water into our personal drinking bottles.

By dinnertime a cold rain was falling again. We huddled under the kitchen tarp to gorge on spaghetti and tomato sauce. As we ate, a deer wandered into our camp and grazed on the greenery between our tents. After dinner we saw a bald eagle at the top of a very tall pine tree. We hadn't noticed its arrival, but the raptor sat there silently watching us as we let the beach intertidal zone wash away our dirty dishwater. Our bit of organic waste would feed the seaweed and creatures which would eventually feed that eagle. Although cold and wet, this place was incredibly marvellous in its natural design.

I downed a cup of hot tea and made for bed. Martin joined me shortly. As I lay there writing the day's entry in my journal, I became very aware of some strange sounds outside. Large, heavy raindrops were bouncing off the taut tent roof. I muttered aloud that they sounded like popcorn popping. Nonchalantly, Martin replied, "That's an awful lot of popcorn. The forest must be full by now." I fell asleep imagining we were camped in a bowl full of the puffy snack. It rained all night.

We awoke to a blue sky with just a few wisps of white fluffy clouds. The sun was out and the day was warm. For the first time since arriving on the islands, we could see the mountaintops. Dark-green forests enveloped the steep slopes from the depths of the valleys to the peaks of the mountains. The full majesty of the wilderness was reflected in the calm sea. Gwaii Haanas was inviting us to explore it.

After a quick breakfast we took advantage of a very low tide to visit the marine life in Burnaby Narrows. We spent a couple of hours in our kayaks, drifting on the shallow water, admiring the variety of life below us. There were bat stars – blue, red and brown ones. There were abalone, oysters, mussels, jellies and small fish, all making their living in the seaweed, kelp and sea lettuce gardens. Jess lifted out a sea cucumber, almost 45 centimetres long, slimy and brown with bright-red knobs all over it. We all took photographs. After gently placing the creature back into the water, Jess then lifted out a huge moon snail. Being out of the water, the animal slowly drew its fat, gooey grey body back into its fist-sized shell. That beautiful swirled shell belied its grotesque owner-inhabitant.

When we got back to our camp, I stood on the driftwood- and seashell-strewn beach thinking about the wonders we had just seen. I gazed up and was distracted from my contemplations by an odd dark object in the sky. In a flash I remembered: the solar eclipse! I immediately turned away, worried that I'd already looked at it too long. I called my friends' attention to the event. One couple had brought along safety glasses to observe the eclipse. Using these specialized shields, we took turns viewing the sun, which had become three-quarters hidden by the moon. While we hadn't experienced a dark shadow, we were still satisfied with our exciting activities that morning. Wow, I thought, and we'd only been in the park for less than a day!

As we sorted through camping gear, the sky clouded over again, first deceiving us with a beautiful rainbow at the end of the bay and then becoming dark. The rain followed quickly, and we had another night of popcorn. It was still raining the next morning when we struck camp. All our gear was to be stowed inside waterproof bags. I stuffed our soaking wet tent into a dry bag. Amazingly, everything – personal effects, food, cooking utensils and camping equipment – either fit into the holds or could be strapped to the decks of our long, slender sea kayaks. We paddled off early with the outgoing tide.

I kept my face down to prevent the rain from running down into the front of my paddling jacket. Watching the dark ocean instead of looking up at the mountains, I noticed an interesting phenomenon: the fresh water of the rain drops was bouncing off the surface of the salty seawater, creating thousands of tiny silver pearls. These sparkly spheres would roll along the surface for a few seconds before dissolving and becoming part of the sea. Entranced by the variety of water, I paddled along. Everyone paddled silently with their own meditations.

Eventually, though, we got cold. The constant rain had seeped through our waterproof jackets and mixed with the perspiration created by hours of paddling. Time for a break. We took out on a sweeping arc of beach and happily the rain stopped. However, all the firewood we could find was soaking wet, so it seemed to take forever to get a fire going. Finally, standing in our underwear, drinking hot soup, we held sticks hung with our wet clothes over a smoky fire. Eventually our clothing dried out, sort of, but it would reek of woodsmoke for the rest of the trip. We put back in and paddled on.

While there are no organized campgrounds or facilities in Gwaii Haanas, there are places where people have traditionally camped. These sites are set well back into wind-sheltered bays, with freshwater sources nearby. They are perfect refuges when the sea is too rough for boating. We had to find the next such place, but we also wanted to enjoy the kayaking and the scenery while the weather was relatively good.

Each bay we passed seemed to have its own resident bald eagle or pair of them, always perched high up in the trees. On the beaches below the raptors, Sitka black-tailed deer grazed on seaweed. Cute otters scrambled over the rocky shores. We drifted by one headland for a few minutes watching a black bear hunt in the shallow water. The bear would grab something in its jaws, take it ashore and eat it, then go back into the water for more. We continued paddling farther southward, exploring the eastern side of Moresby Island.

At the next campsite, I opened up the tent dry bag and poured out the rainwater that had pooled on top of the compressed nylon. Then I pulled out the sopping wet tent. Martin stretched it out over the pebbly beach, hoping the breeze would dry it out a bit before nightfall. The tent was still damp when we set it up under the trees that evening. We tied the guy-ropes to large stones and tightened them as best we could. That night, although it poured again like popcorn, our tent, wet as it already was, did keep the rain out. We were always warm and dry inside our little sanctuary.

One of our camps was near Raspberry Cove at the southern end of Moresby Island. From there we paddled through the drizzle across to Rose Harbour, a long defunct whaling station on Kunghit Island. A few private homes are still occupied in this off-grid settlement. We spent some time at a guest house, sitting by the warm woodstove, leafing through photo albums that chronicled the history of the whaling community. Then we walked through the community to see the remnants of those old factories that had operated between 1911 and 1942. Scattered about the forest and beaches were thick oxidized chains, a corroded iron boiler, giant oil containers and rusty company signs. Until this stuff eventually decomposes back into the earth, it will continue to be just junk left behind, littering the landscape, I thought.

The highlight of our time on Kunghit was a short hike up through the rainforest to a traditional Haida canoe that had been partially carved out of an old cedar tree. No one knows exactly why the canoe was never finished, but it has been decaying under a blanket of moss for many, many years. The tree is now just a shadow of the canoe it might have become, the canoe slowly being reclaimed by the forest.

On our way back to our campsite we paddled past a rock with several sea lions resting on it. One of them looked up at us, while the others just looked back over their shoulders to confirm that we hadn't come too close. They couldn't be bothered moving; they simply went back to their naps. We paddled on.

We waited for good weather, calm seas and a favourable tide before making our final paddle across to Anthony Island, called SGang Gwaay ("Wailing Island") in the Haida language. Fortunately we didn't have to wait too long. The following day, the sun was high, there was a slight ocean swell and we were in fine spirits to make the three-kilometre crossing from the southernmost tip of Moresby.

We approached the smaller island from the north and entered a charming archipelago of tiny wooded islets. Enchanted lagoons and waterways enticed us. We surrendered to the seduction and paddled our kayaks through the labyrinth, always curious about what we'd see around the next corner. Jess and Alyssa expertly guided us towards a particular beach, the entry way to an ancient Haida village.

The village of Nan Sdins is a UNESCO World Heritage Site because it contains the remnants of the longhouses, ancient totem poles and other artifacts, as well as the spirits of the peoples who once lived there. A young Haida lady, a member of the Watchmen who look after the site, had us entranced with oral stories of her people and the spirits that call this place home. Some of the totem poles identified the family clans of the old houses. Others are monuments to deceased people of distinction. The village VIPs were laid to rest in bentwood boxes placed in cavities atop their totem poles. The carvings on each pole, like labels, identify the spirit, person, clan and history of the souls.

The buildings and totems are being allowed to decay naturally, to return to the earth according to Haida tradition. As a result, mosses have grown over the fallen roof beams and poles. I tentatively walked up to a few of the still-standing totem poles, craned my neck and looked up. Their vivid colours have long since faded to grey, their once-crisp carvings softened to mere impressions of their former characters. Although these souls looking out over the sea have taken on a ghostly appearance, their presence remains – or perhaps that's just my Western interpretation.

Tourists are not allowed to camp on the island, so we spent just three hours visiting Nan Sdins. I would have liked a lot more time to explore SGang Gwaay, but we had to paddle back to one of the other islands before weather and seas turned sour. The Haida spirits seemed to favour us, though, providing us with safe passage to tiny Ross Island just south of Moresby.

There, after a week and some 125 kilometres of paddling, we set up camp for the last time in a delightful forest. I slept soundly through the night rain. The following morning, a heavy fog shrouded the world. We radioed Moresby Explorers, and yes, the motorboat was on its way to collect us. Sombrely, we struck camp and packed up all our wet gear. The fog was just lifting as the boat arrived. Working together, we loaded everything into the large inflatable, our six kayaks strapped to a metal frame over top of the boat. After some four and a half hours of fast, bumpy motoring in heavy seas, our adventure was over. When we arrived back at Moresby camp, a rainbow crowned the bay. A perfect ending to a magical visit.

12
Pacific Rim Reserve

KAYAKING WITH ORCAS

In 1997 Martin, my fiancé at the time, and I decided we wanted to explore Canada's Pacific coast. We had camping, hiking and kayaking in mind. Pacific Rim National Park Reserve was the obvious place to start this adventure. So we flew 3400 kilometres from Toronto to Vancouver, rented a car and took the ferry across to Vancouver Island. The park is on the west coast of the island, requiring a drive through steep, snow-topped mountains.

As Martin doesn't drive, I took the wheel. My first challenge was to learn how to drive in the Vancouver Island Mountains. The automatic transmission protested the steep inclines, and I began to understand the purpose of those low manual gears. We shared the narrow highway with massive logging trucks and RVs. The deep sheer drops and hairpin turns kept me hugging the edge of the road on the up side of the mountains. Martin volunteered no comment, and I was too busy paying attention to the challenging drive to ask him how he was doing: motion sick?

I took a break in the centre of Vancouver Island for a short walk in Cathedral Grove, a stand of giant Douglas fir and red cedar trees. We strolled with our heads bent back, gazing 75 metres up towards the crowns of these 800-year-old evergreens. One tree had a split through the middle so big I could stand inside it. Several other giants lay on the ground, a massive Pacific storm having brought them down earlier in the year. Amazing that something could live so long and then just be wiped out, I thought.

We had reserved a "drive-in" campsite in the Green Point campground in Pacific Rim National Park Reserve. On the way to our site we saw a black bear foraging on the side of the roadway, prompting me to make a mental note to keep our food and smellies (toothpaste, deodorants and other toiletries that might smell tasty to a bear) stored in the trunk of our car.

We parked the car in our "driveway" and set up our three-person dome tent next to the picnic table and firepit. There were plenty of trees providing shelter and a buffer from the neighbouring tent sites, all of which were occupied. Across the road was a trail to the beach. This was the idyllic style of car-camping I'd remembered from my childhood: the appearance of wilderness within reach of the safety of a car and civilization.

For dinner I stir-fried potatoes, onions, eggplant and some pork chops, all in one large frying pan on our camp stove. Crows and jays squawked around us as we dined alfresco at our picnic table. This was cozy. We got everything cleaned up and stashed away before Vancouver Island's famous rain started. Although it rained all through the night, our tent and sleeping bags stayed comfortable.

I awoke the next morning to the odd whistling call of a Wilson's warbler. The rain had stopped but my head was heavy with wisps of a migraine. I would have to take things easy that day. After a breakfast of granola and camp coffee, we explored down the path to Long Beach.

Although it was Canada Day, we shared the beach only with the birds. What was that crow digging up? We tried digging too, and found red worms under the air holes in the sand. We also found seashells and crab carapaces caught up in the tangle of seaweed at the water line. A small fish stranded on the beach suddenly came back to life when I touched it. With cupped hands I tossed it back into the sea to give it another chance. A closer look at what we first took for air bubbles on the sand revealed them to be thumbnail-sized jellyfish. I waded into the ocean and stared down at a couple of red-purple, multi-legged sun stars in the water. We eventually passed another couple who were complaining there was nothing to see on the beach – where were they looking?! "Oh, by the way, look, there's a bald eagle flying above us!" I pointed.

At 16 kilometres, Long Beach is aptly named. Our walk led us around countless coves and bays. On the other side of one rocky point we finally found the crowds of people. We sat on a piece of driftwood near the lifeguard station to eat our lunch. There were families flying kites and children building sand castles. A dog chased a flock of sandpipers. There were wetsuited surfers and kayakers. A few people sat lazily in folding chairs, reading, napping or simply enjoying doing nothing at all. My head slowly cleared as we wandered back to our camp. By the time we got to our tent, my legs were aching from having walked so long on the soft beach, but the soles of my feet were nice and smooth!

Needing a bit more adventure one day, we hired a water taxi to take us to Meares Island, just outside the park. The island's Big Tree Trail is a 4.2-kilometre route, partially boardwalked – that's the popular section. The rest of the path was a muddy slog, and we just had to follow it. Due to the heavy rains, the mud was at least knee deep in places – we didn't stand still long enough to find out how much deeper we might sink. In fact, if we stopped too long, our feet got sucked down. Martin almost lost a shoe down there. We slid over slippery roots and fell into the mud. Yup, we got down and dirty. We quickly abandoned any attempt at staying clean and dry. For three hours we slogged through the moss-draped forest, around massive ferns, spiny plants and hemlocks. So why were we doing this? Well, to gawk at the thousand-year-old western red cedar trees, some with girths of more than 18 metres! The uber-high canopy held the heat and humidity in, so sweat streaked our muddy faces as we tried to find our way through this rainforest. With so much to look at, we didn't always pay attention to the trail signs and got lost several times. Eventually we broke out into the bright sunshine on the beach and breathed in the refreshing sea air. Covered in mud and sweat, we were happy.

In the park, we also explored in ways that were less adventurous but offered more formal education. There were many information boards along the park routes, explaining about the natural environment and human history of the area. The three-kilometre Gold Mine trail and the two-kilometre Rain Forest trail were definitely easier, being on dry land and boardwalks, accessible to people not wanting to get dirty! We got to see more of those giant cedars and hemlocks without getting our feet wet.

The Wickanninish Centre had super-informative exhibits about the ocean, the land and the Nootka people. We learned about how these Indigenous nations used the resources around them to live and thrive. They were very adept and creative, also producing beautiful art. Some of these traditions are still alive today. We completed our visit with a stop for dinner in the adjacent restaurant. The raised terrace and picture windows looked out over the ocean with the beach spread out on either side of us. The limitless view suggested endless possibilities for more adventures.

After getting up close and into the details of the park, we drove over to nearby Radar Hill, where we got a bird's-eye view of the coast, its beaches and islands. This perspective gave us an appreciation of how broad and wild Canada's West is. This is where the massive mountains, trees and endless beaches butt up against the Pacific Ocean. West of here is nothing but water, out to the horizon.

One day we took a boat tour from the municipality of Ucluelet to the Broken Group Islands. Our little craft passed by the docks where fishing boats were offloading their catch into vats of ice. We motored out of the harbour and across Barkley Sound. To the east, above the rugged wave-lashed coast, logging-scarred mountains rose over us. To the west, between what seemed like an infinite number of rocky islands, we could see the expanse of the Pacific. Looking more closely, we discovered that some of those rocks on the islets were harbour seals. Other islands served as resting places for Steller sea lions – we laughed as their little ears twitched to listen for our approach.

We transferred from our boat to a Zodiac to land on Turret Island, where we had half an hour to explore. There were several informal paths through the woods and along the shore of this small island. We wandered along, looking out over the beach where kayakers and a couple of canoeists were camped. We were keeping an eye out for whales, as we had been doing since arriving on the Pacific coast. Unfortunately, there were still none to be seen that day, our last day in the park.

The following week we found the whales on the other side of Vancouver Island, in Johnstone Strait. We were paddling our kayaks on a wilderness camping trip with 12 other people, including two guides from Wild Heart Adventures. A pod of orcas gently swam by, barely causing a ripple. They quietly rose next to us, as though to find out what we were. A huge black eye glistened above the water right next to me! And in a moment it was gone.

The next day, we had a similar experience as we paddled around the nearby islands: we'd find ourselves temporarily in the middle of a group of orcas. Again we stopped paddling as these giants simply passed us by. We fumbled with our cameras, but couldn't get any decent photographs from the kayaks, as we, the sea and the whales were all in motion.

On our way back towards camp, we found a mother orca and her calf rubbing themselves against the pebbles on the edge of a beach! The mother was largely above the waterline. Amazing! As we bobbed in the water watching these two, a male swam by on our other side. These giants were all around us, yet they didn't seem to pay any attention to us. As we didn't want to risk disturbing them, we tried to keep our distance. Eventually our own hunger persuaded us to paddle back to camp for dinner. We couldn't stop chattering about our awesome experiences!

13
Gulf Islands Reserve

THE SALISH SEA
CHOMPING ON WILD KELP

In late August 2017 Martin and I drove our rental car onto a BC ferry in Vancouver for the two-hour ride to Gulf Islands National Park Reserve. The sun had set behind the many coastal islands just after we set sail, and we arrived on Pender Island in the dark. The night air was very warm. As I drove out of the brightly lit hold of the ferry, I realized that there are no street lights on the island. The place was pitch black.

I crept along the dark, meandering forest road, fumbling with one hand to find the headlight switch on the unfamiliar dashboard. Vehicles behind us were honking, their drivers swearing at us through open windows as they tried to pass. In the darkness I couldn't see anything inside or outside my car. As I had no idea where the sides of the road were, I had no choice but to stop where I was. More yelling from the other vehicles. Frazzled, I too swore as I finally got my car's dashboard and headlights on, and saw that I was stopped in the middle of a very narrow two-lane road. I fell in behind the line of cars that had made it past me. Martin, sitting next to me, did his best not to further antagonize me with unhelpful advice (he doesn't drive).

We finally came to a single street light at the turnoff to South Pender Island.

All the other vehicles continued along the dark main road, but our GPS insisted that we veer onto that tiny sideroad. Gingerly I followed that route, creeping across a one-lane bridge, through rock-blasted mountainsides and on into the darkness. We could see only as far as our high beams illuminated. Despite the hostility of the other drivers, I wished that at least one of them was also driving along this lonely road with me.

At long last the GPS announced "You have reached your destination." Martin and I strained to read the house numbers posted alongside the road. Spotting the sign for our bed and breakfast, I carefully manoeuvred into the driveway, around a cluster of trees, and parked in the glow of a house light. We were late, but we were there.

Although I was completely stressed out and exhausted, I held in my frustrations as our gracious hosts greeted us and showed us to our room. It was the best I could do to thank them sweetly and go to bed. I was beyond appreciation of having made it to Gulf Islands National Park Reserve. Sleep.

Despite the challenges I'd personally faced getting there, this national park reserve is actually easily accessible and unbelievably beautiful. Under the warm morning sun, I was finally able to see the world around me and was immediately captivated. The lovely waterways and forested mountains of these islands are absolutely charming. With a steaming cup of cappuccino in hand, I sat back in an armchair on the veranda of our room and, sighing, looked out at the neighbouring islands.

Gulf Islands National Park Reserve is made up of a multitude of small plots of land scattered over several islands, as well as some entire islets, in the Salish Sea between Vancouver Island and the USA. The public is not allowed in many sections of the park, in order to protect some of this unique ecosystem, with its sub-Mediterranean climate, from logging and the expansion of "cottage country."

In spite of the impact of having their own homes on these islands, many residents actively support awareness of and preservation of the island wilderness. Volunteers maintain a series of beaches and hiking trails that link into the national park network. Martin and I set out to take advantage of some of those eco-tourism facilities.

The oceanfront trailhead of the two-kilometre William Walker Trail was just a few metres from our lodgings, so that's where Martin and I started our explorations of the Gulf Islands. The footpath switchbacked up the steep mountainside and around monstrously huge cedars and pine trees. After a breathtaking, sweaty climb, we followed the well-worn path onto a sun-warmed clear-cut plateau.

Shiny-leaved salal shrubs, the first vegetation that naturally regrows in logged areas, covered the open field we found ourselves in. The remains of many massive trees stuck out of the brush all around the trail. I noted one cedar stump, a good two metres in diameter, that still bore the slot that had been cut into it. A logger would have stood on a plank stuck into that slot while he cut down the giant tree towering above him.

There were no chainsaws running while we hiked that day, so the forest was quiet. The only sounds we heard came from the grey jays squawking in the branches above us. A few butterflies fluttered about, and there were only a few mosquitos around. We continued up the trail, crossing several times over a still-active logging road. We passed a few surviving behemoths: towering conifers purposely left standing to preserve some of the woodland's age-diversity.

Martin and I followed the William Walker Trail into one of the national park plots and to the end of the park's 2.3-kilometre Mount Norman Trail. We veered onto that park trail, climbing ever higher up to the peak of Mount Norman.

The woods in the park were markedly different from those in the lower sections of the mountain. This was a second-growth forest with pine trees planted in well-defined rows. The young trees were very tall and skinny, with bushy green caps. The lower branches were grey and scratchy-looking, dead from lack of light filtering down through the high canopy. There wasn't much undergrowth. Probably due to the density of the new plantation, several trees had tumbled down onto the trail. We had to break off dead branches and brush aside a jumble of sharp, raspy twigs in order to clamber over these fallen pines.

At the 240-metre-high summit a short side trail led us to a look-out where we made ourselves comfortable on the benches of a lovely wooden viewing platform. With our backs to the wooded hilltop, we ate our sandwiches while enjoying the almost 180° view. Directly below lay Bedwell Harbour, dotted with white-sailed boats, each perfectly mirrored in the calm waters between North and South Pender islands. Pretty cottages and beaches dotted the far shore. Beyond the low, forested hills of North Pender, past the myriad dark-green islands dappling Swanson Channel, the majestic mountains of Vancouver Island enticed through a hazy sky. We wistfully watched a ferry on its way to Victoria, but that journey would have to wait for another day. We still had lots to explore on the Gulf Islands.

From the lookout, Mount Norman Trail led us down the steep slope, along a pitted dirt road, to Ainslie Point at the end of the harbour. Rather than hike back over the hill to our lodging, we decided to follow the two-lane paved road we'd driven the previous night. In the daylight, we now saw that the street winds between blasted-out cliffs and through a dark forest and then follows along the seashore. On our way we stopped to admire the intricacy of the one-lane trestle bridge that connects North and South Pender. This was the wooden structure we'd barely recognized driving over the night we'd arrived on the islands.

The following day was hot and lazy, too hot to expend too much energy. Still, wanting to use our short time on the islands to experience more of the park, Martin and I walked the easy 1.7-kilometre trail around Roe Lake. We'd been told this was where we'd find the local swimming hole.

The dirt trail was very narrow in places, clinging to the steep edge of a wooded hillside. Eventually we descended into a valley filled with giant ferns. We passed a bright-green, sludgy pond, more like a swamp than a lake. Hoping this wasn't Roe Lake, we continued our search down the path.

A few metres farther, in the middle of the dark forest, we were delighted to find a proper pond: Roe Lake. The water was a deep tan colour, striped by the reflection of tall grey pine trees bordering the far side. Damselflies flitted about the water lilies that crammed the edges of the little round lake.

A parting of the lily pads leading from the shore to the middle of the lake marked the location of the swimming hole. Amongst the weeds on the shore, we found the short wooden ladder that went down the steep muddy bank to the gap in the lilies. Martin isn't into swimming unknown waters, but I'd come prepared. I stripped off my sweaty hiking cloths to reveal the bathing suit I wore beneath, and splashed into the cool lake. I noted, and thought it odd, that there were little hard-shelled snails floating between the lilies. So I swam about in the cool, weed-free centre of the lake until the heat of the day was drained out of me. Refreshed, I climbed back up the ladder and joined Martin sitting on a rock in a small clearing. He'd found a pretty place for a picnic. The sun dried me off as we contentedly ate our sandwiches.

A group of teenage girls arrived at the swimming hole while I was getting dressed. They squealed with apprehension upon seeing the snails on the water. I assured them that these were not leeches. Timidly, one by one, they climbed in for their swim. As Martin and I left the lake, we could hear one girl still protesting, insisting that leeches were attacking her.

The following day, Martin and I rented sea kayaks at Port Browning on North Pender Island. Not being familiar with the local tides and currents, we also hired Kyle, a guide, to keep us safe. Kyle led us through the maze of pleasure boats docked and anchored in the marina. We kayaked past moss- and lichen-covered cliffs and along small coves dotted with upscale cottages. Holidaymakers sunning themselves on the warm afternoon waved at us as we quietly paddled by.

In another small bay we came upon one of the many middens left by the Coast Salish peoples of long ago. Kyle explained that middens are beaches made completely of the leftover seashells from countless meals eaten over the ages.

In the seaweed-choked waters we also saw the remains of old clam gardens: rock and sediment walls built at the low-tide line. Clams and other sea creatures once were grown and harvested in the pools between these artificial terraces and the shore. But these gardens have long been neglected and are now overgrown.

Using the end of my paddle, I pulled up a giant kelp leaf that was floating by. I chomped into it. Yum, tasty! The flesh was plump, juicy and sweet. The only salty flavour came from the bit of seawater on the wet leaf. Martin and Kyle laughed at me as I ate a few more mouthfuls before tossing the remains of my snack back into the ocean.

We paddled around another corner. There, looming above us, was the trestle bridge that crosses over the man-made canal between the two parts of Pender Island. The full scale of the high wooden structure really became evident as we slipped along with the strong current flowing beneath it. I marvelled at the workmanship and the effort it must have taken to get those huge beams into place.

After the bridge we kayaked close to the steep bank of South Pender. Sea urchins, shellfish and red sea stars clung to the underwater cliff walls beneath us. We glided over this colourful ocean world, around tide-sculpted rocks, past small headlands and on towards the beach at the Beaumont marine campsite in Gulf Islands National Park Reserve.

From the water we could see some of the remnants of an old canning plant. Next to the broken-down stone walls, gnarly, bright-orange, papery-barked arbutus trees, a broadleaved species of evergreen, leaned out over us from the sun-baked banks. Way up above us, at the peak of Mount Norman I could just discern, between the trees, the underside of the wooden lookout we'd eaten lunch at a few days ago.

At the end of Bedwell Harbour, past the sailboats and cargo ships, rising out of the distant clouds, snow-capped, rocky peaks framed the scene. On that idyllic summer afternoon, I understood the allure of these islands. I could have floated there forever.

The enchanted waters of the Gulf Islands had one more attraction in store for us: sea lions! On a rock between the marina and a set of cottages, four females lay basking in the last of the day's warmth. We lingered to see whether they'd move, but they seemed comfortable in their repose. The sun was sinking fast, however, and having no lights on our boats, we had to get off the water. With strong, steady strokes we paddled back to the dock at Port Browning and returned our kayaks. The sun was already behind the mountains, casting long, dark shadows, when we thanked Kyle for the wonderful tour.

14
Mount Revelstoke

THE SELKIRK MOUNTAINS
ALPINE WILDFLOWERS

I arrived in Revelstoke by coach in early August 2017. The temperature had been in the mid-30s for most of the summer and there had been no rain for weeks. As a result, wildfires were devastating the forests near this small city of 7,000, and the air was thick with smoke. Bravely, ever hopeful, I decided to see what I could of this mountain of a national park. I rented a car and drove into Mount Revelstoke National Park just outside the city, on the Trans-Canada Highway about halfway along the 1000 kilometres between Vancouver and Calgary.

The park is relatively small, just 260 square kilometres, encompassing the 1939-metre-high Mount Revelstoke and four other major peaks. The park is so small and mountainous that there are no accommodations of any kind. There isn't even a campground in the park. However, Glacier National Park's campground is just an hour farther down the highway, and that's where I set up "base camp" for my explorations.

The day after claiming a creekside campsite and setting up my tent, I drove back to Mount Revelstoke National Park. There is a 10-kilometre path to the summit of Mount Revelstoke, but hiking in the extreme heat and heavy smoke seemed foolhardy. Instead I drove my air-conditioned car 26 kilometres up the gently inclined Meadows in the Sky Parkway. The 13 switchbacks made my 1600-metre ascent comfortable. Also, there are the many lookouts that afforded generous views of the city of Revelstoke and the meandering Columbia River down below. Being a midweek day, there were few other people jostling for the best belvederes and I could take my time. As I drove slowly upwards out of the lush green rainforest, the smoke-filled air became ever more nauseating, but the higher I went, the more wildflowers edged the roadside.

So I put up with the air pollution and continued upwards. The parking lot at the end of the road was surrounded by a welcoming riot of colourful flowers.

The alpine meadows were in full bloom with purple lupines, fuchsia monkey flowers, pink willowherbs, red paintbrushes, yellow mountain arnicas, white Sitka valerians and daisies white and blue. As I strolled along the various trails that meandered around several subalpine lakes and tall stands of pine trees, I was delighted by the various combinations of colours. There were pockets of blues and yellows, yellows and reds, reds and whites and then stretches of fuchsias. This high mountain peak seemed to have pierced into a heavenly rainbow.

Despite a breeze, the air was smoky and warm on the mountaintop. I slowly wandered along the secluded Eagle Knoll Trail and came upon a wooden bench in one of those natural alpine gardens. There was no one else about, and this was the perfect lunch spot. As I ate my sandwich, I drank in the colourful scene. Bumblebees were dining on flower nectar. A chipmunk scampered up to my feet to nab a pine cone. I was content and at peace in this little corner of paradise.

The forest below, however, was not at peace. Wildfires had been raging for weeks around Mount Revelstoke and Glacier national parks, filling the air with so much smoke that visibility was reduced to less than a kilometre. The glorious mountain vistas advertised in the Parks brochures didn't exist on the day I was there. At the Summit Fire Lookout, 1933 metres above sea level, was a signboard depicting the shapes and names of nearby peaks. Although disappointed by the lack of mountain scenery, I considered that a bright sunny sky would have subdued the intense colours my camera captured. Of course, clouds would have been a preferable filter.

To make the best of the day, I decided to drive back down to the base of Mount Revelstoke and explore the lower, less smoky areas of the park. Amongst the various trails I visited, the Nels Nelsen Ski Jump Trail stood out as unique. The hill is no longer used for ski jumping but the trail up to the platforms still exists. The rocky path is just 1 kilometre long, and with 78 metres of elevation gain it is a very steep slope. There were, and still are, no elevators as at modern ski jumps. So, like the ski jumpers of the 1920s, I hiked up to the platforms. Of course, I was carrying just a light backpack on a warm summer day, unlike those early skiers who ascended carrying heavy wooden skis on their shoulders in the wintertime.

The trail leads up past three jumping platforms, the first of which was the launch for Canada's first female ski jumpers, including Isabel Coursier. Isabel set a women's world record of 25 metres in 1922. Before her, Canadian "glider girls" wearing skirts would ski-jump holding men's hands. As I read the information plaques on the platforms, I admired the bravery of those cutting-edge women, pushing their socially imposed boundaries. I wondered what future generations might think of the progress people are currently making. Was I contributing to the knowledge and advancement of human limits? I hoped so.

Breathing heavily, I continued my slow ascent to the top level of the ski hill. At the end of the path I found a metal cast of Nels Nelsen's ski suit, tilting out over the void beyond the edge of the jumping platform. The structure was designed for daring tourists to lean into, to appreciate some of what those intrepid ski jumpers had experienced. After carefully checking the secureness of the bolts and fasteners of this unique viewing structure, I gingerly lowered myself onto it and peered down between the metal mock skis. A lump formed in my throat as I considered the depth of the valley below me. This would have been the Norwegian-born Canadian Nels Nelsen's view as he performed his world record breaking 73-metre jump in 1925. I shuddered as I contemplated the jumps of more than 250 metres now performed! No, I thought, I won't be ski jumping, thanks, not even as a "glider girl."

Ten days later I returned to Mount Revelstoke National Park. Due to a couple of days of light rain, the air was clearer. I drove up the parkway, hoping for that promised mountain vista. This time I wasn't disappointed. The signboard was true after all: there were snow-capped Rocky Mountain peaks all around! The flowered alpine meadows now backdropped by those rugged grey mountains were even more stunning than on my first visit.

In the clear, fresh air, I hiked along the 5.5-kilometre mountain-top trail to Miller Lake. The trail led me out of the alpine meadows, through lush evergreen forests and over rockslides where the mountain fell straight down. As I had to pay close attention to where I was stepping on the rocky, cliff-hugging path, I made a point of stopping often to look at and appreciate the wildflowers on the high side of the trail, the deeply forested valleys below and the distant mountain peaks.

In a nook in the middle of a dark forest, I stumbled upon the turquoise-coloured Miller Lake. The little oddly shaped lake calmly reflected the snowy mountain peaks above it. A few other people were lounging in the warm sun, on the large grey boulders by the water. I too made myself comfortable on a rock, ate my picnic lunch and enjoyed the beautiful day. I lay back and dozed off for a while.

I had one last thing to do before leaving the lake: I had to test the water. At a small bit of sandy beach, I waded in. The water was icy; too cold for a swim. I lingered, hoping for the courage to dive in. But I had dawdled too long and the sun was sliding down behind a mountain. I had to get back to my car before dark. So I laced on my boots and hurried down the trail. I left Mount Revelstoke National Park in the dark. Yes, it had been a good visit.

15
Glacier

FOREST FIRE!

Glacier National Park of Canada is not to be confused with Glacier National Park in the United States. The American park, in Montana, is the US continuation of Canada's Waterton Lakes National Park. Canada's Glacier park is in eastern British Columbia, about two-thirds of the way from Vancouver to Calgary.

Given that the Trans-Canada Highway runs through it, Glacier ought to be an easy park to visit. However, I've found it to be one of my more challenging parks to get to. In 2016 Parks Canada had posted a bulletin on their website advising that many of the trails in the park were closed due to the presence of grizzly bears. As I couldn't find anyone to travel with me at that time, the potential of facing a grizzly while exploring on my own worried me. I cancelled my trip. In August of the following year, Parks published a similar grizzly bear advisory and there were forest fires burning in the far reaches of Glacier. I decided, however, that if I didn't take my chances and go to Glacier that year, I might never get to explore it. So in 2017 I went.

The sun was just a faint yellow blur in a smoke-overcast sky when I arrived. In spite of the thick haze, or perhaps because the smoke was preventing dissipation of the ground heat, the air temperature was an energy-draining 32°C. I made a stop at the Rogers Pass Discovery Centre to confirm that it was still safe to camp in the park, and to purchase my permit.

Despite the poor environmental conditions, the dark-green forested Illecillewaet campground was almost filled with campers. I was lucky because some had just vacated a choice site and I got to set up my small dome tent right next to the narrow, cascading river called the

Illecillewaet – "swift current" or "big water." The breezy stream provided me with a bit of fresh air. I noted that the washrooms and the kitchen shelter were also nearby.

Just up the winding campground road was the trailhead for most of the big scenic hikes. However, the thick wildfire smoke hung like a heavy fog over the beautiful mountain peaks that were advertised in the park brochures. Grey fingers of haze reached down the vales, through the giant hemlock and cedar forests of the lower mountainsides towards the campground. I decided to stay low, below the smoky cloud canopy, and explore the park's valleys.

Rogers Pass, providing a connection from eastern Canada to the Pacific coast, bisects Glacier National Park. How Albert Bowman Rogers determined in 1881 that this narrow, steep, zigzag gorge, at 1330 metres elevation, would be a good place to bring the Canadian Pacific Railway through, I cannot fathom. The route loops almost 360 degrees back on itself along the cliff edges of the deeply crevassed valley. Hiking along that original rail route, now the Loop Brook Trail, I found remnants of towering stone pillars that, in conjunction with wooden trestles, had supported the original railway. Collapsed snowsheds, a type of wooden awning meant to protect the railway from avalanches, still mark the failure points of the route. Annual heavy snow and rock slides eventually forced the closure of this line in 1916. The CPR now runs safely through tunnels deep beneath Rogers Pass. The Trans-Canada Highway runs alongside, through its own tunnels and under a few modern concrete snowsheds.

After seeing their impact on human activity in Rogers Pass, I wanted to see some of those infamous snows and glaciers. I chose to hike the Great Glacier Trail because it rises just 321 metres. I was hoping the end of the trail would still be below the smoky cloud cover. Also, this was one of the few trails not yet closed due to the presence of grizzly bears.

My first stop, just beyond the trailhead, was at the remaining foundations of Glacier House, once a posh resort for early 1900s tourists wanting to visit the famous Great Glacier near the CPR. When the rail line was rerouted through the new tunnels, bypassing the resort, the hotel became less popular. Furthermore, the glacier, now called the

Illecillewaet Glacier, had been retreating. By 1927 both the railway station and the Great Glacier were too far away for most elite tourists, and the luxury hotel was demolished.

I continued my three-kilometre hike along the trail towards the glacier. The trail inclines gently along the rushing Asulkan Brook and through a fairy-tale-like forest. Brilliant green moss-covered erratics – giant boulders left behind by ancient glaciers – littered the damp forest. I was half expecting pixies (and hopefully not bears) to peek out from behind the hemlocks.

The trail became steeper where it exited the woods and veered towards the headwaters of the Illecillewaet River. I followed the switchbacked route over an old rockslide. Fat, sweet huckleberries growing among the rocks along the way made for delicious excuses to rest. Farther up, a few stunted, windswept conifers marked the edge of the rocky glacial moraine I was labouring along. The day was hot, 30 or so degrees, and the back of my shirt under my light daypack was quickly soaked with perspiration. Over the sound of my own heavy breathing, I became aware of a continuous roar coming from somewhere above me. I stopped at a cliff-edge vantage point and spotted the source of the din: a huge waterfall fanning out over a rocky mountainside. Gorgeous. I hoped the trail would lead me close enough to the fall to benefit from the mist that bounced off the cliff.

I arrived at a broken wooden post that I assumed marked the end of the trail. Several small groups of people were ambling over the slick, rounded mounds of bedrock. I stopped to chat with them and eat lunch. Like the others, I spent some time photographing the waterfall, which was still quite far above and to the northeast of us. Glaciers, however, were still nowhere to be seen.

Adamant to see a glacier, I didn't linger too long. As none of my new friends wanted to climb anymore, I clambered farther uphill on my own. While there was no trail anymore, I trusted that the periodic small piles of stones marked a passable route. Using hands and feet, I scrambled up the steep, polished bedrock and around car-sized boulders. With one foot pinned on each side of a deep, narrow crevasse, I slowly ascended through a long trough that had been scored into the rock by the glaciers. Arriving at the crest of the mound, I noticed I had ended up well above the waterfall – no cooling spray to be had.

Farther up, to the east and across another valley, I could see the toe of a glacier – the Vaux. The ice wasn't sparkling white as one might have expected. Instead it was a dirty grey, barely distinguishable from the granite mountainside to which it clung. The extreme heat of the last few weeks had been melting the glacier and exposing the rubble that had been scraped up by centuries of ice movement. I assumed that ash from the wildfires was also settling down onto the glacier, contributing to its muddy appearance. This was not quite what I'd hoped to see.

Decision time. Do I continue climbing in hope of seeing the Illecillewaet Glacier, or be happy with what I've already accomplished? I had scrambled well over a kilometre past the end of the trail. My shirt was soaked with sweat. I was getting tired and I noted it was getting late. I still had the long, hard climb back down to complete before dusk. Bears might be more active in the valley after dark. The answer was obvious: I had to go back.

Near the trailhead, just after walking over a nice wooden bridge crossing Asulkan Brook, I veered off the Great Glacier Trail and onto the Meeting of the Waters Trail. The sun was setting and I had just enough time to enjoy the view of the confluence of Asulkan Brook with the Illecillewaet River. I sat a moment on a bench overlooking the rushing waters, resting from my five-hour adventure. I was drained. The cool, misty air rising up from the rushing waters was comforting. Reluctantly, I stood up again and continued. The walk took me by a very handsome old stone bridge over the Illecillewaet River. I had crossed that bridge earlier in the day, but from the trails on the overpass, the beauty of the stonework hadn't been visible. I was quite pleased I'd taken this scenic detour back to my tent. These last few attractions had completed my exciting day. And I hadn't encountered any grizzlies.

I woke up the next morning to the strong smell of smoke. Fire! Hurriedly, I split open my lightweight summer sleeping bag and poked my head out the tent door. There were curls of smoke seeping between the trees and around my tent. How close, I wondered. Coughing in the harsh air, I quickly dressed and ran over to the park kiosk to find out what was happening. The fires, I was told, were not threatening the campground, but the wind was blowing the smoke this way. Although smoke can be more dangerous than fire, there was no evacuation requirement. Still, I found the air too uncomfortable to breathe let alone do any physical activity. So I struck camp. An internet search told me there was no vacancy at any of the lodgings in Revelstoke, west of Glacier National Park, so I tried to escape eastbound to the town of Golden.

The line of cars was moving very slowly down the two-lane Trans-Canada Highway. At the eastern boundary of the park, fires were raging up the steep slopes on both sides of the road. A constant stream of helicopters dangling huge sacks of water and fire-retardant were flying by. To avoid chemical drips onto passing vehicles, traffic was stopped whenever fire-retardant was being transported overhead. I could see the plumes of ash billowing up from the burning forest where the helicopters were dropping their loads. There was nothing I could do but slowly, patiently continue driving and hope to avoid getting further caught up in the situation.

Golden lies in the next valley, between the Columbia Mountains and the Rockies. The air there smelled of smoke but was definitely clearer. I splurged on a restaurant meal and a night in a hotel. I also took advantage of the opportunity to buy a new sleeping bag because in my haste to evacuate Glacier National Park, I'd permanently broken the zipper of my old bag. This purchase turned out to be quite fortuitous. A light rain fell during the next two nights, bringing the temperatures down with it, to just 4°C. Camped out in Glacier again, I snuggled into my new sleeping bag and layered the old one overtop. I was comfy and warm for the rest of the week.

Though the rain was not enough to put out the forest fires, it did clear the sky of smoke. For the first time during my visit I could see and admire the snowy mountaintops in Glacier National Park. Plus, the lower daytime temperatures were perfect for hiking.

As I prepared for my big hike, a neighbouring camper asked me to help boost his car battery, which had been drained by a space heater he'd plugged in overnight. He'd borrowed a set of jumper cables from another neighbour, but that person's car was a hybrid gas-and-electric vehicle and he'd been told those types of cables can't be used to boost a gas-powered car. I've no idea why, then, the cables were loaned. In any case, after much manouevring on the narrow dirt road, I got my rental car to his and provided the needed boost. It was 10 a.m. when I finally arrived at the trailhead.

The trails, I discovered, were all closed. Parks Canada had barricaded the trailhead and had officials sitting there to ensure no one passed. I was told that a female grizzly had lost her two cubs, and they were wandering around the lower trail system. Only hiking groups with a minimum of four adults were allowed on the trails. Adopting a positive attitude, I waited. Eventually a couple from Calgary arrived, and then a family of four including two young boys. We all agreed to hike together up Asulkan Valley Trail, and with five adults we were allowed onto the trails. My patience had paid off.

For about the first third of the seven-kilometre trail, we walked on cushy fir needles through a forest of balsam. The route was comfortable, the day sunny and warm. The forest seemed so peaceful. However, the three large, steaming piles of bear scat we carefully stepped around reminded us to be vigilant. With our bear-bells jingling on our day packs, we purposefully ensured we were constantly making noise so as not to surprise any grizzly bears that might be lurking behind the trees or boulders. Of course, it would have been hard for the two boys to be quiet anyway as they raced each other and generally had fun on the trail. As a result, we did not see any grizzlies.

Eventually the trail broke through the treeline and angled steeply upwards. Slowing down, I gave up the lead to the couple from Calgary. Unlike me, they were very used to climbing mountains. The path became rocky and switchbacked alongside Asulkan Brook. We stopped often to graze on blueberries that grew alongside the trail. We stopped to admire the waterfalls cascading off the side of Mount Abbott, and again to spot the distant, grey-streaked toe of Asulkan Glacier.

Suddenly a surprised hoary marmot whistled a warning at our approach. Scrambling over to scrutinize the large rodent, one of the boys tripped over the rocks and skinned his knee. As I bandaged the boy's injury, the creature leerily watched us, but it quickly disappeared into a hole when we stood up to continue our climb.

Farther up the trail, we stopped again, this time to eat our picnic lunches. We sat comfortably on a pile of huge boulders in the brook, the whitewater splashing around us. I passed around my binoculars so we could see whether an odd-shaped object at the top of a nearby moraine was a hut or a house-shaped rock. Rock, we decided, without much conviction. As we climbed onwards, the trail became ever steeper and I stopped often to catch my breath. Although I had my hiking staff to help me, I became the slowest of our group.

The trail led us over two bridges that looked like they were just a couple of aluminum extension ladders laid down over the rocky brook. There were no handrails and the contraptions rattled precariously as I crossed over them. From there the trail hugged mountainside scree before leading up to the top of a steep glacial moraine. I fell far behind as the rest of my group scrambled quickly up the slope. Since there was no longer any need for us to hike as a group at this high altitude, I didn't mind climbing by myself. However, I was tired, and I considered quitting my ascent – I'd already seen a lot, perhaps enough.

I took shameless advantage of a ptarmigan hen and four chicks that were scurrying back and forth across the path in front of me. They made for a good photo opportunity and yet another excuse for me to stop and catch my breath. That 10-minute rest did me good, and I resolved to finish the climb. I couldn't see any of my group anymore, but I carried on confidently, if slowly.

I eventually made it to the crest of the moraine. The trail followed a very narrow ridgeline from which both sides dropped off steeply into the valleys far below. As the path was rocky, I had to pay more attention to my footing than anything else. The next time I looked up there was a wooden post in front of me. Surprise: I had made it to the plateau!

The others of my group came over to congratulate me and offer celebratory snacks. After a final short rest, I'd recovered enough and was excited again to explore the mountaintop.

On the small plateau were the Alpine Club of Canada's quaint

Asulkan Hut and an outhouse. At the far edge of the highland, an inukshuk overlooked the snowy valley below. Far off in the distance, between several mountains and through the smoky haze, I could just discern the Rogers Pass Discovery Centre and a section of the Trans-Canada Highway. In the opposite direction, down below, I could see the tongue of the Illecillewaet Glacier, stained red with algae. Having finally seen this famous glacier, I was content with my explorations of this park and ready to go home.

However, one final challenge lay ahead: the walk back along that rocky ridgeline atop the downward-sloping crest of the moraine. My group descended together. As we walked, we couldn't help but notice the depth of the drop-off on either side of the ridge. We also noted that the trail ahead seemed to fall off the end of the moraine. Until we reached that drop-off, we couldn't see how anyone might possibly get down without falling. When we got there we realized we'd have to hold on to the boulders and clamber down the steep face of the moraine. We worked together, encouraging each other down the scary precipice.

Once down off that precarious part, the rest of the path to the trail-head was just a "walk in the park" – literally. We laughed at ourselves, at how quickly we disregarded the hardship we'd just endured. And we happily noted that we hadn't seen any of those nasty grizzly bears.

As we strolled happily down the path, we chatted about things other than the challenges of the trail. That's when I finally discovered that my new friends were the family who'd lent the jumper cables, and they found out I was the one who'd provided the battery boost to our common camping neighbour. We had become a community, taking care of each other and sharing memorable experiences in the park.

16
Kootenay

THE ROCKY MOUNTAINS

SNOWSHOEING WITH COUGARS

I love to cross-country ski and snowshoe. So when I searched for some national parks I'd not yet visited, yet in which I could enjoy these winter sports, the Rockies called to me. In December 2008 Martin and I took a short vacation to Kootenay and Yoho national parks, in British Columbia. We went before Christmas to avoid the expensive high season and spent our first four days based in the village of Radium Hot Springs, just on the west side of Kootenay park.

I was so very glad I had rented an SUV for this trip. The mountain winter driving really started with Highway 93 through Kootenay park, a narrow two-lane road hugging steep mountainsides. The road was plowed but icy, so I took it slow. Martin sat gripping the armrest next to me the entire way. Halfway through the pass, a tree that had fallen over the highway forced me to squeeze by it in the oncoming lane, right next to a drop-off. That would have been a long way down! Fortunately there were no other vehicles on the twisty road. Or perhaps unfortunately, in case of emergency. I was relieved when we finally drove through a narrow gap that had been blasted out of the mountainside, and into Radium Hot Springs, some 260 kilometres west of Calgary. Just a block before our inn, in the middle of town, we had to wait for a herd of bighorn sheep to move off the road! Our adventure had started.

The appearance of the sheep was like a reward for having completed the strenuous drive. I'd seen bighorn sheep before, but they were always "way up there," as in "you see those white specks at the top of the mountain?" Apparently they like to lick the salt on the roads in the winter. Lucky for us that we got to see them up close. Real close. The rams peered up at us, their horizontal pupils looking eerie. They decided to ignore us and continued on enjoying the roadside salt. I carefully drove around them.

I gazed out our bedroom window the next morning and found hoarfrost covering everything. An infinite number of short, white, jagged ice needles seemed to have grown over the trees, branches, leaves, berries, pinecones and everything else outside. I'm sure this is where people got the idea for frosted-glass ornaments – yet another attempt to bring the wonders of nature into our homes.

We had to get out into that winter wonderland and get to know the park. We walked along the narrow highway, back through the giant crevasse gateway and to the trailheads just outside Radium Hot Springs. That's where we found the Redstreak Trail. Even though there wasn't really enough snow on the trails to use the snowshoes we'd rented, we wore them partway anyway. The trail led up onto the mountainside and became very narrow and twisty around large boulders that had tumbled down the mountain. We wondered, or hoped, or were quite sure that no rocks would come down while we were passing.

At one point, an ewe with two lambs seemed to start following us, although they clattered over the rocks alongside the path rather than walk on the hard-packed trail. We stopped so the sheep could move on undisturbed, but they stopped with us. So we quietly continued on, aware of them always behind us. Periodically a lamb would dislodge a rock that would tumble down the mountainside, disturbing the wintery silence of the forest. And then the sheep were gone. Despite being able to see for miles through the sparse forest, the rocky mountains and the valleys around us, we could see no animals anywhere. We knew they were there, and we knew too that they were watching us. We continued snowshoeing in silence, wondering.

We followed the trail around the mountainside, through an open Douglas fir forest, over some scree and down into the narrow Sinclair Creek valley. Our route took us back along Juniper Trail. The forest had become dense with cedar where chickadees flitted about. Another short side trail along a charming creek led to a glistening waterfall.

With a dusting of snow over everything, we felt like we had stepped into a Christmas card scene.

For a bit of pampering, we decided to try out one of the local natural hot springs. Being outdoorsy and adventurous, though, we didn't opt for the touristy Radium Hot Springs pool with its deluxe change facilities. Instead we followed the cryptic directions, given us by some locals, to Lussier Hot Springs, hidden away up in the mountains just outside the park. Off the main highway and along a one-lane dirt road winding deep into the wilderness I drove. Even if we didn't find the spring, we were enjoying the views of the snow-covered mountains and broad valleys with rocky creeks down below. The forest was snow-covered and so pretty, clean, white and bright. Eventually, we came across a short broadening of the road, where three cars were already parked in a space just large enough for four. I took my place behind them.

Martin and I had come prepared, wearing our bathing suits underneath our winter coats. Stepping down a short rocky path, we arrived at the hot springs. In the −30° weather, the steam was thick over the hot sulphury water. We quickly shed our coats and boots and slipped into the hot water. Rocks had been piled up so that the water bubbling out of the ground would be contained in a natural shallow, deep enough to cover our shoulders while sitting on the pebbly bottom. The rising steam kept our heads warm. Too hot. I moved to a lower pool that the steaming water spilled down into – still too hot. The water seeped down farther into a third bowl, which was just right. Like Goldilocks, I was content. Ahhh.

Of course, no enjoyment of a hot spring is complete without a cooling off. Without enough snow to jump into, I carefully trod over the slippery rocks and lay myself down in the shallow creek to let the cold water wash over me. My dark wavy hair turned white as the steam coming off me caught in it and froze. Enough of that – I quickly hurried back into the hot pool. The seven other people soaking in the natural spa looked at me as though I was crazy. Well, at least I'm not boring.

After hurriedly changing out of our wet bathing suits in the frigid air, we hopped into the suv and turned up the heat. The drive down the mountain became its own adventure when we missed a turn and got lost. There are many roads all over this forest, and no signs. These were logging roads. Eventually I caught up to a timber truck. As the truck was fully laden, he must have been on his way out of the mountains, I reasoned. So I followed that truck for what seemed like kilometres, finally ending up in a logging corral. Our trucker stopped and walked back to give us directions to the highway. He had known why we were following him, and laughed at our plight. We felt embarrassed and very out of place, our SUV dwarfed amidst the dozens of monster trucks. I carefully navigated to the highway on-ramp without being run over by one of them, and made my way back to the inn.

The mountain driving was stressful for me, particularly in winter when roadways are covered in ice and snow. The sun sets early, around 4:30 p.m., so I usually drove "home" in the dark after a day's adventure – there are no street lights in the parks or anywhere else outside the villages. To add to the challenge, one evening I drove home in a fog so thick I couldn't tell where the side of the road was. Other nights, we drove home through whiteouts caused by blowing snow. I always drove slowly, with the fog lights on. I was afraid to stop, because if there were a car behind us it wouldn't be able to see us in time and might plow into us. I followed what looked like the tracks of a vehicle ahead of us, hoping it hadn't driven over the cliff. I strained to find the line that marked the edge of the pavement, or better yet the centre line. Martin watched for road signs to determine where our turnoffs where. We always managed to get home safely, but I was totally exhausted every night.

There was still so much more for us to see in Kootenay! So we squeezed in one more hike: the five-kilometre Dog Lake loop trail. We were the first to leave footprints in the freshly fallen snow as we set out that morning. At a T-intersection along the trail we stopped to inspect a box – a camera – mounted on a tree. Well, some researcher now had a close-up of our noses. We wondered what types of critters the photographers were targeting in the winter.

The trail took us down into a valley and across the Kootenay River. From the suspension bridge we spotted a bull moose, with his huge antlers, ambling along the edge of the fast-running glacial water. We paused to watch him disappear into the forest. We continued on, gazing appreciatively at the snow-covered mountains above us. We were alone on this trail in the beautiful pristine white wilderness.

Eventually we got back to the T-intersection where the wildlife camera was mounted. There on the snowy trail, on top of the footprints we had left earlier, was another set of tracks. Not a bear or a wolf, which I'd recognize. I couldn't identify these tracks. Curious, we wondered whether the camera had caught our mystery beast. Luckily, back at the trailhead we met the researchers who owned the camera. After we told them our story of the footprints, they were anxious to go get their pictures, of a cougar! We wondered how close the cat had been behind us. What if it had followed us? What if it had been interested in us? What if we'd seen it? There are no answers to "what if" – only more questions. No matter, though, because we had made it back safely. Brave in the car, we admitted we would have loved to have seen the cougar, even though we knew it was a foolhardy wish. Perchance to see such a majestic cat from the safety of the car? No such luck!

17
Yoho

THE ROCKY MOUNTAINS
NORDIC SKIING IN −30°C

Yoho National Park was the 24th park I visited. By driving from Kootenay National Park to Yoho, Martin and I got to experience the difference in weather patterns created by the various mountain chains. Kootenay had been cool with very little snow, while Yoho, on the other side of the range, was in a deepfreeze zone, buried in snow. The temperature was minus 30-something when we arrived at the visitor centre in Field, BC, a small village of artisans along the Trans-Canada Highway in the middle of Yoho National Park. We picked up some trail maps and information about the park before driving on to Emerald Lake Lodge.

Emerald Lake Lodge, dating back to the early 1900s, is a picturesque stone and timber building with a row of quaint wooden cottages along the lake, nestled deep in the Rocky Mountains. We felt like we'd stepped into another old-time Christmas card. Deep snow covered everything in this enclave of rugged grey mountains. Twinkle lights peeked out from the snow-laden boughs of the evergreens that towered over the resort. Indeed, it was the week before Christmas 2008 and we had six days to stop, relax and enjoy this romantic spot.

There were two other couples at the lodge when we arrived late in the afternoon. It was already getting dark. To give us all the advantage of the quiet winter isolation, we were installed in the pretty, wooden cottages at the end of the snow-packed road, about a five-minute walk from the main building. The route was so charming, with lanterns lighting the way between dark pine trees, that we looked forward to the daily, though chilly, trips to the dining room. No one, however, had expected it to be quite so cold.

Late the next morning, Martin and I woke up to a frosty room – the electric baseboard heaters had been no match for the extreme cold outside. The pipes in our cottage had frozen and we had no running water. The toilet no longer functioned either. Hastily we dressed, not just because of the cold room but also hoping to quickly warm up our chilled clothing.

Stepping out of our cold cottage, we were accosted by the crisp, clear air. Wow, that hurt! I took a moment to check the thermometer outside the door. The red-tinted alcohol had frozen in the bottom of the tube, below the −45°C mark.

Hurriedly we ran over to the reception desk in the main lodge. The people from our neighbouring cottages were already there, reporting the same problems as Martin and I had experienced in our cottage. The resort transferred us all to cottages right across from the main lodge. Even though the utilities were still functioning in these new cottages, we were largely dependent on the fireplaces to keep our rooms comfortable. I felt rather guilty at the amount of wood we burned throughout that week.

Each night before going to bed, we'd pile the logs supplied by the resort into our fireplace. But the winter nights are long, so by morning there'd be just a few embers left. Each morning I'd hurriedly pull on a fluffy fleece jacket before getting out of the warm bed and stoking our fire with more wood. Once our room was warm again, Martin would get up, open the curtains and gaze out at the ice-peaked, rocky mountains on the other side of the frozen little lake. He'd marvel at the bright sun and brilliant blue sky reflecting off the stark white snow. The intense light, he knew, was deceiving; it was freezing outside. Amazingly, chickadees peeped and flitted about the bird feeders on our balcony. "How do those tiny bodies survive in this cold?!" he wondered.

At around 10 a.m. we'd bundle up in thermal long underwear, wool sweaters, fleece jackets, down-filled coats and felt-lined boots to run across the roadway to the main lodge for breakfast. These meals were serious affairs, with steaks, game meats and heavy sauces providing us with the energy we would need to cope with the frosty day.

However, for the first couple of days at the resort, the temperature didn't rise much above −40°. The bitter cold and the early sunsets forced us to stay inside much of the time. We spent hours in the warm glow from the stone fireplaces in our cabin and in the main lodge. Martin and I put together a 1,000-piece puzzle, and we each read a couple of novels during our stay. The nights were very dark and quiet as the temperature dropped again. We would snuggle into the fluffy down duvets and sink into deep sleep, in keeping with the rest of the world around us.

On the third day, the thermometer defrosted and registered a balmy −30°. Desperate to stretch our legs and get some exercise, we braved the cold and went for a hike around the 5.2-kilometre Emerald Lake Loop trail. The frosty snow squeaked under our boots. Although we would have liked to have hiked at a faster pace to keep warm, the deep fluffy snow obscured the edges of the boardwalk, so we had to slow down and pay attention to where we were walking.

The world we'd stepped into existed only in shades of black and white. We crossed over rushing black creeks, between dark trees and bold shadows, under steely mountains and grey rocks and through stark white snow. Frozen "Emerald" Lake was pure white. Only the sky had colour in it: a brilliant bright blue, the shade of blue that only exists in very, very cold temperatures. Despite the general lack of colour, the scenery was spectacular! Cold, but spectacular.

Emerald Lake Resort had an outdoor hot tub tucked away in a stand of tall pine trees. Early that evening, in the dark, Martin and I dared to make use of it. The water bubbled at a scalding +40 degrees, steam rising up into the frigid −40-degree air. We eased ourselves into the spa and soaked in the heat. Finally relaxed, we leaned back and admired the stars that were sparkling between the swirling clouds of steam above us. The pruning of our skins eventually forced us to give up this magical experience. We laughed at this crazy escapade as we raced back the few metres through the extreme cold, to the warmth of the changing rooms.

Heavy snow had built up on the power lines leading to Yoho National Park, causing the electricity to go on and off for the rest of our stay.

One night, with no heat, the pipes in the main lodge froze and burst. When the power came on again, the pipes defrosted, causing the kitchen to flood. The Filipino and Aussie staff were completely stunned by the extent of the cold – temperatures they had never believed possible – and the damage it created. They were also awed by how casually we, their Canadian guests, accepted the situation. The other two couples, Asian tourists, abandoned us. Martin and I stayed on, as the resort's only guests.

In the main lodge, the staff set up a card table and armchairs in front of the huge fireplace in the second-floor sitting room. There Martin and I sat, with blankets covering our backs, eating our dinners. The kitchen had been repaired and the chef and cooks did an outstanding job feeding us. I got the impression the staff didn't mind carrying our meals up there to us, as we were in the warmest place in the lodge, other than the kitchen.

One morning Martin and I decided to go for a drive to the nearby village of Lake Louise, in Banff National Park. We were pleasantly surprised when our rented SUV started perfectly, without a block heater or jumper cables, in this deepfreeze. We drove down the Trans-Canada, through the infamous Kicking Horse Pass. The pass got its name from an 1858 incident in which Sir James Hector was kicked by his horse while exploring a route for the Canadian Pacific Railway. "Kicking Horse Pass" is another one of those colourful Canadian place names that make me smile.

In Lake Louise we rented Nordic skis to take back to Yoho with us. We were told the ski lifts and gondolas on all the mountains in the area had been closed due to the extreme cold. The other tourists in the shop wondered out loud whether we were foolish to attempt cross-country skiing, causing us to wonder too. Oh well, we could always abandon the attempt if the cold proved to be too much.

On this small road trip to Banff, Martin and I also stopped by the renowned Chateau Lake Louise. We wandered around and took some photographs of the famous CP hotel, with its bland concrete-looking walls standing out brazenly against the beautiful winter wonderland surrounding it. However, we preferred to stop for lunch at the pretty

Deer Lodge nearby, a hand-hewn log building from 1923, which seemed so much more suitable to this alpine environment.

As we sipped our afternoon coffee, the famous Canadian Pacific Holiday Train, decorated with colourful lights, painted Christmas scenes and a huge wreath on its "nose," rolled by on its way across the country. The train's mission is to raise food and money for food banks in both Canada and the US. I'd never seen the Holiday Train before, but thought it very appropriate to enjoy in such a lovely, historic location. We happily made our donation to the worthy cause.

Finally, on our last day in Yoho the weather had warmed up a bit, to about −20°C, and we set out at mid-morning for our first ski. We took the lodge's shuttle bus to the Natural Bridge, where the Kicking Horse River has ground a tunnel through the rock. The shuttle dropped us at the lookout, but it didn't linger and neither did we – we had to move in order to stay warm. Unfortunately Martin's automatic bindings had frozen open, so he couldn't ski. He had no choice but to walk the six kilometres back to the lodge. He stubbornly refused to hitch a ride from a passing vehicle.

As my own bindings were functioning well, there was no reason for me to give up this opportunity. So I set out on my own, skiing down the 1-kilometre Tally Ho Trail and then along the Emerald Lake Link trail. Bright rays of sunlight pierced the dark pine trees, lighting my route in the shadow of the mountain to my right.

The snowmobile trail-groomer passed me twice, disturbing the pristine silence of the winter forest. On the other hand, he provided me with a groomed (though not track-set) trail to follow, plus the security of someone knowing exactly where I was. The latter benefit was especially important given I would be passing through some avalanche zones. These areas were well marked with signs warning skiers not to stop there. I barely glanced up at these steep, snowy, treeless slopes as I hurriedly passed – safely, as it turned out. No avalanches that day. Outside these danger zones, however, I paused often to gawk at the extraordinary mountain scenery.

The sky was a brilliant blue. The icy mountains refracted the bright sun so that the light bounced off of the crystalline snow. If I stared too long without my sunglasses, I'd be blinded by the frozen beauty. How awesome that I should be granted the privilege to pass through this rapture.

Martin was waiting for me in the shelter at the resort's parking lot. He was chatting with the shuttle driver. When I finally arrived, the men looked at me with such horror, making me wonder what was wrong. Apparently my eyebrows and lashes were frosted white. Icicles hung from the frozen edges of my hat and from my nose. My jacket collar was stiff with frost. Underneath all that ice, my face was bright red. The men were worried I was frostbitten. I assured them I was fine – more than fine, actually. I was energized and alive! I was panting from the fast pace I had set, my blood surging through my veins. And I had the biggest grin on my face! I had been generating so much heat while skiing that the perspiration was freezing on everything it came into contact with, creating my abominable snowman appearance.

Not wanting to miss out on any opportunity to enjoy the outdoors, I went out skiing again in the afternoon. Martin's bindings had thawed, so he was able to ski with me this time. We followed an 11-kilometre path, breaking trail, right up to the base of the sheer mountains at the far end of Emerald Lake. Steep grey cliffs created a sheltered alcove around us. We stopped to brush the snow off a wooden bench to reveal the Kicking Horse Ski Club logo etched into the seat. This was a truly lovely spot to contemplate the wonders of the world. All around us, light sparkled from infinite crystals of snow and lifted our spirits.

Looking back towards the lodge, however, we could see the lights coming on, reminding us it was time to head back. The sun was setting, the mountain shadows darkened the valley, and the temperature was falling to dangerous levels again. In the depth of winter, this enchanting valley was one of those paradises we were allowed to visit but really should not stay in.

We arrived at our cottage in the dark, but very satisfied with our adventures. What a great start to the winter. The next day, we left for home, ready to start celebrating Christmas and looking forward to more Nordic skiing in the relatively warmer temperatures of southern Ontario.

18
Banff

MOOSE ON THE ROAD

By 1982 I had still not yet seen anything of Canada west of Ontario. Banff was the first national park to be established, and it is arguably the most internationally renowned, so it seemed to me to be an appropriate place to start getting to know the rest of my country.

As I was a university student at the time, and living at home to keep my expenses down, I asked my parents to join me on this exploration. My dad refused to go, citing that since he had seen the Alps, he already knew what mountains look like. My mom uncharacteristically agreed to go with me. She had never seen the Alps, and was also interested in getting to know her adopted country. Many years later, after my mom passed away, my dad visited the Rockies with his new girlfriend and came to understand how wrong his original concept of these mountains had been. In the Rockies there are no gentle, cow-filled, pastured valleys or pretty chalet restaurant atop every mountain. The Rocky Mountains are a wild, remote wilderness. Banff National Park, in the middle of those mountains, has only one notable nod to civilization: the town of Banff.

As we didn't have a car, my mom and I relied on buses, and walking, to get around. We took a three-hour coach ride from the Calgary airport to Banff, checked into a small old hotel on the main drag and went out to explore the town.

Like many people, I found it odd that such a cute, bustling alpine tourist town should exist inside a national park. National parks, I thought, were designed to preserve the natural beauty of the land. No doubt, however, the alpine setting of the town is very pretty, with its colourful flowerbeds, ponds, rock gardens and rustic garden shelters.

Even the museum is in a picturesque log building, and the natural history displays inside are just as interesting as the building itself. And the entire scene is set within the towering Rocky Mountains. My dad might well have mistaken this for a Bavarian village in the Alps.

From our hotel, mom and I took a series of sightseeing coach tours, the first one including a boat ride on Lake Minnewanka. Outside of the alpine village, this lake is a natural wonder, its turquoise water sparkling in the sun, set in an alcove of snow-peaked mountains. There were tiny white dots on the mountainsides – bighorn sheep! This was the stuff of postcards. I made a note in my journal that I'd have to return sometime to do some canoeing on this pretty lake.

The tour continued on to show us highlights of the Bow River, with its wide waterfalls and tall, sandy hoodoos. We passed the majestic copper-roofed Banff Springs Hotel, where we saw elk grazing on the golf course. At the buffalo paddock among the trees, we were even able to get glimpses of some of those famed bison. Despite the manicured facade of this park, there sure was a lot of wildlife around, especially larger animals. I was surprised at the apparent coexistence, or perhaps "endurance," between wilderness and human civilization.

Ascending mountains, I learned, is the thing to do in Banff. For those of us who don't want to climb up every peak, there are gondolas to take us to the summits. Mount Norquay is one of the ski hills in the park that runs lifts even in the summer. This mountain isn't ice-capped like the taller ones in the neighbourhood, but mom and I were happy to have brought our ski jackets, because the wind was cold up there. Looking down off the mountaintop, we gained an appreciation of how utterly vast these untamed valleys are. If there were people down there, we couldn't see them – they were insignificant. I considered that when I had been at the base of the mountain, I too had no idea of how unimportant I was.

A few days later we gave in to the innate desire to climb. We opted for the "moderate" walk up the 5.5-kilometre footpath to the top of Sulphur Mountain. Somewhere along that 655-metre climb, we lost the trail and continued our ascent along the road. As my mom started becoming lightheaded from the altitude, we took more frequent short breaks to catch our breath and take in some snacks and water. Stubbornly, she refused the rides passing cars offered – she wanted to be able to boast that we had climbed the mountain. And eventually we did make it to the top.

At the peak we found one of those alpine restaurants with large picture windows all around – my dad would have loved that! The view was well worth the climb. Elated, we could see the town far below. Having acclimatized to the altitude, my mother and I wandered along the short, level trail leading around to the other side of the restaurant. Looking out from there, we saw nothing but snow-covered mountains and endless valleys of forests. If there were people down there, it seemed that no "outsider" would ever know.

That was how I got my first real understanding of how vast this wilderness was, and how insignificant I was to "existence." This awareness of my irrelevance was quite disconcerting, and yet somehow I found comfort in knowing that this was how the world should be, and is. I began to think that humans do not need to (and fortunately cannot) tame and control everything.

When we finally made it back into town, mom and I splurged on a dip in the Upper Banff Hot Springs. We figured we deserved a pampering in the natural sulphur spa – it was just the right thing to soothe our tired muscles. There were many, many other people in the large pool, yet everyone quietly respected each other's peace. Steam from the 38°C water rose up between the tall pine trees and dissipated into the heights around the pool. I felt like I was in heaven. When our skin had sufficiently pruned, but before relaxation succumbed to sleep, my mom and I departed the spa and silently walked back to our hotel room. We were both contemplating the marvels we had experienced.

Our adventure in the Canadian Rockies continued by way of a coach tour north along the scenic Bow Valley Parkway, 51 kilometres to Lake Louise, and then along the awe-inspiring 232-kilometre Icefields Parkway towards Jasper National Park. Rows of giant grey mountains lined both sides of the highway. Snow and ice sheathed the peaks, and dense green forests covered the steep lower slopes right down to the wildflower-filled meadows along the winding two-lane road. Fir, pine, aspen and poplar were abundant, but there were no maple trees in this part of the country.

There even were bears foraging along the sides of the highway. From the safety of our bus, we gawked like the tourists we were, not fully aware of how dangerous these creatures can be. They looked like cute teddy bears. Sadly, they ignored us and wandered into the bush out of sight. Better for the bears that way, I supposed.

Farther down the road, mom and I saw our first moose. These things are huge! As it crossed the road in front of us, this particular male stopped to stare directly through the coach's windscreen and straight down the aisle that was three steps up off the ground! The massive rack on its head added to the bulk of the animal, giving the impression that it should fall over for the extraordinary weight balanced precariously so high up over its long, spindly legs. "Like a couch on stilts," is how I described it later.

Our tour stopped at the famed Chateau Lake Louise. This hotel, originally built in the late 1800s as a stop for the CP Railway, has been rebuilt and enlarged several times. The present-day square monstrosity, with its massive, blank, cement-like walls, I thought, seem incongruous with the rugged mountain setting. The enormous structure blotted out the scenery. I considered that perhaps the building's most important purpose was to keep the hordes of tourists housed together in one place, rather than in a multitude of small hotels that might take over all the land.

Mom and I stepped into the Chateau, and I was impressed at how posh, and European, the public areas were, with fancy ceilings, marble and dark wood fixtures. We peered through the hotel's shop windows at the luxury goods offered for sale, but we were more interested in seeing the lake outside. Quickly we exited the back of the building, and walked into a picture postcard.

Lake Louise, framed by those ice-topped mountains, lay before us. My mom and I wandered by the hotel's colourful formal gardens, over the vast manicured lawn and down to the pretty, turquoise lake. Lake Louise, like every other lake we'd seen in the park, was picture-perfect. Although there were many other people around us, the landscape behind the hotel was so large that I never felt crowded. No wonder so many people want to be here, I thought, and there's such a huge hotel to house them all in. I too wished I could stay a while, to hike around the lake and enjoy the tranquility. However, there was still more to see down the road.

A stop to walk to the lookout over Peyto Lake provided us with more jaw-dropping vistas. The viewing platform hangs from a cliff high above this little alpine jewel, turquoise with mountain minerals. Could I possibly take any more photos? Yes I could, and did.

Our coach continued northward, through unending photo opportunities, into Jasper National Park.

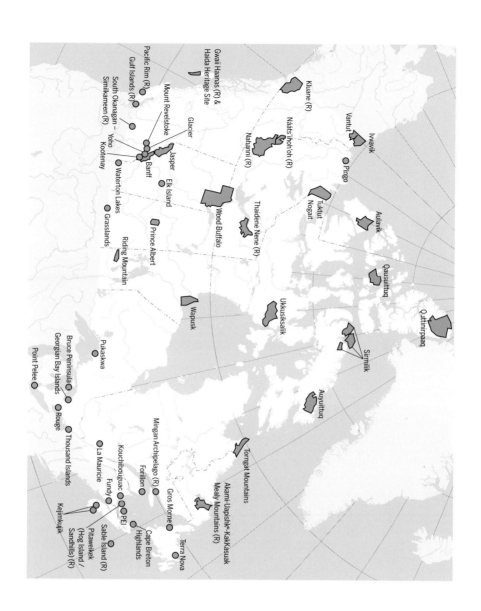

Pacific Rim (R)

Gwaii Haanas (R) &
Haida Heritage Site

Gulf Islands (R)

South Okanagan –
Similkameen (R)

Mount Revelstoke

Glacier

Yoho
Kootenay

Banff

Jasper

Waterton Lakes

Elk Island

Grasslands

Prince Albert

Riding Mountain

Wood Buffalo

Nahanni (R)

Náàts'įhch'oh (R)

Kluane (R)

Vantut

Ivvavik

Pingo

Tuktut
Nogait

Aulavik

Thaidene Nene (R)

Wapusk

Ukkusiksalik

Qausuittuq

Quttinirpaaq

Sirmilik

Auyuittuq

Point Pelee

Bruce Peninsula
Georgian Bay Islands

Pukaskwa

Rouge

Thousand Islands

La Mauricie

Kouchibouguac

Mingan Archipelago (R)

Forillon

Fundy

Kejimkujik

PEI

Pitaweikek
(Hog Island /
Sandhills) (R)

Sable Island (R)

Cape Breton
Highlands

Gros Morne

Terra Nova

Akami-Uapishkᵘ-KakKasuak
Mealy Mountains (R)

Torngat Mountains

193

Aulavik - muskox

Aulavik - muskox at the Thomsen River

Aulavik - camp on the tundra

Vuntut - distant base camp

Vuntut - wolf in the flowers

Vuntut - mountain of caribou

Pingo - Canadian landmark

Pingo - view from Highway 10

Ivvavik - Marlis overlooking the Firth River

Ivvavik - camp on the Firth River

Ivvavik - lone caribou

Ivvavik - negotiating Firth River rapids

Kluane - on Sheep Mountain

Kluane - glacial highways

Chilkoot - creek crossing

Chilkoot - Dan Johnson Lake

Qausuittuq - pair of Peary caribou

Qausuittuq - hiking back to camp

Qausuittuq - Peary caribou close up

Tuktut Nogait - hunting blind

Tuktut Nogait - La Roncière Falls

Tuktut Nogait - hiking

Naats'įhch'oh - reflections on Backbone Lake

Naats'įhch'oh - perfect day on Backbone Lake

Naats'įhch'oh - hiking by Backbone Lake

Nahanni - Virginia Falls

Nahanni - view from Sun Blood Mountain

Nahanni - view into First Canyon

Wood Buffalo - salt at Salt Pan Lake

Wood Buffalo - buffalo in the woods

Wood Buffalo - black bear at the cabin

Gwaii Haanas - kayaking

Gwaii Haanas - totem poles

Pacific Rim - kayaking with orca

Pacific Rim - Broken Group Islands

Gulf Islands

Gulf Islands - to Vancouver Island

Mount Revelstoke - self reflections

Mount Revelstoke

Mount Revelstoke view

Glacier - glacier

Glacier - Asulkan Trail

Kootenay - sheep in Radium Hotsprings

Kootenay - to Dog Lake

Kootenay - highway

Yoho - Emerald Lake

Yoho - near Emerald Lake

Yoho - bridge to Emerald Lake Lodge

Banff - townsite

Banff - Bow River hoodoos

Jasper - touring on the glacier

Jasper - Maligne Canyon

Waterton - windy mountain

Waterton Lakes - snowshoer dwarfed by the trees

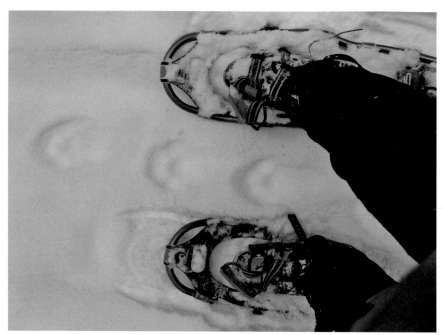

Waterton - following a cougar

Elk Island - Astotin Lake

Elk Island - hiking

Prince Albert - marsh

Prince Albert - Waskesiu Beach

Grasslands - vista

Grasslands - ranch on the French River

Riding Mountain - buffalo

Riding Mountain - beach

Pukaskwa - South White River

Pukaskwa - rocky shore

Bruce Peninsula - hiking in trilliums

Bruce Peninsula - Marlis on
an Escarpment outcrop

Bruce Peninsula - The Grotto

Point Pelee - monarch on goldenrod

Point Pelee - beach

Rouge River - fall colours

St. Lawrence Islands - bridge to USA

St. Lawrence Islands - Boldt Castle

La Mauricie - vista

La Mauricie - Lac du Fou with canoes

Wapusk - young male polar bear

Wapusk - four male polar bears

Wapusk - comfortable polar bear

Wapusk - moose

Ukkusiksalik - Marlis at a Thule tent ring

Ukkusiksalik - Islands in Wager Bay

Ukkusiksalik - caribou wandering by

Quttinirpaaq - picnic at Henrietta Nesmith Glacier

Sirmilik - "Arctic – 1906," Bylot Island

Sirmilik - Marlis with kelp and urchins

Sirmilik

Auyuittuq - ice on the Weasel River and Thor Peak

Auyuittuq - inukshuk and Mount Asgard

Auyuittuq - fireweed

Mealy Mountains - vista

Mealy Mountains - natural compass

Mealy Mountains - ship in the fog and icebergs

Torngat Mountains - Ramah Fiord

Torngat Mountains - Saglek Fiord

Torngat Mountains - fiord

Terra Nova - iceberg in the distance

Terra Nova - vista

Gros Morne - Gros Morne Mountain

Gros Morne - beach

Mingan Archipelago Islands - beach

Mingan Archipelago Islands

Mingan Archipelago Islands

Forillon - lighthouse

Forillon - wild coastline

Kouchibouguac - river

Kouchibouguac - lagoon

Fundy - kayaking

Fundy - Salmon River

PEI - beach

Cape Breton Highlands – The Cabot Trail

Kejimkujik - Lake

Kejimkujik - kayaking

Kejimkujik - canoes

Sable Island - feral mare with foal

Sable Island - hiking in the sand dunes

19
Jasper

THE ROCKY MOUNTAINS
WHITEWATER RAFTING

The townsite of Jasper, in the middle of Jasper National Park, is smaller and less touristy than Banff, where my mom and I had taken a coach from. People actually live in Jasper. With its small roads and odd collection of houses and shops, the town is much like many other hamlets in rural Canada. In the evenings and early mornings, elk roam into town and graze on people's vegetable and flower gardens. Tourists go out of this town for excitement.

My mom and I went out to see the edge of the Columbia Icefield, the huge ice cap on the Continental Divide at the Alberta/British Columbia boundary. Our tour took us to the Athabasca Glacier, one of six glaciers leading off the Icefield. This was the first time either of us had actually been to a glacier. Not only did we get to see a real live glacier, we went onto it!

From a specially designed bus driven directly onto the Athabasca Glacier, we saw drifts of dark rocks suspended in the ancient ice, crevasses, and moulins with meltwater spiralling down into the depths of the glacier. Up there above us, in the towering mountains overlooking the sparkling blue and white glacier, were examples of smaller hanging valleys, cirques, arêtes and other glacial features I had only seen pictures of in my high school textbooks. All the knowledge from those geography courses came rushing back to me: here were the terminal, median, ground and lateral moraines I had been taught were piles of stones left behind as the glaciers retreated.

In southern Quebec and Ontario where I lived, dense forests obscure much of the geological features left over from ancient glaciers. Here in the Rockies I could actually see the geography right out in front of me, and I was thrilled that I could identify the various land forms!

My mom and I stepped off the ice bus onto the rough, grey glacier. Although we weren't allowed to wander far, I was excited just to touch the thing – it was real, not just something in books. The cold seeped up through the soles of my summer hiking shoes – I could feel the ice. Despite the bright sun above, I shivered as I stood in the ice-chilled wind. I couldn't stop smiling, as I realized that this – exploration of the natural world – was what I really wanted to do with my life.

We took another local bus tour to see a beautiful cascading river in the ever-deepening Sunwapta Canyon. The tour also stopped at a viewing platform from which we looked down into the very narrow, 50-metre-deep Maligne Canyon, the deepest canyon in the Rockies. The turquoise water rushing along this "wicked" river feeds into the Athabasca River. So many beautiful places to explore, I thought.

Our tour took us to a belvedere overlooking the powerful 23-metre-high Athabasca Falls, flowing through a narrow gorge. Farther downstream on the Athabasca River was an awesomely long set of rapids. And on the river were several rafts of people shrieking as they were swept over the whitewater (not the falls). I thought that looked like a lot of fun!

I imagined great adventures, riding wild down the raging river, through pine forests and wide valleys, all beneath the rocky, ice-peaked mountains. My mom was dead set against such a reckless activity. She reminded me of the old adage that "only fools shoot the rapids." I, however, was still young and foolish. So I secretly bought two tickets, knowing mom wasn't going to let me waste the money on the purchase. I guessed correctly: after much chiding, she relented and reluctantly came along with me.

I had a blast! The ride was bumpy and exhilarating as we rode the whitewater waves. With eight other tourists and our guide we rode the fast-moving river through the wilderness just as I'd imagined. Around and over rocks we slid, past whirlpools and swirling water. The spray soaked us thoroughly as our raft punched through the biggest of waves.

The fact that there were no safety or support systems along the treed shoreline was exciting – daring! What a ride, what a rush!

Adding to my pleasure, mom later declared she too had loved the ride. We were both tempted to do it all over again, but instead settled down to savour the inevitable anticlimax from such an adrenalin high. We reflected on how much fun it was to have done something outside our normal, safe world! Together my mom and I had each stretched ourselves. This shared experience was the start of our changing relationship from mother-and-child to good friends.

However, while I was in that raft on the river, another idea had started to form in my head. Something my mom would definitely not agree to: wouldn't this be even more fun if I could control the boat, as opposed to just going along for the ride? What a crazy idea! But that day I'd discovered that crazy ideas could be exhilarating. Forget the naysayers, I decided. I'd take up whitewater canoeing when I got home. And I did.

20
Waterton Lakes

THE SOUTHERN ROCKY MOUNTAINS
SNOWSHOEING IN −40°C

It was a six-park year for me in 2014. I visited, for the first time, Sable Island in Nova Scotia, Terra Nova in Newfoundland and Kejimkujik in Nova Scotia. I also went back to properly visit Mingan Archipelago in Quebec and had the opportunity to visit Point Pelee again. I was making maximum use of my Parks Canada annual pass. So, I thought, why not add another park before year's end? I was thinking it would be great to visit one where I could enjoy some winter sports: Nordic skiing, say, or snowshoeing. Waterton Lakes National Park fit the bill.

Due to the amount of travelling I had already done that year, I had accumulated sufficient frequent-flier points for the flight to Calgary and a rental car. Frequent traveller points also allowed for a free stay in one of the two hotels that were open for the winter in the townsite of Waterton. Although Martin doesn't care for the cold, he agreed to come along when he realized that the trip would essentially be free, and that he didn't have to do anything other than pack his own stuff. We would spend the week between Christmas and New Year's Day in southern Alberta.

I'm always impressed by the sudden change in scenery from the flat, treeless prairies in the east to the abrupt wall of treed, snow-peaked mountains in the west. What would the European pioneers have thought, after months of travelling westward across the flat centre of the New World, coming up to … "What is that stretching across the horizon?" A mirage? A wall of clouds or a row of mountains? Heading south from Calgary, I drove nearly 300 kilometres along the edge of the vast continental plain, with that wall of mountains on my right. I wondered, perhaps like the early railway surveyors, whether there was any passage through to the Pacific.

The relatively narrow band of foothills between the prairie and the Rocky Mountains had been the traditional hunting grounds of the Blackfoot. One specific site with a wonderfully colourful name is called "Head-Smashed-In Buffalo Jump." We made a stop to see this historic site. Most every high school student in Canada has learned how the Indigenous hunters drove herds of buffalo over a cliff to plunge to their deaths on the rocks below. This important hunt provided food, clothing and shelter for the people. I was very impressed by the interpretive centre's realistic film depicting such a hunt, right down to the merciful killing of still suffering animals that had not died from the fall. My experience at this UNESCO World Heritage Site made me appreciate how hard life must have been without modern conveniences, and how ingenious the First Nations Peoples were to have survived in this environment.

Highway 6 led us due south, out of the arid, windswept yellow prairie and abruptly into the silent, snowy mountains that bar the border between Canada and the USA. There is a way into that fortification! We drove through a narrow mountain pass, like a gateway, into a dense pine forest shrouded with a blanket of snow. The Rocky Mountains towered over everything. Rays of sun streamed down between the icy peaks. I might have felt claustrophobic had I not already associated woodlands with security and protection – sanctuary. We had entered nature's cathedral. This was Waterton Lakes National Park.

Just after the park gate, the road follows alongside Lower Waterton Lake. There Martin and I came across several cars stopped on the side of the road. Each vehicle had its lakeside windows rolled down, allowing billows of warm air to escape into the cold valley. Binoculars and long camera lenses pierced the steamy clouds. We took our place along the roadside and joined the watch from the warmth of our car: elk, hundreds of them, were grazing on the other side of the narrow end of the lake. I dug out my new ultra-zoom compact DSLR camera and aimed to photograph those with antlers. But all elk heads were down, busy grazing. The animals took no notice of us. So we idled, engine running to keep us warm, and watched the elk until I could no longer justify burning gas and polluting the environment with so much car exhaust. Had this been a standoff, the elk would have won. The sun had sunk behind the mountains and the temperature was dropping fast. I wanted to find our hotel before dark.

The hotel was made up of a cluster of quaint wooden guest apartments set up around a main lodge that housed the reception desk, a lounge with fireplace, a sports equipment rental shop and a restaurant. As this was the only eatery open in town that winter, we spent a lot of time there, at a table in front of that huge fireplace. A giant buffalo head, dressed for the season with a Santa hat, was mounted over the stone hearth. The lounge also featured a long, curved wall of picture windows from which we could comfortably admire the wondrous winter scene of pine trees and mountains. At night the arc of the windows was accentuated by pretty twinkle lights.

On our first full day in the park, we discovered that other than the main road in, the Akamina Parkway is the only driving route open in the winter. The parkway has several switchbacks leading up the side of the valley, offering broad views of the Waterton townsite and of the mountains along the length of Upper Waterton Lake. Under a bright blue sky, the vista was fabulous, the sunlight glistening on the icy mountains, the snow-covered trees and the lake below.

I had to stop at one hairpin curve partway up the hill because several bighorn sheep were blocking the road. They were busy licking road salt, completely unperturbed by our presence. Since we weren't going anywhere, I decided to photograph them. However, I didn't want to step out of the warm car into the freezing cold. So I manoeuvred the car to be parked perpendicularly to the road, across both lanes. As I photographed from my open window, a car came down the road and stopped at the other end of the hairpin curve. The driver followed my example and also parked crosswise to take pictures. I'm sure that driver, like me, was thinking we could never get away with parking like that for any other reason. Eventually the sheep moved far enough to one side that our cars could get by one at a time. We nodded our mutual understanding as we passed each other.

At the top of the Waterton Lake valley, the narrow two-lane parkway continues to meander alongside a creek flowing from Cameron Lake. I drove very slowly, my attention being split between the narrow, snowy, twisty road and the glorious scenery. Against a bright blue sky, a strong wind swept wisps of snow off the mountaintops. Martin and I kept gawking at each awesome new view of the same mountains from different angles along the winding road. "Look at how the sun's rays stream over the edge of that ice-capped mountain!" "Now look at how the top of that mountain glows gold in the light!" "Oh, see how the dark pine trees create a ragged edge along the shaded, steep side of the mountain!" I kept stopping to take photographs – I now have way too many pictures of mountains.

The end of the parkway was closed, allowing for a double, track-set Nordic ski trail down a slight slope to Cameron Lake. On weekends, we learned, families from nearby towns come with snowshoes, sleds and Nordic and backcountry skis to enjoy the easy route down to the small lake. Parallel to the closed road, the narrow Dipper Trail winds through a forest of giant pine trees, heavily laden with snow. Martin and I skied down that three-kilometre trail to the frozen lake, where we joined other visitors having fun in this winter wonderland.

The interpretive centre at Cameron Lake was locked down for the winter, but there were picnic tables scattered around the frozen waterfront. Several families had shovelled the deep snow off some of these tables and were enjoying winter picnics. Steller's jays as blue as the sky were perched on tree boughs around the site, hoping for handouts of bread crumbs or granola. A few people skied onto and around the edges of the frozen, windswept lake. The entire scene was magical, ensconced in a pine forest surrounded by steep granite mountains glistening in the sun.

We had several very cold days when the wind chill fell well below −40°. Despite the cold, there was a constant snowfall of very fine, light flakes that accumulated over several days to more than a metre of dry powder. Time to go snowshoeing!

We decided to explore the route to Bertha Falls, a five-kilometre round trip from the edge of the townsite. However, there was too much snow on the access road up to the trailhead parking lot, and even with winter tires I couldn't drive up the hill. So I parked in the lot at the end of the road and we hiked back to the trailhead.

Setting out, we spotted a narrow, thigh-deep trench where people had previously snowshoed through the forest. We assumed this was the trail to Bertha Falls. The latest storm had already padded the trench with light, fluffy fresh snow so that even with snowshoes, our steps sank deep. Puffs of powder swirled overtop of our snowshoes as we struggled along. This was hard going.

We stopped often on the continuous climb up the trail. Our many pauses, to take photographs and look at the spectacular mountain scenery, were really just feeble excuses to catch our breath. However, we had to keep these breaks short because of the biting-cold wind that was being funnelled through the narrow channel of Waterton Lake. Despite wearing layers of thermal long underwear and fleecy sweaters under our winter coats, plus balaclavas, hats, gloves and overmitts, we could not stop moving for more than a couple of minutes before our extremities became stiff with cold. This hike was a chore.

The trail turned sharply westward, away from Waterton Lake, and followed a high, narrow ledge along a creek to the falls. The creek valley was very narrow and steep. Dark-grey storm clouds obscured every-thing above – we could only assume there were mountains towering overhead. The snow was now coming down hard, blanketing the low-er parts of the forest that were still visible. The footprints we left were immediately obliterated. No one would know where we had hiked. We finally arrived at a wooden footbridge over a creek. To our right was a wall of snow: Bertha Falls, we assumed. The snow was so thick that we couldn't see the ice of the frozen falls.

While Martin and I were a bit disappointed by Bertha Falls, the lack of view meant we weren't exactly tempted to linger and take photo-graphs. We had to keep moving! We turned around and almost ran down the trail, taking advantage of the descent to add speed, create more warmth and get back to our car quicker. What had taken us 90 minutes to hike up took us only half that time back down – we were motivated to get back.

Upon arriving back at the parking lot, we discovered that sometime during the day, a snowplow had blocked the exit with a half-metre-high windrow. Our rental car was trapped. Without a snowshovel, we had to improvise. Using the ends of our snowshoes, we dug an opening through the snow pile just wide enough to get the car out. Fortunately the windrow wasn't hard packed yet.

A short time later we were sitting in front of the fireplace in our hotel, warming up with Spanish coffees. And grinning from ear to ear at our crazy achievement.

Either because we like a challenge or perhaps because we're just die-hards, we decided to go on another snowshoe hike the following day. This time we did the easier route, to Crandell Lake, with its gentler grades, wider trail and a lot less snow. A couple of fallen trees required crawling on all fours to get by. The only threat that day, we thought, was the bitter cold. Again, mountains towered around us, their peaks lost in the snow clouds. There were light flurries softening the sky. As we approached the lake, we came across fresh cougar tracks on the trail. The paw prints were not yet filled with the fresh falling snow, so we knew the wild cat was close by. We made a point of chatting and mak-ing noise as we peered into the forest, foolishly hoping for a glimpse of the majestic creature. We nervously walked under rocky overhangs, wondering if it was up there ready to pounce on some unsuspecting prey, like us. Of course (fortunately?), we never did see the cougar – these predators are masters at camouflage.

We did, however, see what we thought were a pair of wolves as we drove back to our hotel that evening. While there aren't that many people visiting the park in the winter, several cars had already collected at the roadside to watch the animals. With my zoom lens I took some close-ups, which I later zoomed in on even further electronically. In the park office I showed my pics to the staff, who decided we had been looking at very large grey coyotes. The coyotes, we were told, would probably have been after some of the deer we'd seen in the same area earlier. We all agreed that wolves, rare in the park, would have been a better story, but coyotes were pretty good too!

On our last day in the park Martin and I were "house bound." We had tried to drive southward down Highway 6 to the US border, hoping to see the eastern edge of the park where the prairies abut the mountains, but we had to turn back. Strong 60 km/h winds whipped up the light snow, creating complete whiteouts. I couldn't see the road for minutes at a time. I was worried not only about the potential of driving off the pavement but also of another foolish driver like me blindly running into us. We made it back to our hotel without incident, but I was exhausted. There was nothing left to do but sit back and read a novel in front of the fire. With wine at hand, we whiled away the rest of the day. This was our time to relax.

THE PRAIRIES

21
Elk Island

DEATH ON THE TRAIL

As the first wildlife sanctuary set up by Parks Canada, Elk Island National Park was designed to preserve and grow a herd of elk. Although I saw several islands in the lakes, I didn't see any elk. Parks assured me they were there. I found it surprising that these beasts, with such unwieldy antlers (per the brochures), could be so well hidden in the aspen forest.

My best friend since Grade 6, Lili, and her family had introduced me to Elk Island, just a 45-minute drive east of Edmonton. That was in September 2015. The aspen trees were just starting to turn yellow on that sunny, cool autumn day. The air was already sweet with the decay of fallen leaves. Lili with her husband, Andrew, and their teenagers, Olivia and Roman, took me for a walk along the four-kilometre Simmons Trail loop. We had to watch that we didn't step into any of the many fresh bison patties dotting the mown grassy path.

American bison are also known as buffalo. There are two types of them in the park: plains and wood. We didn't see any during our hikes, but we did see them on the way to the trailhead. On Bison Loop Road in the park, we were able to step out of our vehicle to photograph the beasts. They were huge. There were about a dozen of them: bulls, cows and calves. They were obviously used to people, and didn't bother with us. Some tourists even sat in the red Muskoka chairs Parks had placed along the roadside from which to admire the scenery. Roman stayed in the car and surprised us with an excellent sketch of a bison. Olivia looked bored – she'd seen this all before and more than once, I gathered.

The following day I returned on my own to further explore the park. Elk Island is a relatively small park, completely fenced in, and bisected by a four-lane highway. As I drove into the park along that highway, I saw bison grazing along the fenceline. At the same time, the radio station I was listening to started playing Bob Marley's "Buffalo Soldier." I loved the coincidence, even if the term doesn't actually relate to buffalo, the animals. (Buffalo Soldiers was the nickname given to several US Army regiments, formed soon after the Civil War, that were composed of Black soldiers.)

As there were very few people in the park on that midweek school day, I opted to be cautious and only hike a medium-length trail. I carried my day pack with my lunch, a litre of water, rain poncho/tarp, fleecy jacket, first aid kit and miscellaneous other emergency equipment. And my smart phone – there is cellular access throughout (most?) of the park.

The 13-kilometre Moss Lake Trail is a very easy walk, slightly hilly, and mown the entire way. The aspen and underbrush had grown in so densely alongside the path that it created thick hedgerows obscuring any views of what may have lain beyond the trail. Occasionally, on hilltops and at lakesides, I got a view of the surroundings: aspens, birch and a few conifers dotted an old, burned-over landscape. There were large marshes filled with wild grasses, and ducks swam in the open water around beaver dams.

Sitting on a bridge over a small stream connecting two ponds, I ate my lunch in silence. The wind rustled the leaves above me. The only other sounds were of the occasional blue jay, creaking like a door hinge in need of oiling, and friendly chickadees chattering with each other in their woodland home. I continued my walk, alone. Grasshoppers jumped out from under my long stride. I stepped around a dead garter snake, and then came across a large but squashed yellow-spotted salamander. Wild buffalo had trampled the poor creatures to death. As bad things come in threes, I wondered whether these were omens and what the next death would be. I hastened my already quick pace and almost ran down the trail, hoping not to meet any of the murderous buffalo.

After three hours of fast-paced walking I was back at the trailhead. Although there were many fresh tracks, patties and other scat on the trail, I hadn't seen any buffalo or elk the entire time. I hadn't even seen any other humans in the park, and my rental car was still the only one in the parking lot. I sat back in the driver's seat and reflected on my adventure: I never did find the third death. Happy and relieved, I drove back to Edmonton for the night.

Having toured Edmonton before, I was bored in the city. For all the entertainment available there, I'd rather be in the woods. So the following day I drove out to the park again. I risked a short walk alone on the Lakeview Trail and the Living Waters Boardwalk. Along the way I met some Australian tourists who were looking for beavers. We found a muskrat instead. At our approach the little brown creature scurried through the water and disappeared into the mud under the boardwalk just ahead of us. My new friends were thrilled to have seen some wildlife, and I was happy it was alive.

Later on I walked over to a platform overlooking the weed-choked end of Tawayik Lake. Finding solitude, I sat on a bench and caught up on my travel journal, and then finished reading a novel I'd started a few weeks ago. I sat there in peace for about four hours. I might have dozed off a few times, I don't know, nor did I really care. At one point a flock of swans flew overhead. Other than that, the day was quiet.

To transition back into civilization again, I stopped by the café at the park's golf course. I purchased a drink on the patio, and looking out over Astotin Lake, I toasted the park. A few golfers walked by chasing after their balls. Ah well, "Time to go home," I thought. And I quietly left the park. Satisfied.

22
Prince Albert

THE BOREAL FOREST

STRANDED IN THE WILDERNESS

I was desperately in need of a vacation. In my 23rd year working at one of Canada's major financial institutions, I was entitled to five weeks of vacation. However, Martin, having just started a new job, was allotted only six days. In a compromise, we agreed I should go alone, but to a destination which didn't much interest him. As I had been to all the Canadian provinces and territories except Saskatchewan, and Martin had already been there many years ago, he wouldn't feel like he'd be missing anything by not accompanying me. So 2009 became the year I could finally say I'd been to all the provinces.

Of course, my way of getting to know a province included visiting its national parks. I flew 2200 kilometres west, from Toronto to Saskatoon, rented a car and drove another 2½ hours north, following the directions of the GPS I'd borrowed from my dad. The traffic was fast: 130 to 140 km/h – in Ontario we don't usually drive more than 120.

I arrived in Prince Albert National Park early in the afternoon that July day, and checked into a small hotel in the townsite of Waskesiu, within the park. The hotel faced the lake, but a stand of dense trees obscured the view. From my window at the back of the hotel, I noticed that there were rows and rows of one-room cabins, shacks really, along a grid of dirt roadways. There was barely enough room for a car to be parked between the cabins. I watched as people washed their dishes in washbasins behind their cabins – there was no plumbing. How odd, I thought, that people should consider such sparse facilities to be an attractive vacation option. If I were going to rough it, I'd go all out and camp in a tent. But I know, different people have different interests.

The day was very hot, so I spent the afternoon at the crowded beach on Waskesiu Lake. Sitting by myself on a shaded bench, I ate the sandwich I'd purchased from a beachside kiosk. Most of the other vacationers were sunbathing. A few hardy kids ventured into the cold water, but I didn't go in myself. I was still winding down from the work I'd left behind. I lingered, not doing much of anything, 'til sunset when the mosquitos started rising out of the roadside shrubs.

In the morning I rented a mountain bike and tore up 7.5 kilometres of the Red Deer Trail. I had energy to expend. Parts of my route took me along a few closed road allowances and down a sparsely used secondary highway. I came to a sudden stop on the paved road, surprised by an elk that jumped onto the road in front of me. Upon seeing me, the animal froze in place and stared. After a moment of contemplation, the elk sauntered off to the other side and started to graze on the roadside grass. I would have expected to see wildlife in the forest I passed through, not on the road. Of course, in the woods I'd only seen trees and the trail I cycled along. Wildlife has a habit of staying hidden when one is looking for it, and surprising us by showing up where we least expect it. I smiled, feeling privileged to have gotten a glimpse of this elk. "Thank you for letting me see you."

I spent another day hiking the various park trails, through Boundary Bog, along the Waskesiu River and around a peninsula on the lake. The bear-bell on my day pack jingled in time with my gait, ensuring I wouldn't surprise any bears. As a result, of course, I saw no wildlife at all. Nor did I come across any other people. However, I enjoyed the solitude and the stillness of the forest. I paused for lunch in a remote spot along the lakeshore. A sandhill crane stepped out of the reeds nearby and created a brief stir as it lifted its wings to a full 1.5-metre span and flew away. My spirits lifted too.

As tranquil as that day of hiking had been, the next day, of kayaking, was frantic. The weather forecast had been for a favourable, warm, calm, sunny day. Perfect for paddling, I thought as I rented a kayak that morning. My destination was the cabin of famed conservationist Grey Owl, at the north end of Kingsmere Lake.

I met a young couple from Saskatoon who were also renting a kayak, and we agreed to do the trip together. We helped each other load the boats onto our cars, using foam noodles to cushion the car tops. Then we drove to the boat launch near the north end of Waskesiu Lake.

A short, calm paddle got us to the Kingsmere River, which flows between the two lakes. Just a bit upstream, we found the start of a 1-kilometre narrow-rail portage that bypasses some rapids on the river. We spent an hour balancing, pushing and pulling the kayaks, one at a time, on the heavy two-wheeled rail cart to the other end of the portage. I also portaged my two dry bags with emergency gear (tarp, sleeping bag, food, first aid kit etc.).

The wind had picked up and the waves were choppy on Kingsmere Lake. Not being experienced paddlers, the young man and woman took a break after 15 minutes of hard going in their tandem kayak. They beached and got up to stretch their cramped legs. As I floated just offshore, they wisely decided to return to their car. Later that evening, I found out they had rolled their kayak on their way back to the portage. Fortunately no one was hurt, but apparently they were very shaken up by the time they got the boat back to the rental marina.

Now paddling alone, I stayed close to the shoreline. The wind grew even stronger, and the lake became violent with whitecaps. Water washed over the deck as the waves hit my kayak broadside. I kept my head down and rode over the steep waves, the bow crashing down with every other stroke. My boat was stable and I was dry in my paddling jacket. I spotted rocks and trees, one after another, on the shore. I used these landmarks to note my progress as I passed them. I was advancing, but very slowly. After three hours of hard paddling, I had covered only about 12 of the 16 kilometres to the end of the lake. I took a break at the Sandy Beach campsite, a remote wilderness spot usually used by backpackers.

The sky turned dark as I ate my lunch at the picnic table. This didn't look good, I thought as my safety training kicked in. I hauled my kayak far out of the water and tied it to a tree. Then I draped my tarp over the picnic table and stashed my belongings underneath, just in time. The rain came pouring down. I sat in my dry spot under the table, contemplating the inevitable night I was going to have to share with the

277

mosquitos that were sheltering under my tarp with me. This was not going to be a comfortable night.

Two hours after the downpour started, it suddenly stopped. The air became dead calm, the lake like a perfect mirror reflecting a now cloudless blue sky. The bells in my mind rang out warnings: this was the calm before the next storm! But it was only mid-afternoon and I could see the end of the lake just a few kilometres to the north. I knew I could comfortably get to my destination in minutes on such calm waters. However, I also knew I would surely be trapped there for a miserable night out with the mosquitos.

So I did the "right" thing and paddled back to the portage as swiftly as I could. My retreat took less than half the time of the original paddle. My strokes were light and quick, my kayak skimming over the silent water. As I flew down the length of the lake, the water-mirror showed me that a few light fluffy clouds had arrived. I raced the kayak back along the rail-cart portage, oblivious to the hardships of the task, and back down the river to my car.

That was when the real storm started. With a crack of lightning and a roll of thunder the sky suddenly darkened and the rain came down again. Two big guys who had been fishing off a nearby rock offered to help load my kayak onto my car. I was soaked and exhausted; I had no strength left in my shoulders and arms. For the first time in my life I wasn't reluctant to play the helpless woman – I gratefully accepted their offer. After thanking the guys I sat alone in the safety of my car, just staring out at the pouring rain. I was relieved; I had avoided a rough night. Instead, I got to melt in a long hot shower, enjoy a delicious steak dinner and sleep in a warm, dry, mosquito-free bed that night.

I slept like a log as the storm raged outside, right through 'til dawn. After a big breakfast, I splurged at the local spa to soothe my aching muscles – I'd never appreciated a massage as much as I did that day. And as if there'd never been a storm, the sun had come up and the weather became hot again. I took the rest of the day off, relaxing on the beach, a fit finale for my experience of Prince Albert National Park.

23
Grasslands

LOST IN AN OCEAN OF GRASS

After visiting Prince Albert National Park, I drove 600 kilometres southward, through Saskatoon and Swift Current, over the vast, undulating prairie, to the hamlet of Val Marie, just outside Grasslands National Park, near the Montana border.

I would be staying at the Convent Inn, built in 1939 as an actual nuns' residence, converted several times over the years, eventually becoming an inn in 1997. As I was travelling alone, I took advantage of the unique opportunity to find out what it would have been like to live in a nun's tiny quarters. The room was so small I could barely find a spot to store my suitcase. Judging by the size of the closet and single table, the sisters would have had very few personal belongings. I was rather tickled by the appropriateness of me, a woman travelling alone in 2009, staying in a convent, even if I was almost a century late.

In comparison to the tight confines of my accommodations, the prairie outside the Convent seemed boundless. Whereas the room felt claustrophobic, one could lose one's sense of self outside the building.

My first venture into the park was to drive the Frenchman River Valley Ecotour, an 80-kilometre loop. For the first hour or so, I felt lonely on this remote road that was fraught with the potential of inadvertently taking a wrong track and ending up in the middle of nowhere. However, there were just enough route markers to remind me that I wasn't lost, yet. I was further comforted in the knowledge that I had a full tank of gas, five litres of water and a lunch with me. I was prepared to explore and get a feel of the landscape.

As the grassland is hilly, the route by which I'd come quickly disappeared behind me. There was nothing to indicate which way was north, south, east or west or which direction I had come from or was going to. There was only endless prairie all around. Everything looked the same: low hills of swaying, yellowish grass. I was grateful for the odd landmark I did come across. For example, a solitary tree, though dead, was still useful. A rocky ridge was also a nice change, but the ridge-top offered only more of that limitless sea of grass. A few car tracks scratched the land, suggesting directions to something that might once have been of interest to people who'd passed here before me.

I followed one set of tracks down a steep route into the Frenchman River valley. Offering a sense of location, the small river had once drawn people to it. Its water had provided at least a promise of prosperity. However, the abandoned Larson ranch was all that remained of a failed attempt at taming this nearly resourceless wilderness. As I walked around the site, a few rabbits hopped into holes in the boarded-up house. By the narrow stretch of green that marked the river, I found drifts of blooming wildflowers. A sage grouse was hiding in a bush. The river, more like a creek, meandered and occasionally disappeared under the gravel. A young couple were camping on one of the small green spaces – the first people I'd seen in the park. In this vast empty space, we were drawn to each other, to communicate, to socialize as people must do. They too were here to "feel" the emptiness and find whatever might be there that fills the apparent void. I drove on.

I stopped to explore a prairie dog town. I walked around the burrow mounds, careful not to step into any of the holes. There were hundreds of them, and I couldn't predict which hole a prairie dog might peep out from. The wind carried the sharp chirps of these cute little creatures as they popped their heads out of their burrows to watch me and warn each other of my presence. And they were fast – I didn't even have enough time to focus my camera before my targeted rodent disappeared into the dry earth.

Hiking in the park was an even lonelier experience than driving in it. After about 500 metres, over the first hills, I stopped to look around me – there was nothing to suggest where I was. I felt like I was lost. There was no footpath; only the occasional metal T-bar pole to mark the route. I followed from marker to marker, up and down the dry, hilly plains. From down in the valleys I could see nothing but the grassy hills rising high around me, capped by the blue sky above. A single small puff of white cloud drifted by, seemingly lost, like me, from the rest of its kind.

The view from the crests of the hills revealed nothing but more undulating prairie stretching out to the distant horizon. I was reminded of being on a ship in the middle of the ocean. Down in a trough there's only a curving wall of water to be seen; up on the top of the swells, only an endless expanse of water. And the grass swayed in the wind as waves on the sea. I was adrift, alone.

Looking more closely, however, I did see things. Grasshoppers jumped to avoid my tread. Ground squirrels scampered through the tall grass. A couple of mule deer grazed in a greenish gully. There were buffalo out there in the distance, near 70 Mile Butte. Over the next hill I came across an antelope standing tall and proud, watching me as I passed. So this is "where the buffalo roam and the deer and the antelope play." A couple of hawks circled overhead. (Not today, boys, I'm not dead yet.) These solitary, distant sightings provided me with some entertainment and reminded me that I was not alone here after all.

I drove out of the park and down a remote highway. Wheat filled the fields out to the horizon on either side. I passed just one lonesome house on the long route back to Val Marie. As I drove, kamikaze ground squirrels kept running under the wheels of my car. My heart sank and I cried out each time the tires crunched. I tried driving slower, faster, zigzag, and straight, but there was no way of preventing the casualties. Those squirrels were on a suicide mission and I was their unwilling enabler. I felt horrible. Perhaps only those hawks would be happy, for the easy meals I was providing.

I had company at the Convent that night: two couples had arrived on motorcycles. They were on a road trip across the country and staying in Val Marie for just the one night. We ate together at a trestle table in the dining hall. I was curious about their open-air, hair-in-the-wind biking experience. Specifically, I asked the women how they managed to put up with the grasshoppers on the road: "Doesn't it hurt when you hit them?" They laughed. "No problem – we sit behind *them*," pointing at the men. The guys admitted that even with leather chaps, it's painful when they hit the insects at high speed. Their experience made me appreciate the car I was travelling in.

Rain that night rendered the park roads impassable. The dust had become "gumbo," a thick mud that would jam up any tires. In hope that the sun would dry out the dirt roads by the afternoon, I drove more than 200 kilometres along secondary highways, around remote ranches and farms, to the isolated East Block of the park. As the ground was still damp, I left the car in the parking lot instead of driving along the track. I went walking, but I wasn't alone. Herds of apprehensive deer watched me. Farther along, a couple of fox cubs played with some flying insect. There was a bald eagle sitting on a post, and more antelope. There was a lot more life in these grasslands than first meets the (human) eye. I left the park content with what I'd experienced and learned.

En route to Regina, I stopped to refuel from a giant, 50,000-gallon gasoline drum in the village of Mankota, population 200. The "station" had no kiosk or attendant – you just insert your credit card in the machine and pump the gas yourself. I noted the awful mess on the front of my car: the grille and hood were thickly plastered with dead grasshoppers. Gross. The car looked like someone had barfed on it. There was also a layer of grime on the windshield that the wipers hadn't been able to clear. Even with the gas station's squeegee, I couldn't get the windows clean. I thought of my new friends with their motorcycles, and was even more grateful for my car, disgusting as it now was.

I felt I couldn't return such a filthy car to the rental agency in Saskatoon. So when I arrived in the city, I took the car through a carwash that advertised a special bug removing solvent. The carwash attendant assured me everyone in the prairies is used to the grime of dead grasshoppers. The rental agency was surprised I brought their car back clean.

24
Riding Mountain

THE CENTRAL FORESTS
CRASHING MOUNTAIN BIKES

In June 2010 Martin and I flew to Winnipeg to start our next adventure. Although Manitoba is a neighbouring province to Ontario, we flew there to avoid the 2200 kilometre drive from Toronto. On arrival we rented a car and drove 270 kilometres northwest to the hamlet of Wasagaming, on Clear Lake, in the heart of Riding Mountain National Park. We had come to see the fabled prairie buffalo and do some mountain biking.

My first reaction upon arriving was that we'd somehow driven to the wrong park. Wasagaming looks almost identical to Waskesiu in Prince Albert National Park, Saskatchewan! The long beach, the road layout, even the style of buildings, shops, cabins, cottages and gentrification in both townsites were so similar that I had to be careful about where my accommodations were! Here, though, I had rented a cabin instead of booking a hotel room.

We were fortunate in our selection of cottages in Wasagaming. Not only did ours have a screened-in porch where we could take refuge from the continuous onslaught of mosquitos but it had been recently renovated. Many of the rental cottages around ours were just shacks that had been built generations ago, some with no running water, drains or electricity. They appeared rundown and patched up to keep them from falling completely apart, and yet they were all occupied during our stay in the park.

The nearby enclave of privately owned cottages didn't look much better. These were the original lakeside cottages that had been clustered together to allow the wilderness to reclaim the terrain. However, with their piecemeal additions, these shacks were now so tightly packed in against one another that there was nothing natural left around them. What might once have had a wilderness appeal now looked, to us, rather like a shantytown. Others must have had the same impression, because apparently there's a movement to replace these "cottages" with upgraded, modern "monster" cottages with treed lawns. Some people complain that gentrification dissolves the original atmosphere of a place, maybe their own childhood memories. But I would suggest that the original cottages here had once also been the epitome of a vacation venue for the well-to-do (not everyone can afford a cottage). This so-called gentrification seems to be regenerating the original cottagers' expectations of what a country retreat should be.

These were observations Martin and I made as we pedalled our rented mountain bikes through the townsite, along the lakeside trails and into the wilderness. Our objective was to cycle most of the way around Clear Lake, but the summer so far had been particularly rainy, causing the underbrush to thickly overgrow onto the trails. Bushes scratched and grass blades cut our legs as we pushed our way along the North Shore Trail. The vegetation almost obscured the path, hiding some pretty bumpy rocks and roots. The mud was often thick too, further slowing our progress. I bulled my way forward, Martin shaking his head at me as he followed in my wake, sanely walking his bike around obstacles that I tenaciously forced my way over or through. Partway around Clear Lake, I stopped, completely exhausted. Taking the time to rest and contemplate, I realized our bike tires were ruining the muddy treadway by gouging deep ruts into it. This is not proper trail user's etiquette. Martin was thankful I'd conceded defeat – he wasn't enjoying this crazy trek. Bloodied and bruised, we headed back the way we'd come.

On our return trip, I slowed down and took notice how pretty Clear Lake was. Covering about 3000 hectares, the lake was dotted with sailboats and fishing vessels. There was a reedy wetland at the west end and several sandy beaches around the south shore. The entire valley was surrounded by low hills covered with spruce and a mix of aspen and other deciduous species.

From the Southside Trail, I found a small offshoot leading to a tiny, secluded pebble beach. Martin followed, pushing his bike under a low tangle of branches and over some old, broken boards. The sun was high and the lake sparkled before us. A few motorboats zoomed about in the far distance. We were completely alone in this pretty little cove. I couldn't resist the opportunity to cool off and soothe my scratched-up, mosquito-bitten limbs in the lake. I stripped and walked in. Martin, thinking I'd gone completely mad, refused to follow me any farther. He paced back and forth worrying that someone else might be so foolish as to force their way down the overgrown path that led to this, our beach.

I walked out to where the water reached my waist, intending to dip in for a swim. However, a pair of vigilant loons in the middle of the lake noticed me and swam over for a closer look. I just stood there in the cool water, silently taking in this magical moment, the loons and I sharing a curiosity for one another. Eventually I had to break the spell because my feet were freezing. I turned away and walked ashore, leaving the lake to the loons. The sun quickly dried me and I got dressed, much to Martin's relief. Unhappy with my antics, he hurriedly walked his bike out of the brush to the main beach and waited for me there.

Cycling back up the unkept trail away from the secluded bay, I failed to duck in time to avoid a low-hanging branch and got clotheslined. My bike careened off a narrow board that had been laid over a wet section of the trail, and I fell face first into a deep mudhole. I was sore and my bike was mangled, but in the thick brush there wasn't enough room to inspect, clean or fix anything. So I hauled myself and my defunct bike out and paused at the edge of the main beach to pop the rear wheel back into its bracket. Martin stood on the large public beach with a group of teenagers, staring at me in disbelief. I must have really looked bad because one of the guys exclaimed "Shit!" at the sight of me. One of the girls chastised him for being so rude. I reassured her by replying that "shit!" had been my exact reaction when I fell into the mud.

I wasn't quite sure whether or not I was pleased to have worn shorts that day – my exposed legs were gashed and muddy, but so were all my clothes. I withdrew from the gawking spectators and, with much poise, kicked off my shoes and walked straight into the lake, this time fully dressed. I waded in knee-deep and splashed the cool water onto my legs, arms and face, clearing off the blood and mud. My filthy T-shirt and shorts would continue to bear my badges of honour. With my back to the beach, perhaps only the loons noticed the big grin on my face!

I love swimming wherever and whenever there's an opportunity, and as there was a heated pool beside our cottage, I made much use of it. Every morning before breakfast, when there was no one else around, I went for a swim in that pool. The lake had its charms, but the pool wasn't as cold. Furthermore, Martin always had fresh, hot coffee ready for me when I got back. Ah yes, this was good. This was the perfect way to prepare for any day of adventure.

On the last day of June, we drove into the bison compound, a vast fenced-in piece of prairie into which American buffalo had been reintroduced. The park signage informed us that bison and buffalo are two names for the same animal. From the lookout, we could see the dark masses of a herd in the distance. So I drove us a couple of kilometres down a winding two-tire track across the grassy plain towards them for a closer look. The buffalo had wandered onto the roadway, stopped and sat down as if to indicate that we weren't to trespass on their land. I turned off the engine and happily complied. We lingered a bit to admire the huge, shaggy animals and take photographs from our car windows. When we'd finally had enough, I carefully drove in reverse, back down the long laneway, leaving the buffalo to their homeland.

Since the beginning of time, bison has been one of the traditional sources of meat in North America, but unfortunately we overhunted them almost to extinction. Now efforts are being made to reintroduce them to the wild, as in this national park. Buffalo are also farmed, as a sustainable source of lean meat. To complete our experience with the buffalo, we dined on a delicious bison stew in a nearby resort, the meat having come from a farm in Quebec. Definitely, bison is tastier and leaner than beef, I opined.

On Canada Day Martin and I dressed up for a two-hour dinner cruise on the *Martese*, a 95-passenger vessel that has been taking people on tours of Clear Lake for many years. As we ate our wonderful dinner, we enjoyed the view of the lake, the forests and the crazy trail we'd cycled along a few days earlier. Cruising was a far more civilized way of enjoying the beauty of the wilderness that surrounded us. I stood at the rail with the breeze fluttering the skirt of my long red crêpe-de-chine dress, taking in "the big picture." We admired the low, wooded hills and peeked into shallow bays as the *Martese* slowly made its way around the lake. Towards the townsite we watched people strolling and cycling along the boardwalk, children and dogs playing on the beach, and boats floating in the water – everyone was enjoying this fine evening. And Martin was happy again.

The sun was still up at 10 p.m. as we drove out of the park to the village of Onanole to watch the Canada Day fireworks, since fireworks are not allowed in the national parks. We joined the long queue of cars and took our place to park in an open field. Rows and rows of cars and pickup trucks covered the pasture. There were two rocking chairs on the back of the truck parked next to us – kids were helping their grandparents up there to watch the spectacle in comfort. This was Canada Day fireworks, Western style. The main attraction started and we were treated to a beautiful show. In the distance, Mother Nature was putting on her own show of lightning and thunder, but she held back the rain until we got safely back to our cottage. Then nature took over, as it should: the rain poured down all night, washing away the smoke of the man-made fireworks and the prints we'd left along the trails.

CENTRAL CANADA

25
Pukaskwa

THE GREAT LAKES – SUPERIOR
KAYAKING BIG WATER

In August 2006 Martin and I went to discover Lake Superior for ourselves. Covering more than 82,000 square kilometres, this is the largest freshwater lake in the world. We were going to explore the northern, Canadian shore, some 700 kilometres along the Trans-Canada Highway from Thunder Bay to Sault Ste. Marie. En route we would stop for a one-week kayaking trip in Pukaskwa National Park, with Naturally Superior Adventures.

We made a few other notable stops along the way. First, just east of Thunder Bay we visited the Terry Fox Memorial, this section of the Trans-Canada Highway being named after a Canadian hero who attempted to walk westbound across Canada after losing one of his legs to cancer. The memorial, set in a beautiful rock garden of native plants overlooking Lake Superior, marks the end of Terry's historic feat.

A little farther east we toured some amethyst mines. We were shown how these purple crystals grow underground, and how they are extracted. The long, broad swaths of semi-precious gemstones were strikingly beautiful. Several pieces of rough-blasted amethyst offered for sale in their shop were very tempting, but already having a small collection in my tropical fish aquarium at home, I left the samples behind.

Onwards along our 465-kilometre drive to Wawa, the two-lane highway wound through rocky Canadian Shield outcrops and forests of conifers. Occasionally we would get glimpses of Lake Superior between the hills that separated the Trans-Canada from the lake. I put the car into cruise control at about 120 km/h; we rarely saw another vehicle on the road. However, at one point a car came into view in my rear-view mirror, catching up to us quickly. And then it passed us, this tiny little Smart car! Who knew those could go that fast?!

We left our rented car in the town of Wawa, and someone from Naturally Superior Adventures transferred us to Rock Island Lodge on Lake Superior. The lodge sits on a large rock peninsula, with big picture windows providing awesome views of Superior's infamous raging surfs and deadly storms, or its gentle waters and warm sunsets, as Mother Nature decides. This ideal spot at the mouth of the Michipicoten River is the home base of Naturally Superior Adventures (gotta love that name!), our outfitter for the next week.

Before we were allowed to start our kayaking trip in Pukaskwa National Park, Martin and I, and a third adventurer, Kelly, had to prove our paddling and wet-exit skills to our guide, Jason. We met on a small sandy beach and donned wetsuits, paddling jackets and personal flotation devices. Fortunately, the water in the Michipicoten was warm, making our kayak half-rolls comfortable: paddle to the middle of the river, flip your boat, rap three times on the upturned hull, pull the kayak-skirt tab and swim out to the surface. Easy. We were having so much fun that the serious, important exercise became more of a game. Eventually we stripped down to our bathing suits and dove into the cooler lake water for a swim.

Later that evening, we sat on the deck of the lodge and enjoyed a delicious Lake Superior whitefish dinner. Everyone was excited, sharing stories of past paddling adventures, and wondering what Lake Superior had in store for us. We were all experienced individuals and I knew we would be a great group.

After our last night of dining amid tables and chairs, sleeping indoors and hot showers, we made an early start for Pukaskwa. We had our waterproof packs loaded in the van and our four kayaks secured to the trailer by 7:30. I was pleased not to have to do the driving for a change; I enjoyed the opportunity to look at the passing scenery during our two-hour trip to the north end of the park. We crossed several interesting-looking rivers and I wondered what lay around the bends, behind the dense forests, and where the water came from. I imagined canoeing down there to find out. Perhaps another trip?

When we arrived at Hattie Cove, in Pukaskwa National Park, the wind was blowing at a steady 60 km/h and the waves were very high and choppy. Keith, the captain of the boat that was to transfer us to the remote southeast end of the park, told us we weren't going anywhere that afternoon: "Lake Superior was in one of its dangerous moods." So we set up camp alongside the wooden steps that led down to the lake, to wait until Superior permitted us to paddle.

The northwest end of the park has a car campground, a visitor centre and various hiking trails, in addition to a long, sandy, log-strewn beach. Kelly, Martin and I set out on a walk to the end of the beach but discovered that there was no end. The sand, pebbles and driftwood stretched continuously on before us no matter how far we walked. We watched as powerful waves forced giant logs, like battering rams, into the driftwood already on the beach. The three of us cautiously walked in relative safety high up on the beach, along the trees. The setting sun, the corresponding drop in temperature, and hunger, eventually forced us back to camp. Jason had a delicious stir fry ready for us, which we enjoyed at a picnic table overlooking the turbulent lake. We wondered if – hoped that – we could paddle the next day.

The delay in getting onto the water had also given us time to participate in a "smudge" ceremony of purification in a teepee at the interpretive centre. Our Indigenous guide explained her Ojibwe traditions while we helped tie small bundles of tobacco. Then we burned braids of sweet grass and inhaled the soft-scented smoke with a wish and a prayer for a safe journey on *gichigami*, a "great lake."

Gichigami was a bit calmer the next morning, so Keith came around with his power boat to collect us and all our gear and kayaks. However, the water was still very rough and each time the little boat crashed down from a steep wave, it felt like my jaw would clench and teeth would break! I was very thankful for having taken motion-sickness pills before the ride. The little boat plowed on for two hours to get to our designated put-in at Cascade Falls. Once there, Keith determined that the water was too choppy for the boat to safely access the dock. Instead he dropped us onto a beach on Otter Island, not far from the mainland. Ahhh, solid land! We spent the rest of the morning land-bound and no one complained.

There is an old lighthouse on Otter Island, dating back to 1903, now automated. We explored a dank shack nearby, and the lightkeeper's cabin, which now serves as the park's emergency shelter. There's an emergency helipad there too – good to know. The rest of the island is covered with wild blueberry bushes. We gorged on the ripe fruit while gathering another litre bottle full of them. We were set for a traditional Canadian breakfast of blueberry pancakes with maple syrup the next day.

Finally we got to do some paddling, if just a short trip across to Cascade Falls. We put our heads down and bravely made our way over the still choppy water, safely reaching the mainland. We set up our three tents and the kitchen tent on a sandy beach.

Once all the chores were done, we went for a short hike to explore Cascade Falls. At the top of the steep, rocky climb we found a nice deep swimming hole from which the waterfalls flowed. We dove in. Sun-heated rocks radiated like a furnace, warming the water in the still part of the pool while the cascading water along the edge was cool. This was wonderful.

We cooked most of our meals on a camp stove or over campfires. Breakfasts of oatmeal, cereals or blueberry and wild raspberry pancakes, with strong coffee, gave us strength for hours of paddling. We enjoyed lunches of hot soups, bread and crackers, cold meats, cheese and various spreads. Every evening, dinners of one-pot stir-fries, curries and stews were devoured with gusto. We even made s'mores for dessert, the fire-roasted marshmallows melting a piece of chocolate between graham crackers, reminding me of nights long ago at Girl Guide camps. Amazingly, we were able to drink water directly from the lake – what a wonderful surprise that this could still safely be done in southern Canada! Then again, we were keenly aware of the sad significance of that surprise: most freshwater is too polluted.

We got up early on each of our six days on Lake Superior. Jason constantly checked the radio for the most current marine forecasts. We discovered that those often had no relation to what was happening at our specific spot on the huge lake. We had been hoping to take advantage of the purportedly "normal" calm morning waters. Some days, however, we were stuck on land until late afternoon before Gichigami settled. Then we would paddle anywhere from 8 to 22 kilometres, slowly making on our way back to Hattie Cove.

Some days, Lake Superior was so calm that our paddles created the only ripples. Other days, we had hard slogs through choppy waters and strong headwinds. In some sections of the shore, we paddled between many tiny, tree-sheltered islands. In other places we would cross the exposed fronts of wide bays from which Superior stretched out to the horizon. So wide was the expanse of "nothingness" to our left, westward, that we clearly saw the curvature of the Earth. Our kayaks seemed way too small to manage on such a large, endless body of water.

We often paddled close inshore, under the arching canopy of trees. Noble bald eagles regularly flew from their perches at the top of tall pine trees as we quietly passed under them. Cute, curious otters would cheekily swim around our kayaks, then defiantly dive out of sight. Occasionally a big splash would cause us to look up, too late, as a fish jumped – we speculated that these must be large fish to cause such a commotion on the surface.

I did some short sidetrips on my own, paddling up small rivers that flowed into the lake. This was my opportunity to see what was around those corners. In the tree-protected waterways I found tranquility. Sometimes loons greeted me with their haunting calls. Always the tunes of songbirds drifted through the forest. This is where I was most at peace.

I discovered that I definitely preferred paddling in such narrow rivers, as opposed to large, open waters. For me, even canoeing on whitewater rivers, where the river morphology is predictable, is preferable to paddling the chaotic currents on large lakes and seas. Big water is just too powerful and has way too much energy for my comfort. On this adventure, however, I always had to rejoin the rest of the group to continue lake paddling on the aptly named "Superior."

We were landbound one day when Gichigami decided to show us something of its powerfully dangerous storms, with rain and high, white-crested waves. We heeded the warnings to stay off the water, and decided instead to explore the sanctuary of the forest that abutted the lake. Not too far from our camp we found an old, overgrown trail. Carefully following the route, sometimes more by instinct than any semblance of a footpath, we stumbled upon a moss-covered log fishing cabin. As its roof had long ago fallen in and saplings grew from within, the hut obviously hadn't been used in many, many years. Although the cabin had been built far from the reach of the stormy Gichigami, sadly it now offered shelter only to the mosquitos. And those bloodsuckers were very happy to see us. Swarms of them forced us out of the woods and back to the wet, windy beach.

When eventually the storm cleared, we draped our damp clothes over small trees, and sat ourselves down on driftwood to dry in the sun. However, the mosquitoes that had been hiding in the forest during the storm also took advantage of the good weather, and came out to feed on us again. So, as soon as we were dry, we headed back out onto the lake, leaving the mosquitos behind and putting an end to our blood loss.

We stopped to inspect the Pukaskwa Pits, ancient hollows lined with stones on a moss- and lichen-covered rocky beach. These pits were built by Indigenous Peoples so long ago that no one knows anymore what the structures had been used for. We wandered around carefully so as not to disturb the site, wondering about the long history of people living in this rich and beautiful land.

At our next campsite, on large, flat granite rocks of exposed Canadian Shield, we had to use boulders to hold down our billowing tents so they wouldn't take flight in the powerful wind. Despite the wind, however, the sun bore down onto the treeless granite, creating that oven-like effect again. The result was a warming of the pools of rainwater that had been caught in the depressions and crevasses in the shield rock. We used those natural hot tubs to rinse off the sweat and dirt of the last few days.

That night, at about two in the morning, I was awakened by so much light shining into my eyes. The full moon was shining right through the tent walls. I went out to explore. Everything was silent in the silvery light outside. The light glistened on the lake, creating a perfect reflection of our beached kayaks. The sky was so bright I could take a photograph of my own moon shadow! Chuckling to myself, I crawled back into my sleeping bag with a contented grin on my face. Life was good.

As we approached Hattie Cove we started seeing hikers on the waterfront trail as well as sailboats and other kayaks. Keith motored by to check up on us. He had become concerned upon hearing reports of a bear attack. Having been isolated from society for a few days, we knew nothing about the emergency. Apparently other kayakers had had to retreat onto the water and helplessly watch as a black bear savaged their tent and all its contents. The bear had gorged on the contents of their food packs. When the kayakers returned to the remnants of their camp, they found they had no choice but to abandon their trip and return to Hattie Cove.

We had been fortunate not to have had any problems with bears, or any other creatures (other than mosquitos), at our campsites. We had always kept our sites clean, no food or unwashed dishes lying around. Martin and Kelly always did the dishes while Jason and I stashed everything carefully into the kayaks or high up, dangling from the trees. Perhaps too, as we had been farther away from civilization, any nearby bears did not associate us with food. In any case, we noted it is always worthwhile to respect wild animals and not tempt them with our human "goodies."

The sun was already hot when we started our last paddle on Lake Superior. The south winds at our backs created large whitecaps which bounced off a rocky point we had to navigate around. Our tiny boats were pushed about seemingly randomly, water sloshing over the decks. Amazingly, we actually did make progress. With our heads down and steady, strong strokes, we noted how we passed each successive landmark: that boulder, that tree stump, that log, that point of land. My muscles were aching, complaining about the stress, but like the others, I pressed onwards. There was no time to complain and no point in it anyway. We had to paddle.

We finally made it around the last bluff and into the shelter of Hattie Cove. With relief we gently zigzagged our way between the many rocks and islands that dotted the edge of the channel to our takeout point by the visitor centre. And then it was over. For all the hard paddling that seemed to last forever, in the end it seemed to be over too soon.

A day later we were enrobed in domesticity again: hotel rooms with hot showers and flush toilets, restaurants with tables and chairs, cars with air conditioning, and clean clothes and dry shoes. The contrast to the lifestyle we'd opted for during the previous week was extreme. Although I was pleased to know I could live with so little, I recognized that, come winter, I would be grateful for the comforts of civilization. People invented all this comfortable "stuff" for a reason.

As I drove our rented car along the 227 kilometres from Wawa to Sault Ste. Marie, Martin and I made like most tourists, starting with photographing the giant Canada goose statue at Wawa. We stopped at Superior Provincial Park to walk along the deserted beach at Old Woman Bay. Such a pretty spot. We wondered why there wasn't anyone else enjoying it. We finally found other tourists hiking along the short trail to see the Agawa pictographs, ancient rock drawings overlooking Gichigami. We joined the crowd, carefully making our way along the narrow, slippery-wet walkway between surf below and cliff above. This ancient Indigenous art must be a lot tougher than we are, to have survived Lake Superior's furies for so long, I thought.

The only thing we had left to tough out was the flight back to Toronto. During our week of kayaking, we had been completely cut off from all news of the world. At the airport we discovered we were no longer allowed to pack liquids, including toiletries and my contact lens solutions, in our carry-on bags. We had no idea why, but we, like most of our fellow travellers, had to hurriedly repack and dump the water from our drinking bottles. While the airport staff were patient with us, the place was chaotic with panicked passengers. I was tired and stressed out by the time I got to my seat on the plane. I cried with exhaustion. How did we get so far from simple existence living? What were we doing to ourselves and the world?!

26
Bruce Peninsula

THE GREAT LAKES – HURON
HIKING ON THE CLIFF EDGE

As Bruce Peninsula National Park is close to my home in southern Ontario, I've hiked there many times, especially along the Bruce Trail. The Bruce Trail is so named because it leads from Queenston Heights on the Niagara River in the south to the tip of the Bruce Peninsula in the north. The "Trail to the Bruce" runs almost 900 kilometres along the Niagara Escarpment, a 510-metre-high dolostone and shale cliff. The Escarpment has been named a UNESCO World Biosphere Reserve because of the work the local communities do to preserve and protect the area's white cedar trees that are up to 1,300 years old, as well as over 100 species of flora and fauna listed as threatened or endangered. There are even wild orchids, over 36 varieties, on the Bruce Peninsula!

My first time in the park was with Harbourfront Canoe School in 1990. I was a part-time hike and canoe trip leader for Harbourfront, but on this occasion I acted as a backup leader. We took a group of hikers, 18 adults, on our bus to celebrate Thanksgiving on the Bruce. We arrived late on the Friday night and set up our tents in the group campsite. It was a typically chilly October weekend. Everyone bundled up in their thermal long underwear and fleeces inside their sleeping bags.

The following morning we made pancakes on our propane stoves. These hot treats were served up with luscious pure maple syrup. Good, plentiful food makes for happy campers, no matter what the weather.

Coffee was made camp style, in a kettle on an open fire – my job was to keep that fire going. I happily volunteered for fire duty because it meant I could always stand at the source of the heat: smoky, but warm.

Jeff, one of our leaders, liked to show off his scientific method of separating the coffee grounds from the liquid. He'd tie a bandana to the kettle handle, and swing the entire kettle around in a vertical circle at arm's length so centrifugal force would push the grounds to the bottom of the pot. On the last time round, however, the kettle broke free of its handle. The boiling-hot pot went flying through the air, between several trees, and landed upright in the bushes! Somewhere between reliefs – that no one was hit and that the coffee was still in the pot – everyone fell about the place laughing. Besides the issue of having no handle on the kettle anymore, we agreed never to use the Jeff method again – way too dangerous.

Our first day of hiking was perfect: a beautiful sunny autumn day. Everyone enjoyed the outing, hiking northwards on the Bruce Trail, along the upper edge of the cliff. To our left, a wall of mixed forest crowded us against that edge. We dared to step out onto the long rock overhangs to admire the tree canopy below us. The cold nights had already changed the colour of the leaves into a tapestry of reds, oranges, yellows and browns. This colourful carpet contrasted sharply with the turquoise-blue waters of Georgian Bay far below. Off in the distance, a few forested islands dotted the Great-Lake-sized bay. Some of those islands belong to Fathom Five, a national marine park I had still to visit. I contemplated the opportunities.

All day the air had been sweet with the decay of the summer's flora, but as evening approached, the wind picked up. The temperature had dropped considerably by the time we arrived back in the park's group campsite. The brisk air and exercise had rendered us all famished.

We wrapped our huge precooked turkey in aluminum foil and set it in the campfire to reheat. Potatoes and large chunks of butternut squash were likewise cooked in the fire. Someone had prepared a large salad to accompany the main course. We had even brought along pumpkin pies: several of us took turns trying to whip the cream with forks, as we'd forgotten to bring a whisk. Dinner was eaten with great gusto, and haste, standing behind tarpaulin windbreaks. This was a very rustic Thanksgiving feast.

Somehow, being exposed to the elements as we were, that Thanksgiving Day was so much more meaningful. We were keenly aware of the hardships the first settlers would have had out in this wilderness.

We were thankful we had warm houses with all conveniences and luxuries to go home to.

Our second hike, continuing to the north end of the Bruce, was much more challenging than the previous day had been. The trail was considerably rougher. We had to climb up and down the cliff face a few times and scramble over boulder beaches. Furthermore, the weather had changed: rain poured down from a dark sky all day long. The rocks were slippery, the trail muddy. We walked with our faces to the ground, watching that each step was secure. Hiking staffs were a great help to those of us who had them. We didn't linger to explore the dark, damp caves we passed. Neither did we stop to watch the roiling water and giant white waves crashing violently onto the rocky shoreline beside us. The roar from below, and from above, was deafening, so no one spoke much.

The plan had been to hike the final 18 kilometres from Cyprus Lake in the park to the northern trail terminus. By the time we got to Little Cove, we were all soaked, with either rain from the outside, sweat from the inside or both. Our "breathable waterproof" jackets had been no match for that storm. All but six of us dropped out of the hike, opting instead for a warm, dry bus ride to Tobermory, the hamlet at the end of the trail.

Five guys and I were in agreement that since we were already wet, more rain no longer mattered. Tenaciously we hiked on, stopping only to wolf down granola bars and bottled water, to fuel our pace. To keep warm, we hiked as fast as we dared along the treacherous trail. We kept our faces down to avoid the onslaught of driving rain. If there was anything interesting to observe along the way, we missed it. Our only thought was to complete the miserable hike as soon as possible – and to be able to boast that we'd done it. An hour, or six kilometres, later we arrived at the stone cairn that marks the north end of the Bruce Trail. But we were way too cold to stop for victory photos. We just wanted to find our bus, get back to camp and change into dry clothing.

After a few minutes of searching, we found the rest of our group – in the laundromat. They were standing around, men and women, all half naked. Their wet clothes were in the driers. We too stripped down to our underwear, and added our coats, shirts, pants and socks, into the machines. One chivalrous guy felt sorry for me and put over my shoulders an extra windbreaker he'd brought along. We laughed at what the locals might have thought of us, had they been able to see us through the steamed-up laundromat windows!

Many years later I wanted to finish hiking the entire Bruce Trail, and I had just a short section of it left to do in Bruce Peninsula National Park. So I joined a group of 30 people doing the "end-to-end" (trail start to finish) set of hikes, led by Peter and Don, hike leaders from one of the Bruce Trail Conservancy clubs.

That particular spring long weekend on the peninsula, our group was joined by another end-to-end group, ballooning our crew to almost 50. We aimed to hike an average of 20 kilometres on each of three days. This time I got to enjoy wonderful weather during my entire visit.

The section of trail we were hiking along was a bit farther inland, and Georgian Bay wasn't always in sight. Although we were in the middle of the woods, the trees were just budding and the forest seemed sparse. Partway down the other side of a hill we'd just crested, we spotted a black bear. It had obviously noticed us first, because it was running, almost falling over itself, down the hill away from us. Our single-file procession along the narrow trail came to a halt to watch the bear. The bear was just out of hibernation and had been looking for fresh green vegetation to eat – not interested in people at all.

A woman near the back of our group caught up to those of us up front, and looked around to find out why we'd stopped. Upon seeing the bear she screamed at the top of her lungs, scaring the wits out of all of us and especially the poor bear, who just wanted desperately to get away from us. The bear tumbled between the leafless trees, rolled the rest of the way down the hill and then ran out of sight. Within few moments the panic-stricken lady had calmed down and blushed. This had been the first time she'd ever seen a bear in the wild, and she'd reacted as she'd seen done in melodramatic movies.

We gently explained to this person that black bears are primarily vegetarians, enjoying fish too but very rarely eating meat. They only kill if provoked (although who knows what might bug a bear), but even then they usually only maul, not eat, their victims. The lady apologized for her overreaction. The forest went quiet again and we hiked on in silence.

Other critters such squirrels and chipmunks scampered through the newly sprouting ground cover. God's rock garden was coming into bloom, with trillions of trilliums everywhere, Ontario's provincial flower. Scattered around the forest floor were clusters of large yellow lady's slipper orchids. Back on the rocky cliff edge we had to carefully step around the poison ivy growing in the middle of the trail. Peering over the cliff, we could see where rocks had long ago broken off the escarpment and tumbled into the turquoise waters below. Georgian Bay was so tranquil and clear that we could see the huge slabs of escarpment dolomite deep under the crystalline surface.

During the afternoon of our second day, a couple of people decided they'd had enough. They were tired and nursing blistered feet. So without letting Peter, who was leading, or Don, who was our sweep (designated end-person), know they were quitting, they turned up the dirt road at Halfway Dump, intending to take a shortcut to Highway 6 and hitchhike back into the campsite. Unfortunately, about 20 people behind them blindly followed, not realizing they were no longer on the blazed Bruce Trail. As there had been a gap between those 20 hikers and the last 10, those last 10 were oblivious to the fact that 20 had gone AWOL.

At our end point for the day, at Cyprus Lake in the national park, Peter stopped to wait for the rest of the group to catch up. After 10 minutes Don arrived signifying that everyone should be accounted for. But we were 20 people short. No one could figure out how we could have lost that many people on a clearly marked trail along the escarpment edge. Don and I volunteered to go back and look for signs of what might have happened to the missing hikers. We hadn't gone far when we saw the vagrant group coming towards us.

The couple that had wanted to take a shortcut eventually realized, after several kilometres on the dirt road, that they had not taken a shortcut after all. In fact, that unpaved road up to Highway 6 is about

10 kilometres long, and the campsite is about another 15 kilometres after that! By comparison, the Bruce Trail from Halfway Dump to our campsite in the park was only seven kilometres long. So much for taking shortcuts without first consulting maps.

On our final day we hiked from our campsite to Tobermory, the same 18 kilometres I had previously hiked in the pouring rain. This time we had gloriously sunny warm weather. We stopped to explore the Grotto, a large cave with a water bottom, the back of which is visible by scrambling down the rocky cliff face. We slowed to admire the vistas of the turquoise bay. We sat on a rocky outcrop for a casual picnic lunch, sunning ourselves under the cloudless sky. We stopped to photograph the many wild native orchids. We chatted away and eventually arrived at the end of the trail. We toasted the wonderful day and our completion of the Bruce Trail. We photographed each other at the cairn – we made it!

27
Georgian Bay Islands

THE GREAT LAKES – HURON
ISLAND BOUND

There are three national parks on Lake Huron's Georgian Bay: the 30,000 Islands of Georgian Bay Islands National Park on the northeast side, and Bruce Peninsula National Park, with Fathom Five National Marine Park attached to it, on the southwest side. That suggests the size of Georgian Bay: 15,000 square kilometres. Given the proximity of the six million or so people living just a few hours away in the Greater Toronto Area, it's probably a good thing to have so many parks nearby, distributing the potential impact of so many people.

On the Victoria Day long weekend in 1997, I went on a canoe-camping trip with my then boyfriend, Martin, to Thirty Thousand Islands. After a two-hour drive to Honey Harbour, and a bit of exploration of the neighbourhood, we ran out of time to paddle to the islands on that first day. So we set up our tent in a private campground on the waterfront. The evening was calm and the sun was setting over Georgian Bay as we sat at a picnic table enjoying the local whitefish we'd barbecued for dinner.

When camping in good weather, I love to indulge in the luxury of doing my "toilette" outdoors by the lake or river, on a rock or log. I borrow a dishpan or soup bowl filled with clean water. If there's hot water available, I'll temper the cold water before washing my face. I have developed a similar routine for brushing my teeth, but using a mug instead of a bowl. The used water gets tossed into the bush. Unfortunately, that night I learned the hard way that I must manage my contact lenses inside the tent: even the slightest of breezes was sufficient to blow a lens off my finger as soon as it was out of my eye. Luckily I'd quickly found the lens I'd lost, beside the picnic table. Then I did the previously unthinkable: I cleaned and stored the lens overnight in sterile solution, and put it back into my eye in the morning! Risky, but no harm done.

We rented our canoe from the marina at Honey Harbour. After loading our waterproofed camping gear and "trimming" the canoe (balancing its cargo), we paddled off over the rough waves to Beausoleil, the park's largest island. The trip was a bit of a slog, but after a couple of hours we were on the leeward side of the island and took out at a gently sloped, pinkish granite slab, part of the Canadian Shield. The Shield contains some of the oldest rock on the planet, and on Georgian Bay it is exposed due to erosion by prehistoric glaciers. Although this shallow, smooth rock looked inviting to land our canoe on, it was actually very difficult to avoid scraping the bottom of the boat while trying to step out of it without getting one's feet wet. Not only that, but the granite below the waterline was slippery with a thin, slimy coating of algae. We managed to protect the bottom of the canoe, but we did get our feet and pant-legs wet as we slid off our chosen rock.

We immediately set up our tent in a designated "primitive" campground, changed into dry shoes and got dinner going. Our standard first-night dinner has always been bacon-wrapped beef tenderloin with scalloped potatoes and salad. Red wine from a plastic bottle completes our meal. After that, we don't need to worry about meat and salad greens spoiling due to lack of refrigeration. On this particular evening, however, we sat huddled on a log outside our tent and scoffed down our dinner as quickly as possible. The wind had picked up and the weather turned miserable despite the rosy forecast the previous day. That's apt to happen on Georgian Bay. So we layered on the thermal long underwear, fleeces and jackets, and the only thing left to do was crawl into our sleeping bags and hope for the weather to improve.

The following morning was worse than the night: the wind had brought rain. Now it was cold *and* wet. The waves around the island had become white-capped, quashing our plans to circumnavigate Beausoleil Island. We were island-bound.

Unperturbed, we decided to explore on foot. We'd hike around the island, stringing together several trails that would give us a good

10-kilometre walk. So off we went, in rainproof jackets and hiking boots with gaiters. In our waterproofed day packs we carried supplies to have a picnic lunch, with any luck, in a park shelter.

We walked quickly, about five km/h, just to stay warm. The views over the bay were dismal as the rain was bucketing down. Normally Georgian Bay is a playground for leisure craft, water-skiers and sport fishers, but there were no boats out that day. We didn't linger on the rocky shores, in the driving rain.

In the relative protection of the forested sections of the broad, flat trails, we slowed our pace to catch our breath. We passed by and through a few deserted campgrounds, no tents anywhere. It seemed we were the only people on the island. We laughed at ourselves: "How foolish others would think we are, canoe-camping in this weather!" In my typical positive approach to life, I jested that "at least there are no mosquitos to bother us today."

Somewhere on that soggy island, at the junction of two paths, we came across two dripping-wet people huddled under a tree, eating snacks. "Wow, there are others as crazy as us!" Of course we stopped to speak with them. After just the few words of greeting, the guy spoke up: "Marlis! What are you doing here?!" It was Rick, my boss, vacationing with his girlfriend. Neither of us had mentioned in our Toronto office anything about plans to visit Georgian Bay Islands National Park. How was it possible we'd both be on the same deserted island, on the same trail, in the pouring rain, at the same time? Very odd! We introduced our significant others, and shared tales of paddling to this island. However, as it was too cold to stand around too long, we soon hiked off towards our respective campsites, muttering on about the odds of such an encounter.

A couple of years earlier, when I was working in another department of the same company, my husband and I had joined a hiking trip in Zion and Bryce national parks in the United States. As we were taking an elevator to our group meeting point in a Las Vegas hotel lobby, Rick stepped into that same elevator a few floors down. He too had been heading to Zion, but with another group of people. Two chance encounters with the same person was just too weird. For several years

307

after our meeting on Georgian Bay, I made a point of letting Rick know where I was travelling to, and that he was not allowed to go there at the same time. Our colleagues were starting to wonder about us.

Back on Beausoleil Island, the rain stopped the following day, but it was still very cold and the wind strong. All our stuff was wet and we were miserable. Not knowing what the weather would be like for another day, we decided to cut our losses and leave the park.

The paddling back to Honey Harbour was hard. There was a strong headwind. Waves sloshed over the sides of our canoe, filling it with water. We put our heads down and plowed on. I was in the stern and periodically would stop paddling and bail out the accumulated water. The trip seemed to take forever. By the time we pulled onto the shore at the marina, we were exhausted. We stood on the shoreline and looked back across the water. Oddly, no longer being in that treacherous situation, we thought the journey back had been surprisingly short. We felt as though we could have paddled longer. Martin and I laughed at our folly. How quickly we'd forgotten our hardships.

Later that day, sitting cozily in a warm, dry restaurant overlooking the bay dotted with those pretty islands, Martin and I thought back on our adventure in the park. We agreed we'd no longer trust the weather on May long weekends! Some years it's warm and sunny, other years it's absolutely dismal. And when it's so miserable, we really don't want to be stuck outside camping anymore. Ever since that visit to Georgian Bay Islands National Park, we chose to stay in cottages or hotels for our adventures on May long weekends.

28
Point Pelee

BUTTERFLY MIGRATION

I first visited Point Pelee National Park in 1991 with a girlfriend whose family is from Leamington, Ontario, right near the park. I was living alone at the time, and my friend's family invited me to share their Thanksgiving dinner. I took advantage of the opportunity to see the park, and asked them to show me around. That afternoon, we drove to the small, 15 square kilometre park. The Carolinian forest on the island had already prepared for winter, so there were no leaves on or under the trees. The land was as grey and bleak as Lake Erie around it. We walked out along the sandspit to the southernmost point of the Canadian mainland. We stood at the very tip with our coats buttoned up tight, holding on to our hats. The bitterly cold wind tore at the trees behind us and the rough surf threatened to wash the sand off the beach. Only a few gulls lingered, crying in the gale. It was such an unpleasant day that my visit was a very short one.

Twenty-two years later, Martin and I decided to cycle the 550-kilometre Lake Erie Waterfront Trail. We pedalled approximately 55 kilometres a day, on weekends through the summer, westward from the Niagara River to Windsor. We travelled each section eastward, with the prevailing wind behind us, and only on nice days. As we got farther from home, we started staying overnight in bed and breakfasts and pedalling two days in a row regardless of the weather. By mid-September we were cycling near Point Pelee, a 3½-hour drive from our home near Toronto.

On a Sunday morning I woke up in our lodging with a slight migraine, a precursor of unsettled weather. Then I found that my rear bicycle tire had gone flat overnight – another bad omen. True to my tenacious character, I took some painkillers, inflated the tire and set out for the day's ride. However, within minutes of our arriving at the trail, the sky had gone dark and a light rain had started. Martin convinced me to abandon the effort. He dangled in front of me the opportunity to visit a national park. He had never been to Point Pelee National Park, and he didn't really want to pedal in the rain with a cranky cycling partner.

By the time I parked the car at the southernmost parking lot in Point Pelee National Park, the sky had cleared. We took a chance and pumped up my bike tire, again. Then, from the visitor centre, we cycled two kilometres due south along the main trail through Point Pelee. We walked the last half kilometre, over the hard-packed sand, to the end of the spit. Like the last time I was here, Lake Erie was rough, washing over the point of land. The waves crashing onto the rocks on the west side of the spit sounded like an angry ocean. We hurried over to the eastern, leeward, side of the point and took a few steps north into the Carolinian forest to get out of the cold wind.

The Carolinian forest is the Canadian name of the part of the Eastern Deciduous Forest of the US which reaches up into southern Ontario. Only in the very southern fringes of Canada are chestnut, butternut, black cherry, winterberry holly, common pawpaw and sourgum trees found in the wild. On Point Pelee we were delighted to walk under tulip trees, sycamores, black walnuts, red mulberries and sassafras, also part of the Carolinian zone.

And that's where we also found countless monarch butterflies silently flitting about. These beautiful large insects were everywhere, their distinctive orange and black wings contrasting with the blue sky, green trees and purple asters along the footpaths. We had to be careful not to step on the ones resting on the sandy ground. They didn't seem to take any notice of Martin and me, the only people in the park. Most of the monarchs were settled in the trees, awaiting the right weather to continue their migration over the Great Lakes to their Mexican winter residence. That these tiny, fragile beings could fly so far seemed impossible.

Above the butterflies, swallows swept through the air, with gulls gliding far overhead. Turkey vultures and broad-winged hawks circled

310

over the tip of Point Pelee. All were on their respective fall migrations. Witnessing the strength of these relatively small creatures reminded me that I too must have hidden strengths. If a butterfly could journey so far, so could I.

As Martin and I started back to our car, my tire went flat again. Pushing my bike, we walked slowly, enjoying the beauty around us. Our silence was rewarded with the sight of a deer grazing in the bush next to the trail, and farther along, a pair of wild turkeys crossing the road. We stopped to inspect the turtle nests that Parks had covered with wire screening to protect them from predators.

With our bikes securely strapped to the rack on the car, I drove back north along the only road in the park. We made a short stop at the marsh. This small habitat is almost all that remains of the vast wetlands that had once bordered most of the north shore of Lake Erie. Most of the swamps had been drained long ago, to accommodate rich farmland. We walked along the 1 kilometre floating boardwalk, reading the placards that explained how marshes clean the air and water. Apparently these wetlands are home to many species of fish, insects, amphibians, reptiles, mammals and birds. However, most of those little creatures stay well hidden, and we saw just a few red-winged blackbirds trilling in the reeds that day. We contented ourselves with the vistas of cattails swaying in the breeze.

I decided that my migraine and the flat tire had been just slight inconveniences. In return for my positive outlook, we had been rewarded with the opportunity to enjoy what Point Pelee had to offer. For such a small park, there sure was a lot to experience (obviously the reason for the park). The sun was out and the world was smiling on us.

29
Rouge River (Urban)

BRIGHT RED FORESTS, AND SNAKES

In May of 2015 the Rouge became Canada's first national urban park. This park consolidated almost 8000 hectares of parks, wilderness and farmland just east of Toronto, Canada's largest urban area.

As I haven't discriminated against any of the various types of parks, such as marine and reserve ones, in my quest to visit all the national parks of Canada, I thought it appropriate that I include this new type of national park: urban. On Thanksgiving Day in 2015 Martin and I went for a visit.

My original thought was to cycle the trails in Rouge National Urban Park. However, while researching the infrastructure of the park, I discovered that cycling was permitted primarily only on the many roads that cross through or run alongside the park. I quickly changed our plans to walking, and discovered why most of the trails are not open to cycling.

Our 13-kilometre route included a 4-kilometre loop and two 4.4-kilometre return trips at each of the north and south ends of that loop. These trails meandered around the Rouge River and Little Rouge Creek. We walked mostly through woodlands: groves of hardwood, cedar, conifers and mixed forest. There wasn't, however, much underbrush beneath the trees because so many people and their dogs had trampled off the trails, killing off most of the small plants that should have been thriving on the shady forest floor.

On the warm autumn day we visited, the sumac bushes and maple trees had already become a glowing red, the birch trees were blazing yellows and the oak leaves had turned brown. This tapestry of brilliant colours was offset against the dark evergreens and a bright blue sky above. The leaves that had already fallen carpeted the trail and rustled as we walked through.

There were log steps down several steep slopes to the river and creek. On some very narrow stairways, there were banisters for security. Our climbs back up to the tops of the valleys were rewarded by vistas of the clear water meandering through the red valleys. The shallow waters sparkled over rocks, and pools reflected the sun above us. We watched a father and son paddle a canoe downstream. At the south end of the park, we saw metre-long salmon struggling to swim upstream to their spawning grounds, and spent (also stinky) fish lying dead on the riverbanks.

Some of the paths ran around grown-in marshes. Bulrushes and reeds grew so high there that we could barely see the birdhouses mounted on tree poles around the edges of the marshes. The inhabitants of these houses had already flown south for the winter. Only a few starlings were left, flying around us. Canada geese still floated in the middle of the ponds, wearily watching the dogs people were walking.

And then there were the many baby garter snakes on the gravelly sections of trail. These yellow- and black-striped snakes are non-venomous, and their main usefulness in life seems to be controlling the mouse population. That day, when children weren't poking at them, the garters basked in the warmth of the autumn sun.

Everything, and everyone, seemed to be out to absorb the last of this year's warmth. We passed hundreds of people, young and old, families and individuals. We exchanged greetings with all; some with just a smile, some with wishes of good morning or good day, and others with "Happy Thanksgiving!"

30
St. Lawrence Islands

THE ST. LAWRENCE RIVER
WONDERLAND, STRIFE AND PLAYGROUNDS

As a child I had been to Thousand Islands National Park with my family. My memories are vague: we camped at the Ivy Lea campground and did a boat tour of the islands. Images of a Cinderella story fleck my memory – a visit to the unfinished Boldt Castle on Heart Island, just outside the park on the US side of the St. Lawrence River.

Fast forward to the spring of 1995: Martin, my boyfriend at the time, was an avid cyclist, and I enjoyed mountain biking. As Martin had never been to the Thousand Islands, I proposed that we explore a portion of the 40-kilometre Thousand Islands Parkway. We agreed to make a long weekend of it: some cycling, some sightseeing and also taking that same boat tour I had done as a child. The cycling part of the plan was to pedal 30 kilometres from a hotel in touristy Gananoque to historic Mallorytown and back, in a day.

We had perfect weather for our weekend of exploration. After an easy three-hour drive along the Trans-Canada Highway to Gananoque, we checked into our hotel and enjoyed the warm afternoon walking around town. We loved the picturesque waterfront, with all the small boats bobbing in the river. We wandered into a pleasant little restaurant for a romantic dinner.

The following morning we set out on our hybrid mountain bikes along a path that paralleled the Parkway through Thousand Islands National Park. The pavement of the path was very bumpy with cracks and potholes, and warped in all directions, but it was preferable to the Parkway itself because we didn't have to be careful of vehicular traffic. On the bike path, we could look around and enjoy the scenery as we pedalled.

The Thousand Islands Parkway is very broad, with wide grassy shoulders and meadows on either side. A soft breeze stirred the warm, sweet air. Butterflies flitted about. Birds trilled from the tall reeds in the swampier sections. Martin, being an immigrant to Canada, didn't recognize some of the birds. He asked me, "What are those black birds with red wings called?" How do you answer that without sounding flippant? "I'm not pulling your leg. They're called red-winged blackbirds. Really."

To our right, on the south side of the route, was the fast-flowing St. Lawrence River. Occasionally woodlots would obscure our view, but for the most part we could see islands and sometimes even clear across the river to the US side, where small towns and fancy cottages lined the river. Lakers shipping goods between ports on the Great Lakes and the Atlantic Ocean plied the narrow St. Lawrence Seaway alongside the river. Vacationers in pleasure boats hurried to and fro amongst the many (1000?) islands.

Although we took our time, or perhaps because we rode for too long without taking a break, my legs were aching on our return trip. After about 40 kilometres of almost continuous pedalling, my muscles had turned to jelly. Never mind cycle, I could barely walk as I pushed my bike along. Martin waited patiently for me. I forced myself forward to the gas station/general store we could see in the distance. Finally, a place to stop and rest. We had lunch at the food bar attached to the store. Even after a half-hour break, my leg muscles wouldn't work. I was concerned about causing serious injury if I forced myself to continue cycling. We needed a ride "home."

I normally don't hitchhike. In fact, I've only done so in emergencies. And this was one. I approached the next person who stopped to fuel up his car, and asked him to give us a ride to our hotel just 20 kilometres away. As it turns out, the person I asked was not a tourist. He was on his way to his home on one of the nearby islands. He asked us to wait at the station while he drove his sedan home and returned with his pickup truck, which our bikes would fit into. We didn't have to wait long. He was a cyclist himself and was more than pleased to help us out. In fact, on our way back to Gananoque, he insisted on giving us a tour through various islands interconnected with small bridges. Playing guide, he pointed out all the parks and historic sites en route. A large part of the War of 1812 was played out here, with British and US armies fighting for control of Upper Canada.

By the time we got back to our hotel, I'd forgotten about how feeble my legs were, and I fell out of the pickup truck. The gentleman gallantly helped me to my feet, and then helped Martin stash our bikes in the hotel's storage shed. After many grateful "thank-yous," I went to bed to rest. But not before I'd eaten a huge, delicious, protein- and iron-rich steak for dinner to help me recover.

We had planned our trip well. The next day, I was very happy to be sitting in the tour boat, being driven around the many islands. Some of the Thousand Islands are just massive rocks in the river, some with a single tenacious tree growing on them. Others are larger, with parks and cottages. I only had to get up and walk – light exercise – to see Boldt Castle. Indeed, the mansion still presents like a fairy tale set in the midst of majestic gardens on a small, rocky island. Due to the protection of so many other nearby islands, only calm waters lapped the shoreline of this fantasy island. With the mystique of how much more luxurious the estate might have been had it ever been completed, I realized that the Cinderella memories from my childhood were not just dreams.

Fast forward again, to the summer of 2011. Martin, my husband, and I have had a lot more experience cycling and I had grown stronger. We cycled the 750-kilometre Waterfront Trail in 15 days, from Fort George at Niagara-on-the-Lake, through the length of the Thousand Islands Parkway and down the St. Lawrence River to the Quebec boundary. Cycling an average of 50 kilometres per day, this time I pedalled the length of the Thousand Islands Parkway with ease.

We learned more about the War of 1812 from the brass plaques commemorating the various historic sites along the Parkway. Indigenous Peoples had once lived and played in the woodlands. Then Europeans arrived and fought each other, conspiring with and against the original peoples for the heart of North America. So much blood had been brutally shed on this land 200 years ago. Now children play again in these very same places, but the land has been recast into manicured parks and fun beaches. Neither those first people nor the soldiers would recognize the land if they could see it now.

As we cycled along the parkway, Martin and I laughed at our memories of the red-winged blackbirds and of my collapsed legs. I still feel gratitude for the generosity of that man who rescued me.

31
La Mauricie

THE LAURENTIAN HIGHLANDS
HEAT PROSTRATION

In 2008 Martin decided to accompany me on a visit to my 22nd national park: La Mauricie, in Quebec. Being on vacation and wanting to see a bit more of this uniquely cultured province, we took it easy with first-class service on VIA Rail for the 540 kilometres from Toronto to Montreal. In Montreal we rented a car for the rest of our journey in La belle province. The autoroute on the north bank of the St. Lawrence River was quick and easy, though uninteresting for the majority of the time. Only when we turned northward at Trois Rivières did the drive become interesting. The divided highway was beautiful: park-like with broad, grassy shoulders and with dense mixed forest not only on the sides but even in the median, concealing the traffic going in the opposite direction. We passed through the town of Shawinigan and drove on to the cottage we had rented on Lac Chrétien, the stomping grounds of one of Canada's previous prime ministers. This was to be our home base while we explored Le parc national de la Mauricie, just a few kilometres away.

I began each day with a leisurely, cool swim around the small oval lake, followed by a cup of hot coffee. Then Martin would get up and I'd make breakfast. If it wasn't raining we'd eat on our back deck or else at our kitchen table just inside the picture window. Either way, we'd look out over the lake, watching the ducks and loons drift by. Eventually we'd tire of relaxing and I'd drive us into the park for an adventure.

As per my normal method of getting to know a park, we started by driving the length of it, checking in at the visitor centre, stopping at every lookout and walking every short trail along the way. The highway through La Mauricie is 75 kilometres long, with switchbacks over mountains at one end, relatively flat terrain at the other and forest-lined the entire way. Short walks and various lookoffs offered amazing views of the many lakes, rivers and densely forested mountains of the park. The view at Île-aux-Pins was absolutely stunning – we could see the wilderness stretch out seemingly to infinity. Another favourite stop was at Le Passage, from the height of which we could see down the entire length of the narrow Lac Wapizagonke, so Canadien with canoes floating through the wilderness.

Of course, we didn't want to simply watch the world around us; we wanted to participate. So we rented a canoe at Lac Édouard, strapped it to the roof of our car and drove over to Lac du Fou. This lake really is "crazy," oddly shaped with all its many narrow inlets, bays and hidden niches. We spent an entire day circumnavigating the pristine waters, not that there was anything really different around the next corner than what we'd seen in the previous corner.

The woods crowded the shoreline with a mix of trees. Songbirds and cicadas, hidden in the forest canopy, serenaded us. An otter swam up to our canoe, dove under our boat and was gone. We did not have to be anywhere, so we lingered, enjoyed the warm sunny day and paddled simply for the love of paddling. Occasionally we'd come across another canoe and nod a polite "bonjour" as we quietly passed.

At one point in the middle of a bay, I hopped out of the canoe. I'd become too hot and was starting to burn under the midday sun. The water was lovely, refreshing. I swam alongside the canoe for a while as Martin paddled on. When I was comfortably cooled down, I hauled myself out of the deep water and back into the canoe. Martin was worried I might tip the boat over and send him for a swim too. But I'm an experienced canoeist, so I did it easily and without incident. Martin laughed at my inelegant, though effective, boarding method. We paddled on.

Eventually we found a low, flat rock where we stopped to eat our lunch of baguettes with pâté, artisanal cheese and hard apple cider that we'd purchased in the town of Grand-Mère on our way into the park. Yes, we got right into the spirit of the Québécois. We went for a swim and napped on the sun-warmed rock. Late in the afternoon it started to drizzle. We took that as a signal to get up and go. But the light rain was warm, so we happily continued our canoe trip around Lac du Fou. The day was so perfect that even the rain couldn't make us rush back to our car. When we did get back, our time on the water seemed to have been all too short. We'd been way too lazy that day.

Feeling the need to exert a bit more energy, the following day Martin and I went for a hike on the Mekinac Trail. The route starts off deceivingly easy on the level forest floor. Then it crosses a floating bridge over Bouchard Creek, and the trail becomes a long, steep uphill climb. We paused often to catch our breath and wipe the sweat. Fortunately, the higher we got, the cooler the air became, making the climb tolerable. At Lac Rosoy Lookout, at the top of the mountain, there are three fabulous viewpoints – perfect locations to stop for a rest and picnic lunch. We chatted in both French and English with other hikers who also stopped to enjoy the views over the Saint-Maurice River.

On our way back down the mountain, the extreme heat and humidity held in by the dense forest canopy had taken its toll. We were overheated, soaked in sweat and a bit light-headed. Martin and I had started to suffer from what the Parks trail guides termed "heat prostration" – heat exhaustion. Although we had brought along two litres of water each, we couldn't drink enough. At the intersection with Deux-Criques Trail, we wisely decided not to add the optional six kilometres to our hike. We would be happy to have completed the 11-kilometre basic loop.

Thankfully, we arrived at Bouchard Creek before hyperthermia set in. Exhausted and out of bottled water, we splashed the cool river water over our faces and heads. We also soaked our sun hats and put them on our heads dripping to ease the heat. The breeze over the fast-moving river probably also helped cool us down as we rested on the bank. When we were level-headed again, we made use of an overhead rope to help us balance on the rocks crossing to the other side of the river.

Just a short distance farther, we came upon a two-tier waterfall with a wonderful soaking hole at the bottom – a natural spa. I was thankful that Martin had thought to bring along our bathing suits, although I'm sure I would have climbed into the water in my underwear. We changed behind a bush and walked into the water. We found stones to sit on right where the water could fall onto our backs. "Ah, relief." Other hikers joined us. Everyone else had been having the same problem with the heat as we were having. After some time, Martin and I were ready to finish our hike, but by the time we arrived at our car we had overheated again. We took turns guzzling from the water fountain at the trailhead.

Overnight rainstorms brought down the humidity from the previous day. However, by late morning the world was dry again. Martin and I set out on the short, 1.5 kilometre trail to Lac Gabet, rated "moderate." The route was a very steep climb, and because of the rain earlier, it was a muddy mess. By the time we got to the top, dark rain clouds had gathered again and it started to pour. We could see nothing, so we headed back down the trail, joining other hikers who were also giving up the climb. The trail had become treacherous with gushing rivulets of water and mud. Everyone helped each other, offering hands and sharing umbrellas as we slipped and bum-slid down the trail. And of course, by the time we arrived at the trailhead, the sun was shining again. No, we decided, we weren't going to reattempt that muddy climb.

Martin and I stopped at Lac Édouard for lunch. We sat ourselves at the end of the dock, where we hoped the breeze would blow away the mosquitos and deerflies. It being mid-week, we pretty much had the place to ourselves. We ate our crusty rolls with cheese from a local fromagerie while watching dark clouds roll over the mountains on the other side of the lake. There was enough time for us to get in a short swim around a point of land to a beach where a few people sat swatting mosquitos. We swam back to our dock, changed and hopped into the car just before the next downpour.

Too soon it was time for us to leave the park and head home. I drove the more scenic route, le chemin du Roy, one of the oldest highways in North America, southwest to Repentigny where the King's Highway merges onto the major autoroute to complete the remaining 210 kilometres to Montreal. The chemin had taken us along the north side of the St. Lawrence River, through many historic villages. We purchased some more local cheeses and hard ciders, some of which we had for

lunch in a riverside park. The rest we took home with us. As we picnicked, we watched lakers – long, flat cargo ships – ply their way up the
St. Lawrence Seaway towards the Great Lakes. We would follow them
home to Toronto.

THE NORTHEAST

32
Wapusk

VISITING POLAR BEARS

Late in 2006, with my birthday coming, I decided to splurge on a very expensive gift for myself: I booked a four-day tundra buggy tour at Churchill, Manitoba. I was going to see the polar bears of Hudson Bay before they became extinct, extinction being the dire prediction of so many scientists at the time.

I was not disappointed, both in achieving temporary relief from my daily stress at work, and in attaining an amazing once-in-a-lifetime experience. In fact, I noted this as one of the most exciting adventures I had ever had! Even my colleagues got in on the action, watching the live streaming video from the *National Geographic*'s polar bear cam every day while I was at Hudson Bay.

I was with a group of 36 tourists, mostly Americans, some Aussies and a few Europeans. We were just three Canadians on this tour by Frontiers North Adventures. I met most of our group on the two-hour, 1000-kilometre flight from Winnipeg to Churchill. No sooner had we checked in to our hotel rooms than one of our guides came running in, calling everyone to hurry back to the buses. A polar bear was being flown out of town right that moment! Polar bears that wander into town and hang around get captured, tranquilized, put in a "polar bear jail" and taken far from town to be released.

The wind was howling and it was −17°C. We stood outside, behind a rope just a few metres away from a shed from which an ATV pulling a flatbed wagon was emerging. On the wagon lay a 475-kilogram bear, asleep on its back. I'd never been so close to a polar bear before, not even at the zoo. Wow, are they *big*! Several men rolled the bear off the wagon onto a large rope net. They carefully tucked in its massive paws, cradling the snoozing beast in the net. A long rope connected the net to one of two waiting helicopters. The rotor blades started turning, stirring up a snowstorm from which we had to look away. At a signal, one of the helicopters rose, taking up the slack in the rope and then slowly, carefully lifting the motionless beast off the ground. We watched the sad-looking bear dangling in the net at the end of the rope as the two helicopters flew their precious cargo out of sight.

This encounter with a bear on the first day justified my trip: there really were polar bears up here! In fact, during our four days in Churchill, several bears had wandered through town. We had been instructed that if we encountered one while walking around, we should run to the nearest house and just go in – the doors are always unlocked for such an emergency.

Two of the American men in our group could not believe that people would leave their doors unlocked, allowing anyone to walk in uninvited. So that night they decided to test the prescribed procedure, but with a fake bear sighting. The next day they described their experiment as having quietly called "bear" to each other, and running to the church – they were too polite to try entering a stranger's house. However, they discovered, and were very disappointed to find, that the church door was locked. At this point in their story, I interrupted without thinking. I blurted out, "Of course. Churches save souls, not bodies!" As a result I became good friends with these two men, exchanging letters, emails and even a photo album after our trip.

In the afternoon of our first day up north, four of us chartered one of the helicopters that had flown away the polar bear that morning. Hudson Bay Helicopters would happily take us to Wapusk National Park! We buckled in, put on headsets so we could communicate with each other and flew off. I was relieved that the helicopter was heated. Lynn, our pilot, flew us over the local points of interest, some of which we'd visit by tundra buggy in the following days. We flew over the moose marshes, where we saw seven or eight moose. Their dark bodies really stood out against the snowy low willow trees. We hovered high above them so as not to scare them off, and took photos with our long lenses.

When we arrived at Cape Churchill, in Wapusk, I was amazed. Wapusk is Cree for "white bear." White bear indeed: there were 12 massive male polar bears sitting in a row on the seaweed-strewn beach! They were just a few metres apart from one another. Each had created a nest-like indentation by clawing away the weeds to expose the relatively cold pebbles below. They were sitting in their nests literally "cooling their heels" while waiting for the sea ice to form. Unlike bears that hibernate in the winter, polar bears are most active in the winter. The polar bears of southern Hudson Bay semi-hibernate in the summer when there is no ice from which to hunt seals. I'd never heard of so many polar bears in such close proximity; all the pictures and videos I'd seen were always of solitary bears or mothers with their cubs. This line-up of sedate male polar bears was so unexpected!

Obviously, because there were so many bears about, we could not land. Instead we hovered above the bears, respecting their space. Only where there were no bears around did we lower to a few feet off the ground, to get photographs of their giant footprints. By following some of these prints, at a higher altitude, we found eight more bears. Their fur was yellowish against the white snow and ice. A couple of them were inspecting an old shack. Some just ambled along. Two sparred below us. This was amazing – so exciting! There were polar bears everywhere!

In the distance we could see the two peninsulas where there would be more bears waiting to go hunting. Those protected headlands were off limits to us, however, and we happily respected Parks Canada's regulations. On our flight back to town we saw young male bears, females and cubs roaming around, a good distance from the potentially predatory males we'd seen at Cape Churchill.

During the next two days my group explored the area between the town and the cape, via tundra buggies. Tundra buggies are strange vehicles created out of two yellow school buses cut open lengthwise and welded together to make an extra wide chassis. An open-air balcony is attached to the back. This makeshift body sits high up on 1.5-metre diameter tires that are designed to go over the tundra and through the snow and ice.

The buggies follow old military roads that had been permanently etched into the frozen ground in the 1970s. Despite the delineated routes, we bounced through deep potholes and up and down extremely steep slopes. There were no trees or anything else more than a metre tall to help us judge the distance we travelled. Visions of spending a frigid night out there in a broken-down buggy crossed my mind. The fact that there were several other buggies travelling with us was comforting.

After about an hour of slow driving through what seemed like a frozen, barren landscape, we saw our first bears: a mother with two cubs. Everyone on one side of the bus opened the windows to take photographs. Then someone noticed another mother with cubs on the other side of the bus, and down went the windows on that side too. A wickedly cold wind whipped through the tundra buggy, freezing our fingers as we tried to work our cameras. A third bear family walked by us! Everyone on the bus was excited, but the bears ignored us. They just walked on by, having seen these vehicles before.

We watched as a mother bear crossed a patch of ice and waited for her cubs to follow. They were wary of the ice, not wanting to cross. Their eventual slip-sliding over the frozen pond was very amusing. Apparently polar bears are not born knowing how to walk on ice.

Farther along we watched two adolescent males play-fighting, tumbling and somersaulting over each other. On our way back we stopped to watch what we thought were the same three families we'd seen earlier, though we had no way of being sure they were the same ones. Still, we stopped to enjoy their antics and take more photographs.

We made another more stop when our driver/guide noticed some ptarmigan that were trying to hide under a leafless bush. These Arctic grouse are almost pure white in the winter. They are often playfully referred to as "Arctic chickens" because they sometimes seem to behave like confused chickens, and can make for good eating too.

The full moon that had risen in the early dusk was our signal to leave. Unfortunately, as I'd foreseen, one of the buggies broke down on its way back to the tundra buggy corral. Another buggy had to be carefully backed up to the balcony of the stalled one so the passengers could be transferred via the balconies to the still-working buggy. The now double load of passengers was immediately driven to safety.

The remaining drivers then hitched the empty buggy to the one I was in – we passengers stayed safely inside, watching for curious polar bears. Our vehicle geared down and slowly attempted to tow the broken-down buggy, but the cable suddenly snapped with a violent crack. The warmth of the stalled buggy had defrosted the ground beneath it and its tires had sunk too deep into the slushy mud. This was getting quite dangerous. For everyone's safety, we abandoned the other buggy and brought its dejected driver back with us.

At the tundra buggy corral we transferred to regular buses for the 45-minute drive (on solid roads) to town. We arrived in Churchill in the dark, all buzzing with excitement! Later on we heard rumours that the mired vehicle had been rescued.

The following day, our last day in the tundra buggies, we counted 17 polar bears! We saw a bear with a radio collar cuddled up with her cub in a "day bed." We observed a young male on the beach, digging and digging through a thick layer of kelp into the wet sand below, then settling itself down in its cold "nest" for a snooze. We watched a white Arctic fox prance in front of the nose of another groggy bear, which didn't even bother to look up. Farther along we saw that same beautiful fluffy white fox pounce on a lemming.

A bear cub went running up to another tundra buggy and stretched up to have a look at the occupants, who were leaning out of the windows photographing it. Momma came ambling up and everyone pulled their heads back into the relative safety of the buggy. She had no interest in the vehicle; she simply collected her cub and moved on. We were pleased that our presence didn't disturb her, though it was fun to see the curious cub exploring the new things in its environment.

We spotted an Arctic hare in a thicket. Only its black eyes and the line of its long ears gave away its presence. Their pure-white fur is the perfect camouflage in the snow.

As we slowly drove farther along, I noticed an unusual yellow rock on the side of the track. There was a slight movement as we passed.

That was no rock! "Bear!" I called out. We stopped, backed up and watched the sleeping polar bear beneath us.

While we were parked, another bear walked across our track. Our driver/guide explained that this second one was a young male, identifiable because the fur between its hind legs wasn't stained yellow – with urine.

A woman on board our buggy was from Polar Bears International, a research, conservation and education group. She provided us with even more information on the bears we were seeing. The polar bears that live in the southern regions of Hudson Bay have very unique hunting and hibernation habits. They must wait in the autumn for the arrival of ice floes from which to hunt seals. Bears in the higher Arctic can hunt year-round from permanent ice. Some of those more northern polar bears can even hunt beluga whales.

I cried on the flight home, thinking how lucky, how blessed, I was to have had the opportunity to experience these wonders of the world! I mentally hugged the world and all of existence. How wonderful to be part of this. I was ready to return to the trivial challenges at home and at work.

33
Ukkusiksalik

HUDSON BAY

INUIT AND CARIBOU

Ukkusiksalik National Park, just 14 kilometres south of the Arctic Circle, in the northwest corner of Hudson Bay, is the "place where there's stone for lamps and pots." Of all the parks I've visited, this one was the most difficult to get to. It may have lots of stones, but like so many other parks, it has no road access. Nor were there any outfitters licensed to take visitors into the park even in 2019, 16 years after the park was established. And because of the many polar bear dens, Parks Canada requires visitors to be accompanied by Inuit bear monitors, as non-Indigenous people are not allowed to carry firearms in national parks.

I spent over two years working on a way to visit Ukkusiksalik. I gathered some suggestions from my friends Paul and Sue with whom I'd previously travelled to Qausuittuq and Náátsʼįhchʼoh national parks. They had been the last visitors to explore Ukkusiksalik before me, flying into the park in 2014 in a single-engine Otter out of Baker Lake, a hamlet 360 kilometres southwest of Ukkusiksalik. Following Paul and Sue's example, I too arranged for Baker Lake to be my jumping-off point to getting into Ukkusiksalik.

Baker Lake, Nunavut, has approximately 2000 inhabitants, mostly Inuit who hunt and fish, and many of whom work in the nearby gold mines. Although the hamlet lies in the geographic centre of Canada, there are no roads to Baker Lake from anywhere – you have to fly there. And flying to and within the Canadian Arctic is exceptionally expensive because of the frequent weather delays and the relatively few passengers on those routes. An economy round-trip fare can cost an astonishing $4,000! So I was relieved to find that Calm Air, flying the 1600 kilometres between Winnipeg, Manitoba, and Baker Lake, Nunavut, accepts frequent flier points.

Hiring a bear monitor was an added challenge for my project. I'd never done this sort of thing before and didn't know what skills, knowledge or qualifications to ask for, let alone how much to offer and how to advertise for the position. Fortunately Carmen Ikuutaq of the Hunters and Trappers Organization in Baker Lake knew just what to do. I sent Carmen an email stating my dates, proposed itinerary in the park and the types of firearms Parks Canada recommended for polar bear security. She posted my advertisement on the HTO bulletin board a month before my flights. Carmen forwarded the applications, together with scanned copies of firearm licences and police background checks, to my email inbox.

I started my interviews, calling applicants who had phones or used the HTO's phone, and texting on Facebook Messenger with applicants who had no phone access. Everyone responded in the subdued, gentle demeanour typical of Inuit culture. Everyone seemed very nice and needed work. Most were Canadian Rangers, members of the Canadian Armed Forces Reserve, providing a military presence in the Arctic.

I hired my first bear monitor, but two days later he messaged me that he couldn't make it because he had to take care of a friend in need of help. Inuit will always give priority to family and friends above all else. I hired another bear monitor. Two days later that person emailed me from the HTO office to let me know he couldn't make it. I came to understand that he may have had a better job offer from a gold mine. I tried to hire Stephen Kikamat Anautaliq, but he'd already been engaged as a bear monitor by Parks Canada, overlapping my dates. Finally I hired Mark Kingilik, a man of very few words but extremely polite.

Having seen many polar bears in my Arctic travels, I was keenly aware that any encounter with these carnivores could be fatal. I felt I needed to have a backup safety plan. So a few months before hiring Mark, I took and passed the Canadian unrestricted firearms safety course.

In the meantime, my friends John Borley and Carmen Braund had confirmed that they would go with me into Ukkusiksalik. John had explored Vuntut National Park with me in 2018 and had his wilderness first aid certification. Carmen was ex-army, had had her pilot's licence and has a firearms licence. We'd be a good team, with diverse and potentially useful skills and knowledge.

Carmen's partner, Don, was happy I'd taken the trouble to do my firearms training, but insisted I needed practical experience if I was going to be able to protect myself and my team from polar bears. So every Wednesday for five weeks, Carmen and Don took me for target practice at the gun club they belonged to. I quickly became knowledgeable and proficient with a variety of rifles and shotguns. John too had passed the firearms safety course and practised trap shooting (firing a shotgun at flying discs) with us. We'd all become more comfortable knowing we'd mitigated some of the risks we might face in Ukkusiksalik National Park.

Parks Canada had recommended that we aim to get into Ukkusiksalik between the middle of July and August, the sweet spot weather-wise. Carmen, John and I arrived in Baker Lake without incident on July 22. John and I walked over to the HTO office to personally thank Carmen Ikuutaq for all her help, and also to meet with Mark for the first time. Although Mark was just a couple of years older than me, his rugged Arctic life made him appear much older. He arrived at the office with Stephen, Parks's bear monitor. Stephen was eager to help with whatever was needed, and agreed that if Mark couldn't accompany us, he would work with us until Parks personnel arrived in Ukkusiksalik.

Experience has taught me to allow extra days for bad weather before and after any flight in the Arctic. I'd been told that in 2018 a tourist who wanted to visit Ukkusiksalik hadn't allowed for "weather" days and therefore never got into the park. We had planned to spend one night at Baker Lake Lodge, but, as predicted, couldn't fly into the park the next day because of very strong winds. We followed the familiar Arctic traveller routine: phone the pilots at 9 a.m. No go? Phone again at 10, 11 and… until 2 p.m., when the pilots go off duty. Find a place to stay for the night. Repeat the next day, and the next, and… We spent another night at Baker Lake Lodge before we got the "go." Luckily after only a one-day delay, my team climbed the ladder into our tiny plane.

The Otter's fuselage was too low to stand up in, so we literally had to stoop to get aboard. Seating is single file in canvas-slung folding seats that are clipped to the floor. Carmen gleefully took the co-pilot's seat. Behind her sat Mark, then John, and I buckled myself into the back seat. Our eight bags of personal and camping gear, and several sheets of plywood we were transporting for Parks, were stowed beside us. We donned the proffered headsets that were meant to cut down on the drone of the propeller and allow us to communicate with one another.

Although I've never been seriously motion sick on planes, I always take precautionary medication before boarding the little ones. This flight wasn't nearly as turbulent as others I've been on, so I have no idea why, but within 15 minutes I was sick as a dog. The medication hadn't worked. I even had to give up on staring at the horizon to maintain equilibrium in my ears. Instead, I filled a plastic bag. And although I was thoroughly chilled, I was sweating profusely. To keep myself from hyperventilating, I breathed into a paper bag John had passed back to me. I counted minutes: 1001, 1002, 1003… That was the most agonizing hour and a half flight I've ever been on.

A few times, between gasps, I managed to peek out the window. The land below was very flat, green and riddled with lakes and ponds. A flock of startlingly white snow geese flew low over Wager Bay. Our plane was descending – thank God. Someone exclaimed that there was an ATV, and oh, a person too, on the shore! This was unexpected.

Our plane touched down on a very soft, sandy landing strip about half a kilometre from the Parks base camp and came to a stop by a stash of fuel barrels. I was the last thing (yes, I was just a "thing" at that point) to be taken off the plane. I was totally soaked with perspiration and shivering in the 10°C Arctic air. Carmen and John sat me down in a wind shelter between the barrels and a boulder and wrapped me in my sleeping bag and a metallic space blanket. Before the plane left us, Parks staffer Kenny drove up on the ATV, towing a small trailer to transport us to the camp. I was ever so thankful that we didn't have to carry our stuff through the deep sand to the campsite. I was even more thankful that I didn't have to do anything myself.

Just a couple of months earlier Parks had told me they'd set up a semi-permanent, hard-sided dome at their base camp. I had immediately decided we'd camp there for the extra bear protection. Two days before we arrived in Ukkusiksalik, Parks staff told me over the phone that their field team had left an activated solar-powered electric fence, and we could camp within the compound. I hadn't been expecting anyone to be in the park when we arrived, however. Kenny and John the bear monitor, both Inuit from the hamlet of Naujaat, had their two small tents and a kitchen tent already set up. They also had a generator providing power to an electric heater in the dome. And they were building a wooden outhouse. Wow, we were going to be "glamping" on the Arctic tundra!

While I recovered in the warm dome, John and Carmen pitched our two three-person winter tents, and Mark set up his huge old prospector tent. Our kitchen tarp was set up next to the dome, anchored to its floorboards. Everyone was relieved when I finally walked confidently to the tent Carmen and I were to share, to change into warm, dry clothes. I was "back."

I was in Ukkusiksalik National Park! Not only had I completed my mission to visit every one of Canada's national parks, but I was also officially the first visitor to have done so. The awareness of my accomplishment was accompanied by a mix of emotions. My happiness and excitement were tinged with a touch of melancholy. What was I going to look forward to after this? I knew there'd be new parks set up, but until then, what? My companions brought my wandering mind back to the present. We had a park to explore!

Carmen, John, Mark and I walked out of the large electrified enclosure to check out the neighbourhood. We were camped just 75 kilometres south of the Arctic Circle, on a high, sandy ridge on a bend in the sparkling Sila River, which looped around our ridge from the north and west and emptied into Wager Bay to the south. A row of low hills fringed the bay's broad tidal flats. Dark, hilly islands dotted the far reaches of the shining navy-blue water, marking the edge of Hudson Bay.

In the middle of this pristine, uncivilized landscape sits a pair of Parks's red Muskoka chairs. They are conveniently located at the brink of the ridge, looking out over Wager Bay. Carmen and I took a moment to sit down at this windswept spot. The sky was intensely blue, the sun high. Mark, standing beside us with his rifle slung over his shoulder, pointed down to the mud flats. "Caribou" he murmured. We pulled our small binoculars out of our pockets for a closer look. Indeed there were two barren-ground caribou down there, grazing on the vegetation that grew between the wet rocks. Thrilled to see wildlife, we watched for the longest time until they wandered off between the hills.

We set up our night watch. I would take the first shift because I needed some time to sort the camp stuff I hadn't taken care of when we'd arrived. John would take the second shift, followed by Carmen, who was a night owl. Mark would take the early-morning shift. During my watch I'd join John the bear monitor every 15 minutes or so for a walk around the encampment and to scrutinize the seashore for any yellowish-white activity. After satisfying ourselves that no polar bears were lurking about, we'd retreat into the dome to warm up.

Although the sun was still up over the northern hills at midnight, the temperature had dropped considerably. It was near freezing when I woke up John to take over from me. The sky was at its darkest, just twilight, when Carmen's shift started. John the bear monitor, who'd worked with each of us through the night, went to bed in the morning.

Although it might have been nice to have seen a polar bear, it was better that we didn't see any, given we had no hard-sided building for protection. We didn't want to have to shoot a bear simply because we'd put ourselves in a position where they thought we'd make a good meal. Grudgingly we had to admit we were relieved that no polar bears ever came to visit.

So much commotion the next day: Parks personnel were arriving. A helicopter was followed by a plane and then a fishing boat. They were coming to do their field work. There were staff in green Parks uniforms, Inuit officials, and bear monitors hired from Baker Lake and nearby Naujaat. Stephen was among them. The plane left, but the helicopter and fishing boat remained to shuttle people to their various work sites during the next several days. When everyone was settled in, I counted 18 tents, plus the dome, the kitchen tent and a new outhouse in the compound.

I finally met Monty Yank, the park manager, with whom I'd been speaking on the phone for a couple of years, working on a way to visit this park. Jenn Lukacic, Marie Kringuk and Barb Brittan too, who'd helped me get all our permits and mandatory orientation done, had also come. It didn't take long for us to become a friendly community.

While Parks personnel were settling in, Carmen, John, Mark and I took a walk down to the rocky shore. Tucked into the shadow below our steep-edged ridge we found the old Sila Lodge. The wooden main building and five large cabins were all shuttered and boarded up. Such a shame, we thought, that the last economic downturn had spelled the end of the financial feasibility of this eco-lodge. With its wrap-around veranda and views out over the bay, the lodge must have been a lovely retreat. Now the wooden walls were mouldy and the roof shingles were partially blown off of three of the five cabins. A single pot, the only sign of long-ago occupancy, lay on the ground outside cabin two. Broken PVC water pipes were strewn across the lawn behind the lodge. An old bulldozer sat rusting where it had last been parked – we guessed it had plowed the landing strip our plane used at the top of the ridge.

We walked along the water's edge, noting the pink granite rocks speckled with white quartz. Between the rocky outcrops were lovely small, white-sand beaches that belied the frigid temperature of the water. Although we had a bright sunny sky, the Arctic air was cold. We turned our collars up against the stiff wind.

Suddenly a flutter of feathers rose out of the low bushes. We'd accidentally flushed an eider duck off its nest. Mom, pretending to be lame, instinctively hobbled towards the sea, trying to lure us away from her three ducklings that were still too young to lift their heads. Rather than pursue mom as she'd hoped, we hastily retreated. We made a large detour around the area and looked back just in time to watch mom disappear into her nest again.

We walked over to a narrow spit on the bay but were stopped by a large bull caribou that appeared from the lower shoreline. Feeling cornered on the promontory, it squared off with us and lowered its head, metre-long antlers pointed forward. I quietly commanded everyone to back away. We made another retreat, though this one more cautiously, walking backwards, always watching the animal. We hadn't gone far before two more caribou appeared behind the first. Perhaps due to strength in numbers, or maybe simply because we'd given them sufficient room to get off the spit, the three caribou slowly strode around us, grazing along the way. We stood still, watching and photographing them until they headed up into the hills.

The following day, we set off with Parks staff on a hike up the Sila River. We walked along the sandy shoreline and over bald, rounded granite outcrops. A seal, unperturbed by our presence, was sunning itself on a rock on the opposite side of the river.

Where the riverbanks were undercut by the swift current, we walked up and over the gentle green slopes. We tried to avoid stepping on the Arctic willow trees that, at just a few centimetres tall, grow more like ground cover. Some of their three-centimetre-thick trunks are several hundred years old. As it was the height of summer, they were in full bloom: the red catkins are female, the yellow ones male.

The Parks staff had left for their plant research site in the hills, leaving my team to explore the river valley on our own. We wandered upstream past a broad, rugged waterfall.

On several crests overlooking the river, we found tent rings. These circles of rocks were used by Thule people, predecessors of the Inuit, to pin down their hide tents in their traditional hunting camps. After a thousand years of disuse, the rocks are now covered with flaky black lichens, and willows grow between them. Near one site Mark spotted an old collapsed cache, a small rock cavern that would have been used to store caribou meat.

As Ukkusiksalik is well above the treeline, there are no trees (taller than a few centimetres) to obscure the views. We could see for kilometres down the vast valleys through which the two branches of the Sila River flow. Fields of tiny flowering Arctic plants coloured the landscape with swaths of yellows, purples and pinks. Leas of puffy white cotton grass marked low, wet areas where small creeks fed into the braided Sila River. Caribou grazed in the distance. We left them in peace and returned to the waterfall.

Yearning for an opportunity to fish for trout, Mark pantomimed casting a line into the base of the waterfall. John, also a fisher, stood with him, quietly watching the water boil in the pools below each rocky ledge. Mark then knelt down and, with cupped hands, drank from the river. He was taking in the land. John, Carmen and I, with stomachs not familiar with whatever might live in the river, drank sterilized water from our bottles.

The ancient granite outcrop over which the waterfall flowed had a moulin pothole bored into it. We examined this wide, deep cylinder that had been ground into the rock by swirling sands in the meltwaters of long-ago glaciers that had scoured and levelled the land. As they retreated at the end of the last ice age, the glaciers also left behind several erratics, the giant boulders we saw strewn across the tundra.

There was no one at camp when we got back and the electric fence was live, protecting the compound. The solar battery supplying power to the fence was just behind the gate, and a pair of long-handled pliers lay on the ground outside the gate. My team looked to me, wordlessly suggesting that as leader, it was my job to let us in. Warily I reached through the electric fence with the metal pincers and turned the broken knob, watching as the needle on the power meter fell. Sighing with relief I safely unlatched the gate just as John the bear monitor arrived on the AT v. He informed us that everyone else had been flown by helicopter to the far reaches of the park to do their work. He'd been left behind to guard the camp and the supplies at the other end of the landing strip.

Carmen, John, Mark and I huddled under our kitchen tarp, out of the wind. We prepared our simple dinner by adding boiling water to freeze-dried, eat-from-the-bag lasagna. The food was filling and tasty. All agreed lasagna was one of the best varieties of freeze-dried foods. On a full stomach, life is good. Best of all, other than our forks, there were no dishes to wash.

After our few chores were done, John the bear monitor joined us in our little shelter for tea and conversation. He told us about his family and his plans to resume his studies via the internet. However, he'd found his ambitions stymied by the realities of life in the Arctic. Caring and providing for not just food and shelter but also social and emotional support for friends and family were priorities in these isolated communities. Everyone has to work together so that everyone can live comfortably.

That night, and every night that followed, we relaxed our polar bear vigil. Parks staff had returned to camp and had bear monitors, including Stephen and John, taking turns on watch. Most everyone else, when getting up in the middle of the night to use the new outhouse, did a brief scan of the area before going back to sleep. We had safety in our numbers. The only wildlife I saw in the early morning hours was a pair of giant Arctic hares the size of small dogs. Their long ears, ever alert, seemed to be aware of the electric current in our fence, because they loped along just far enough away that they didn't touch the live wires.

In the morning Marie took us on an interpretive walk around the ridge of our base camp. As caribou grazed in the distance, she told us how her family had lived on this land, how her sister had been born on an ice floe, and how her family travelled with dogs for safety. Also, just as she'd always known them, the berries in this area were plentiful and ripe this time of year. Following her lead, we crouched down and saw that the bushes spread out over the arid ground were laden with blueberries, or bilberries. We sampled red bearberries, mountain cranberries or lingonberries and black crowberries too. Although these shrubs didn't grow more than about five centimetres above the ground, they grew so extensively that we sometimes couldn't help but step on the sweet fruits as we walked.

Camp was abuzz when we got back. Jackie Nakoolak, chair of the Ukkusiksalik Park management committee, and Donat Milortok had just caught two monster-sized, nine-kilogram Arctic char in Wager Bay. They skinned and filleted the fish on a sheet of cardboard that protected the picnic table, and passed around fresh morsels for all to sample. The red, raw flesh tasted somewhat like salmon sushi and melted like butter in my mouth. Monty floured the remaining cubes of fish and fried them up with onions. Everyone ate very well that evening and the next day. Later that evening, Jackie joined my team for coffee under our kitchen tarp. Jackie, Mark and John talked fish and fishing.

One morning we awoke to the sound of howling winds, and poked our heads out of our tents to see what was going on. The sky had become dark, darker than the deepest nighttime dusk. Our tents were bowing against an Arctic storm. Hastily everyone got up and gathered more boulders to help weigh down the tents. Just as the Thule people would have done a thousand years ago, we were creating modern-day tent rings. Then the rain started. Not a heavy rain – this area is known as an Arctic desert because there is so little precipitation. This was just a light drizzle, but it was being driven by a fierce wind and therefore penetrated all our rain gear.

Both Mark's and Stephen's tents buckled in the storm. Our kitchen tarp blew down, hanging on by just one rope to the dome's floorboards. Everyone worked together to reset Stephen's tent behind the dome, tying it in place where our tarp had been. Straining against the wind, we reset Mark's canvas tent and tied our kitchen tarp over top for extra waterproofing. From then on, Mark's large prospector tent doubled as our kitchen tent.

Stephen often joined us for dinner or afterwards for coffee, kneeling on the ground in Mark's tent. During that stormy day, Carmen, our musician, opened an electronic keyboard on her tablet and coaxed us to sing along. Mark began shyly, but a contented smile soon crossed his face. As he reminisced, his voice became more assertive. He led us in singing country and pop songs. Mark and Stephen sang in Inuktitut; Carmen, John and I sang the verses in English. Eventually Mark took over Carmen's tablet and played the e-guitar, drowning out the sound of the flapping tarp on top of his tent.

The storm had passed overnight and there was no wind at all when we awoke. The sun was up and the day was warm. Our tents dried out quickly, and the air inside became too hot and stale to breathe. We were forced to get up and out. Outside, however, we discovered that swarms of mosquitos had taken advantage of the calm air. The little bloodsuckers had risen from the scant greenery, desperately seeking protein. They didn't have much time to produce their eggs before the Arctic winds killed them off for the winter. For the first time in Ukkusiksalik, we brought out the bug repellent and donned bug nets over our heads.

Tucking a satellite phone between my ear and my bug net, I called

Baker Lake to find out if our plane was going to pick us up that afternoon. "No" was the answer. The wind was too high at Baker Lake, and the weather was predicted to get worse through the day. We were stuck in the warm sunny park, 360 kilometres from stormy Baker Lake. Aw shucks.

We took advantage of the beautiful weather at Wager Bay to hike up the first of a row of mountains that extended southeast from our camp. At 150 metres high, these were really only hills. The walk over the permafrost to the base of the hill was easy, punctuated only by a few low, marshy patches of muskeg. The sides of the hill were rocky, but long, sloping meadows provided highway-like access to the summit. We were at the top within an hour, and that included lots of photo stops.

A modern-day cairn had been built near the edge of the large, flat expanse of the hilltop. That was the best vantage point, so I set up my tripod next to the cairn and filmed a 360° panorama of the world around me. Scanning up and down along the row of hills, we could see both ends of the bay to where water and sky melded together. Distant islands appeared to be floating on clouds just above the skyline. They may have been a Fata Morgana, but more likely they were an Arctic mirage, a reflection in the mist, of the islands that actually lie in cooler air beyond the horizon – a common Arctic phenomenon. To the north lay a vast open valley with of course lots of grazing caribou. The world seemed to extend forever.

Eventually we had to come off that high – the realities of being only human set in. We "watered the lawn" on the summit and then made our descent. As I sat in my tent taking off my day pack and emptying my pockets of bear spray and air horns, I noticed that my hunting knife was missing. My godmother had given it to me for my 16th birthday. That perfectly balanced German steel knife, with wooden handle and brass fittings, in its leather sheath, must have slipped off my belt while I was squatting on the hilltop. Carmen and Mark spirited back up the hill, as did Stephen, to look for my knife, but all came back empty-handed. Barb tried to console me with what she acknowledged was weak rationalization: I had given up my knife in exchange for my visit to my last park. My heart was heavy.

Our plane came to collect us the following day, our sixth day in Ukkusiksalik National Park. Lots of hugs and kisses goodbye to our new Inuit and Parks friends who were staying behind to continue their work. Parks staff had one last surprise for us: Ukkusiksalik National Park T-shirts – truly exclusive treasures. We were honoured.

Hoping for the best, I swallowed a motion-sickness pill and tentatively climbed into the tiny plane. This time I took the seat right behind the pilot. The flight was fine, but I felt glum. We were leaving this beautiful land. Not only was this adventure over, but my quest to visit every park was over. Until the next national park is created.

34
Quttinirpaaq

THE FARTHEST NORTH
880 KILOMETRES FROM THE NORTH POLE

I had been told that once you've been to the Arctic, you will be drawn back again. After my first experience in the far North, sure enough, just as foretold, I had to go north again. In the summer of 2000 I visited Quttinirpaaq National Park as part of a group of eight backpackers, including two guides from Black Feather. Quttinirpaaq, at the top end of Ellesmere Island, is Canada's northernmost national park, only a few hundred kilometres south of the North Pole.

My group met up in Resolute Bay, Nunavut, on July 12. It was snowing. We were given a brief tour of the town and introduced to this Arctic community of about 200 people, the jumping-off point for so many quests for the North Pole. This day was meant to give us a feel for the many northern adventures that had preceded ours, so we were shown several documentary films. After having seen recordings of the hardships endured by previous, more adventurous travellers, "no problem" we thought, until our guide, Gilles, introduced us to the pile of equipment and food we'd have to carry in our backpacks for the next seven days. Wow, that was a lot of stuff!

Backpackers are minimalists, carrying only the absolute essentials for survival. Our personal stuff was ultralight, taking up minimal space in our packs: a high-rimmed plate, a cup and a spoon (bowls, forks and knives are not necessary); a water bottle; a tiny child's toothbrush with travel-sized toothpaste and a sliver of soap in a tiny plastic bag (most other toiletries are not required for survival); an all-purpose bandana; long underwear; spare wool socks; a single change of clothes; fleece and rainproof jackets; down-filled mummy bag; and a sleeping pad. All clothing labels were cut off, as their weights, though minimal, accumulate. Each of us splurged a bit of space and weight on luxury items such as cameras, binoculars and paperback novels or decks of cards. To this we added communal tents, cooking gear and fuel, and emergency equipment. In addition, each person was to carry at least one day's worth of food for the group. My pack weighed about 25 kilos.

The following day, we piled into a Twin Otter propeller plane, with our packs and another group of adventurers, for our four-hour, 940-kilometre flight to Ellesmere Island. Earplugs muted the loud, continuous drone of the propellers. Conversation was minimal; everyone just stared out the windows at the sea ice and frozen Arctic islands we passed over. The constant vibration of the plane eventually lulled everyone to sleep – I assume our pilots stayed awake.

After about three hours of sitting in the cramped, canvas-slung folding seat, I had to pee. Twin Otters have no washrooms. So I clambered over the pile of backpacks, to the rear of the plane, balanced myself against a wall, and relieved myself, with very little spillage, into a self-sealing plastic bag. The guys definitely have it easier! We landed at Tanquary Fiord, on the northwestern coast of Ellesmere Island, to drop off the other group of backpackers. My group took advantage of the opportunity to stretch our legs. An Arctic hare watched warily as I tried to discreetly empty my plastic bag.

Our flight continued inland over rugged mountains to Lake Hazen at the northern end of the 200,000-square-kilometre island. Our pilots checked whether it was safe to land by circling around the lake. They liked what they saw and set the plane down on a makeshift runway, a more or less flat stretch that had been cleared of rocks. It was early afternoon and there was a chill in the air. Snow-peaked mountains sheltered the broad lake basin. Sparkling in the sun, ice crystals etched the lakeshore.

I watched the Twin Otter fly off towards Alert, just 100 kilometres to the northeast of us, the northernmost permanently inhabited place in the world. Left alone at 81° north, I shivered, wondering what I was getting myself into. I was at Quttinirpaaq, the "top of the world." Our little group pulled together to start our exploration of the remote end of the world that we had been dropped into.

After setting up our tents at Hazen Camp, established in 1957 as a research station, we went to visit the park warden's station/reception centre/emergency shelter/research centre – a very multipurpose building. Looking through some of the small collection of reference material that was available, we were careful not to disturb the few researchers who were busy at work. Several of the scientists grumbled at having to share the building with us. We held our ground under the "Visitors Reception Centre" sign that hung above the door. We lingered a bit longer than necessary, trying to delay our return to the world of mosquitos outside. Yes, mosquitos don't mind the Arctic cold. Eventually we had to brave the hordes of bloodsuckers and return to our tents.

The mosquitos swarmed around us but surprisingly didn't bite. I later learned that out of the 80 or so varieties of mosquitos in Canada, only a few like human blood. In the North, some types don't even need the nutrients from blood to reproduce. Nevertheless, the buzzing drove us crazy. In the course of that week on Ellesmere, I killed hundreds of them, piling their carcasses into little mounds in a corner of my tent each night. I later teased the park warden about all the wildlife I had killed in the park – he laughed and gave me his blessing.

Our plan was simply to follow the valleys around snow-peaked McGill Mountain. There were no trails or designated routes; we just walked wherever it was easiest, along the Snow Goose and Nesmith rivers, down Blister Creek and back to the base camp at Lake Hazen. We had six days to complete our journey.

We started our trek the morning after arriving on Ellesmere, in a freezing cold rain. We kept our faces to the ground to avoid the sting of tiny ice pellets. While the weather was miserable, we were dressed for it. No one complained. In fact, we optimistically noted, "At least we didn't have the mosquitos to contend with." We moved at a steady pace, generating warmth to offset the threatening cold environment. Red-throated loons quacked (yes, these loons "quacked") behind us on Lake Hazen as we hiked up along the Snow Goose River. The river, more like a creek, cascaded over and around rocks and boulders, all edged with snow and ice.

By noon the rain had given way to brilliant sunshine, drying out the world and our clothes. A rainbow crowned the end of the valley we were hiking through. Although the air was still cool, the last of the winter snow had been washed away by the rain. Wildflowers bloomed profusely, determined to prosper in the few short weeks of 24-hour daylight. We were walking through "God's rock garden." However, there were no plants over 30 centimetres tall; this was a world in miniature. We felt like the giants in *Gulliver's Travels*.

As the walking with such heavy backpacks was difficult on the muskeg by the river, we climbed partway up the mountainside to hike on more solid, rocky ground. We passed a nest of fluffy snowy owl chicks as we negotiated our way. Snow buntings filled the air with song. We stopped to watch a small herd of muskox grazing on the lush grasses of the muskeg at the bottom of the valley. We also horsed around with old Peary caribou antlers we found along the way, but we never saw any live specimens of these reindeer relatives.

While we were taking a break, sitting on the ground in one of those flowered meadows, a small rodent ran up to me and hopped over my extended legs. My first impulse was to cry out: "Look, a hamster!" Of course, it wasn't a hamster – it was a lemming. These little creatures had no idea what people are and therefore had no aversion to us. They scampered about the field, and over us as part of their environment. We laughed at the innocence of the place. Then again, we also knew that the harsh reality of survival would quickly set in if we stayed too long. We didn't really belong there. We hiked on.

After setting up camp on our second afternoon, a few of us set out on a short five-kilometre exploratory hike without our big packs. On our way we paused to gaze at two small herds of muskox: a group of nine with a single calf, and another group of eight with several calves. I loved how their long, dark, shaggy fur hung down over their short, white-stockinged legs. Leery of us, the animals turned away, so we continued our hike and left them in peace.

We were looking for the source of the Snow Goose River: the Henrietta Nesmith Glacier. We didn't have to go far: the grey, debris-cloaked giant loomed just behind the next mountainous crag. An hour later we were clambering down into a deep, sandy gully at the glacier's snout. The slick, uneven mountain of ice loomed 20 metres over us, so high it blotted out the sky. As relatively tiny as we were, we felt emboldened (perhaps foolishly) standing up to the behemoth. We reached out to touch its streaks of turquoise, where the meltwaters flowed like tears – so much beauty, yet so cold. As if awakening from a deep sleep, the giant moved ever so slightly. It grumbled at us, and we scurried away like pests.

As marvellous as the scenery was, and as curious as we were to explore it, we were always aware of how vulnerable we were in the remote Arctic. Thus our daily safety routine included letting a base station in Resolute Bay know we were still alive. We did this by using the satellite radio system, the predecessor of hand-held satellite phones. We'd have to unwind two four-metre-long wire antennas and connect them, together with a four-kilogram battery, to a radio. Then we'd put through our call on the designated frequency.

Curiously, for four days in a row, solar flares interfered with the satellite signals, leaving us with no communications. For all we knew, the rest of the world had killed itself off and we were the only people left, sitting on top of the planet (or the bottom, from an Australian point of view). We were left with an odd, lonely feeling. In our solitude we drew together, giving each other the strength to resist the urge to panic at the ridiculous prospect that we were the last people left on Earth. On the fifth day we finally made contact again. "Thank God, the rest of the world was still alive!" We could go home before the winter closed in on us up here.

The weather dictates everything in the North. Our Twin Otter had been rerouted a few times due to high winds and iced-up wings before it could come to collect us at Lake Hazen. As a result of that extra flying time, we had to stop to refuel at Eureka on the midwest coast of Ellesmere Island, on our way south. Eureka is a 1947 weather station with a handful of buildings and row upon row of barrels of aviation fuel. We stood in the field watching our pilots as they rolled a barrel up to the Twin Otter, unravelled a hose and refuelled the plane. This was definitely not Toronto's Pearson International Airport. Once the task was completed, we climbed back up the ladder-steps into the aircraft and onwards we flew. We passed over thousands of glacier-wrapped, mountainous islands in the icy Arctic Ocean. The hours passed without any trace of human habitation below us, and the enormity of the North was impressed upon us.

Finally, back in Resolute Bay, we took our first hot showers in a week. Oh how good it felt to be warm and clean again. We donned the neat city clothes we'd left there a week ago and were ready go back to civilization. Although we knew it was impossible for us to stay in the North, we went home with new insights and heavy hearts.

35
Sirmilik

SNORKELLING WITH ICEBERGS

Sirmilik, "place of glaciers," consists of Bylot Island and parts of the northern end of Baffin Island, Nunavut, about 3000 kilometres north of Ottawa. There is no road access to the park or to Nunavut. The only way to get there is by boat or plane. I explored the edge of Bylot Island from a very comfortable base aboard the cruise ship *Ocean Endeavour* with Adventure Canada and the support of Parks Canada. The ship provided a warm haven in the bone-chilling polar environment.

Although there are glaciers on the inland mountains, much of the lowlands are ice-free. Sirmilik supports a lush ecosystem of Arctic plants that thrive in the short summers, with sunlight 24 hours a day. When I visited in September 2017, however, snow had already put the vegetation into its winter dormancy. In the night sky, the green, glimmering northern lights had replaced the stark midnight sun. The park had a quiet quality.

Our first stop was at Tay Bay on the west side of Bylot Island. Here we split up into groups to explore the park. Hiking through knee-deep snowdrifts, one team spent the morning climbing approximately 400 metres to the top of a mountain ridge. There were no trails or designated routes – they just chose what might look like a good route as they went. Huge boulders, loose rocks and snow-filled trenches were hazards that had to be contended with, but the reward was a panoramic view.

The park was devoid of colour; everything existed only in shades of black and white. Despite the milky clouds hanging low over the land, the fresh snow and ice lay brightly on the dark mountains across the bay. The end of the bay was a solid mass of white ice. All this was perfectly reflected in the calm, mirror-like black water below. The landscape looked like a charcoal sketch.

Other teams explored along the base of the ridge, finding dormant Arctic willows, trees that grow no more than 15 centimetres high, with branches spread out across the windswept permafrost. We were amazed that anything at all could live in this bleak environment. We tightened our parka hoods around our faces to keep the icy wind out. Looking down from the deeply crevassed rocky cliff at the mouth of the bay, we admired another very brave team of explorers. I had to join them.

The hardiest of our group (or the craziest) donned thick neoprene wetsuits, masks, snorkels and swim fins, and bravely plunged them-selves into the icy waters of Navy Board Inlet. Did I mention there were icebergs floating in the water and that the surface of the sea itself was starting to freeze over? The first trickle of ice-cold salty water running down my back made me shiver, but that water was quickly warmed by my body heat. The warm water was then trapped between the neoprene and my skin, and kept me relatively comfortable. Only my lips and the bit of skin around my mouth were exposed to the cold, and they went numb almost instantly – so I didn't feel anything. For about 30 minutes, under the supervision of a diving company, Ocean Quest, my little group of snorkellers explored the underwater world of the Arctic.

In the Arctic Ocean off the coast of Baffin Island, we saw dozens of small, crystal-clear jellyfish floating around. A cloud of tiny krill swam in the crevices of the cliffs that rose up out of the water. Small fish were feasting on the krill, and mussels clung to the underwater rocks. This cold underwater world was pulsating with life!

Below us, in stark contrast to the dormant world above, was a gar-den alive with various types of algae and seaweed, including giant kelp. Technically, the water does not belong to Parks Canada, so we were allowed to pull up some of those three-metre-long yellow leaves and have a taste. Temporarily removing my snorkel, I chomped into the side of a kelp leaf. Yes, it was sweet and succulent! There were black sea urchins clinging to some of the leaves, also enjoying the tasty treat. We tossed some of those into the inflatable boat that accompanied us. The fresh sea urchin roe was a very special treat when we were done swimming. The orange roe was sweet, exploding in a taste somewhat like cantaloupe when we popped the tiny eggs between our teeth.

Oh, but the wind was bitterly cold when I heaved myself out of the Arctic Ocean and into the inflatable boat. The warm water that had been trapped inside my neoprene suit drained down my legs as though I'd released my bladder. Almost instantly, ice crystals started to form on the neoprene. I hunkered down in the bottom of the boat to avoid the wind chill as we motored back to our ship. On the *Ocean Endeavour*, we quickly stripped off the snorkelling gear and wrapped ourselves in warm terry towels. Then we raced upstairs for the pool, the water being supplied steaming hot by the ship's engines. We were stoked!

All that excitement and it was just midday. The sky cleared and late in the afternoon the *Ocean Endeavour* stopped at Canada Point. Parks Canada staff led us in small groups down the pebble beach to see the spot where Captain Joseph-Elzéar Bernier of the polar patrol ship *Arctic* had claimed Bylot Island for Canada. The stone clearly etched with "Arctic – 1906" by Bernier's crew, still evidences his claim.

Although the temperature was well below zero, the sun, low in the sky, cast a warm glow on the cliffs behind Canada Point. Those mountains are slowly eroding, with reddish hoodoos being carved out of the cliff faces. Leading from Bernier's stone to those cliffs was a mysterious line of small rock piles. No one could explain who had made this or why. We came up with many theories, but none could be verified.

In a snowdrift near Bernier's stone, we also found huge, dinner-plate-sized footprints. Polar bear! With binoculars we followed the prints to a den in a snowbank below the cliffs. Our Inuit guides explained that there would likely have been cubs born in that den. I was grateful for Adventure Canada's team of bear guards who were watching out for us. Happily, there were no polar bears around, so we could safely explore this corner of Sirmilik.

I lingered, slowly making my way back to our boat landing site. Wearing rubber boots, I walked through the foamy surf and kicked at the seaweed washed ashore. I marvelled at the fondant-like ice covering the cake-sized rocks on the beach – perhaps the original inspiration for frosting on pastries? And I photographed the snow-covered mud banks sagging down onto the pebble beach. The cold was slowly seeping into my parka, however, and I yielded to the last call to return to the ship. Back aboard, I happily accepted a serving of hot broth, then settled down to record my adventures in my travel journal.

Although at first glance the Arctic appears cold and barren, upon closer inspection I've noticed that there's an amazing amount of interesting stuff to explore, experience and learn about. True, the park was already very cold in September, but we could dress for that. At the end of my one-day visit to Sirmilik National Park, I was completely exhausted but also quite content.

36
Auyuittuq

MOUNTAIN RESCUE

Going to the Canadian Arctic had long been an ambition of mine, although one I hadn't ever considered realistic. No one I knew had ever been there. But after many years travelling more and more "off the beaten track" internationally, my Arctic dream didn't seem quite so outlandish anymore. I was ready to try exploring the polar cold and ice. Hence in the summer of 1993 I set out to accomplish one of my most challenging adventures: backpacking in Auyuittuq National Park on Baffin Island.

My personal mantra has always been not to just do the minimum necessary, but rather to do the maximum I can. So for this, my first time in the Arctic, I had to go north of the Arctic Circle, not just near it. I found the perfect trip, run by an outfitter I had learned to trust on my Nahanni adventure: Black Feather was running a 10-day backpacking trip from Broughton Island, through the length of Auyuittuq National Park and southward across the Arctic Circle to the hamlet of Pangnirtung. This trip sounded exciting!

Using the knowledge I'd gained in my Girl Guide days, I knew I had to train for such a big backpacking trip. Training was important to avoid sore muscles and injuries, but where to do this? I discovered that the Bruce Trail Association offered hiking trips on the Niagara Escarpment, not far from my home in southern Ontario. A group was hiking "end-to-end" – the entire 800-kilometre length of the trail – and the hike leader didn't mind my joining them, even if my heavy backpack would make me the slowest person in his group.

On my first hike with the Bruce Trail group, I carried nine kilograms of accounting textbooks in my backpack. Each weekend I added three more kilos of books until my pack weighed 20 kilograms. Comfortable with that weight, I knew I could carry more if necessary, but I continued training at 20. The weather became hotter during my eight weeks of training, and the 20-kilometre hikes became more and more difficult to complete, but I was never the last person in the group. In the middle of my last day of training, after hiking about 15 kilometres in nearly 30°C, I dumped my pack in the ditch of a road we were crossing. While there wasn't much chance of someone stealing my unattended accounting books, I didn't really care – I was exhausted. I finished the hike carrying just a water bottle. As I drove my air-conditioned car to retrieve my pack, I wondered whether hiking in such heat was appropriate training for the Arctic. I worried I wasn't adequately preparing for the polar challenge.

As the big day approached, I was informed that the ice had broken up between Broughton and Baffin islands, rendering our intended route unfeasible. Black Feather therefore changed our plans. They would take us on their High Adventure trip instead: a 15-day backpacking expedition starting at Tundra Lake outside the park. We would hike around Mount Fleming and into Auyuittuq National Park, then southbound through the park, over the Arctic Circle towards Pangnirtung. There would be no supply drops – we would have to carry the entire way all the food, fuel, tents and gear required to survive in the Arctic. This trip sounded wonderful, but I'd never done anything so extensive before. My anxiety increased.

We were a large group: five men and five women plus two guides, Dave and Julian. Most of us met for the first time in Ottawa, for our 2100-kilometre flight together to Iqaluit on Baffin Island. In Iqaluit we divvied up the communal gear to be added to our individual packs. In case anyone got separated from the group, each person was to carry at least one day's bag of food. In addition to day seven's food bundle, I took on the pots and pans as per my own backpacking tradition. My pack weighed 25 kilograms – I couldn't lift it off the ground, let along swing it safely onto my back. Everyone else had the same problem. The enormity of this endeavour was sinking in, and it made me nervous. Dave and Julian showed us how to help load each other up. We became keenly aware of how extensively we would have to rely on each other, not just for the food and equipment each person carried but also for physical support.

The following day, our Twin Otter dropped us off on the sandy shore of Tundra Lake, about 350 desolate kilometres from Iqaluit. When the sound of the propellers faded out, we became keenly aware of the silence. Absolute silence.

We were alone. There was no one within hundreds of kilometres of us. There were no roads, no buildings, not anything human. Just kilometres of ice-peaked granite mountains, broad, soggy valleys and a never-ending blue sky above. As I stood in a forest of willow trees no higher than my ankles, I realized that my dream had come true: I was in the Arctic, well north of the Circle.

The vastness of the landscape dwarfed us, challenging our sense of humanity. Because so few people had ever been in this valley, I was sure some of my steps were set in places where no other human had ever set foot – a very humbling experience. The group of us instinctively drew together, providing each other with moral support.

And so we walked, more or less single file, following Dave. Julian brought up the rear. We trekked three hours on that first day north of the Arctic Circle. The waterlogged grassy tufts of the muskeg provided cushioning for our heavy steps, but those hassocks were also difficult to step out of because the squishy ground sucked at our heavy leather hiking boots. We found that the sandy banks of the numerous shallow waterways provided better footing.

Wildflowers bloomed in a riot of fuchsia, yellow and white all around us. Fluffy white cotton grass nodded in the wind as we passed.

I was in the middle of the group, just stepping over a little creek, when I saw Dave put down his pack. That signalled our first campsite. Oh good, we're done, I thought. I was tired of all the travelling that day. I didn't even want to walk all the way to Dave, just to drop my pack and walk back again to the creek to collect water. So I decided to fill my bottle right then and there. I knelt down – big mistake! With all the extra weight on my back, I couldn't get up again. In the distance I could see the grin on Dave's face, as he looked back and recognized my dilemma.

I was too proud to have to wait for someone to come and help me up and on with my backpack. So, with a huge grunt and all the strength I could muster, I forced myself up! So there!

Although I never had sore muscles, I was exhausted at the end of each day. I looked forward to sleep. However, the sun never sets in the Arctic summer – it simply rotates above, in a large oval, never falling below the horizon. As a result, the interiors of our thin, nylon, yellow-domed tents were always bright. I needed to wear an eye mask to create some semblance of night. If we were lucky, we camped in the dark shade of a mountain. Except the shade was usually also noticeably colder, so I really appreciated my down-filled sleeping bag.

My first sleeps were disturbed by the sounds of rockslides that echoed around our tents. The racket sounded so close that I would pop my head out to see if I wasn't in the way of an avalanche. I noticed everyone else was doing the same. Sometimes we could see the line of rocks and ice crashing down the mountaintops far above us; other times the thunder came to us from distant, unseen peaks. Always we were far from harm's way. Eventually we got used to the threatening sounds and everyone slept soundly (or was it that exhaustion took over and we didn't care anymore?).

One morning, I woke up with a migraine, an affliction I endured weekly. Someone took about three kilograms out of my pack, to ease my load that day. A big "thank-you" to that person! I hiked in silence, closing in on myself, unaware of the world around me. The only thing I knew was that I had to keep walking, so I did. Time seemed to slow down, and it felt like forever before we finally stopped trekking for the day. Feeling rather nauseous, I skipped dinner and went to bed to escape my pain. Paule, the woman I shared a tent with, being very resourceful, chipped a piece of ice off a nearby glacier and wrapped it in my bandana for me. I may be one of a few people in the history of mankind to have used a piece of 10,000-year-old ice to soothe a throbbing head. In any case, it worked: I felt much better the next morning.

Outside of the park, there are no trails or marked routes. We chose our way towards the park based on what appeared on the map to be feasible routes. The map's contour lines matched exactly the treeless shapes of the rugged mountains around us. No compass was needed, which was a good thing, given that they don't work this far north. The needle touches the base of the compass as it tries to signify that North is straight down, as if to say, "Fool, you're standing on it!"

Within the general route, each of us took whatever line we deemed easiest. Some of us would go around a house-sized boulder one way, others the other way, and some would climb over the top. We usually couldn't see more than one or two people ahead or behind in those monstrous mazes. Conversations were therefore minimal. Each of us concentrated on how best to tackle the challenges before us.

There were natural bridges of snow and ice over torrential glacial streams. I was always nervous on those crossings. Dave would lead the way, marking the designated safe route with our hiking staffs. We gingerly followed one at a time, hoping not to break through a hidden section of thin ice. The occasional sinking knee deep into the snow would cause us alarm, but we always got over those bridges without incident. Julian, the last person to cross, would collect all our poles and hand them back to us on the other side of these crossings.

Sometimes we had to ford creeks, forcing us to remove our boots and roll up our pant legs. With pack straps undone, so I wouldn't get trapped should a mishap occur, I tentatively stepped into the icy water. Fortunately my toes would go numb instantly, and I didn't feel the cold for more than a moment. In rivers that ran thigh-deep, we anxiously huddled into groups of three to give each other stability against the threatening current crashing over hidden rocks. On the other side of those streams, the cold wind on my exposed wet skin always made me shiver. But the wind also quickly dried me and any clothing that might have gotten wet during the crossings. I could get my dry feet into my nice warm wool socks and protective boots almost as soon as I was out of the water.

Just outside of Auyuittuq National Park, we were walking along the crest of a glacial moraine, a small mountain that must have been at least three storeys high – all loose boulders and rocks in a ridge of soft sand. Charles, in front of me, suddenly stopped to take a photograph. I'd been following too closely, and had to stop short, landing with both feet on one rock. Of course, under my weight, the rock gave way. I fell on my back and slid headfirst down the hill, looking up at the rapidly retreating sky. I don't recall calling for help, but I was aware of the racket I had caused as rocks tumbled down the hill along with me in a mini landslide. Fear swept over me as I slid helplessly, like a boulder, oblivious to where I was going. I was part of the rockslide.

Suddenly I came to an abrupt stop. My backpack had become wedged between two large stones. But I was turtled: my arms and legs could only flail, unable to touch the ground beneath my thick pack. Furthermore, the straps of my backpack were the only things keeping me from continuing my fall. I couldn't risk unbuckling the sternum strap and hip belt. I had to wait for the rest of my group to rescue me.

Five people gingerly climbed down to me, taking care that they themselves didn't slide the rest of the way down the moraine. Four people held on to me by my limbs while the fifth unbuckled my pack straps. As my weight transferred to my rescuers, we all slid another metre or so downhill. More rocks rattled down the hill, unnerving us even further. I was rolled onto my stomach but facing down the steep hill. I noted that the bottom of the hill was still a long way away. Carefully I turned myself to face uphill. Someone held on to me until I could support myself.

I had come out of the predicament with just a bruised palm. The thumb muscle was like mush, as if someone had taken a meat tenderizer to it. I had no recollection of how or when that had happened; I had been too preoccupied with fear to feel any pain. I had been fortunate. My rescuers reloaded me with my pack, and we climbed back up to the crest of the hill, rejoining the rest of the group. We tenaciously continued our journey as if nothing unusual had happened.

On the fifth day of our expedition, we entered Auyuittuq National Park, named with the Inuktitut word for "the land that never melts." Perched up high on a steep mountainside, we gasped at the magnificent view. Raw, ice-peaked mountains surrounded us. Straight down in the steep valleys below, the sparkling Owl and Weasel rivers flowed from Summit Lake, in opposite directions, out towards the faraway, unseen Arctic Ocean. In front of us, reaching down from the Penny

Icecap, the long arms of the Turner, Norman and Highway glaciers reflected the sun between mounts Asgard and Loki.

This giant world existed in surreal shades of white and grey beneath the bright blue sky. Ice and rockslides thundered from avalanches around us. Everything seemed so near, yet by its sheer vastness was beyond our reach. I secretly felt we didn't belong, that people shouldn't be there. This was a place for something much bigger than human beings, I thought.

Following the inukshuks that marked the route, we climbed with hands and feet down the rocky mountainside. For hours we squeezed between huge boulders, climbed under rock lean-tos, tentatively trod over treacherous outcrops and leapt over deep crevasses onto sloped wet rocks. Everyone was unnerved by the very real danger. Our trip motto became "This is serious shit!"

The "trail" led us down to the Weasel River, where we picked up an easy footpath, though not without its own challenges. For instance, a wire "bridge" with a suspended seat crossed the river clothesline style. Each person, sans pack, sat in the seat and pulled themselves hand over hand along the overhead wire to the other side. Three of us crossed first. On the other side we collected all the packs that were sent across to us one at a time. I was shocked when we received our guides' packs – they were so heavy that even two of us couldn't lift them off the seat! I was strong, but I knew then how much extra equipment the guides were carrying. This was a reality check on my lack of self-sufficiency in this environment. On the other hand, having lifted everyone else's packs off the seat, I also knew I was carrying more than some of the men, so I was reassured that at least I was carrying my share.

The weather got colder. Rain soaked us, then wind dried us as we hiked under Mount Thor. At 1250 metres and with a 15-degree forward slope, Thor has the largest natural vertical drop in the world. We were humbled as we crossed barefoot through the numerous streams flowing from the mountain.

The sun came out and wildflowers bloomed alongside snowdrifts and in green, mossy valleys. Knee-high Arctic willows scratched at our pant legs as we passed through stands of miniature forests. Weasels, ptarmigan, snow buntings, thrushes, Canada geese and gulls entertained us. We even saw bumblebees, butterflies and moths!

At the end of one day's hiking, my new friend Margaret and I decided we needed a hair wash. We didn't have enough fuel with us, and there was no wood to burn, to heat water with. So we used water directly from glacial runoff.

Using combs, Margaret and I moistened one another's hair. We lathered-in a sparing application of shampoo from a sample pack I had brought along. I was the first to rinse: I bent my head down over a pot as Margaret poured a mug of fresh water over my hair. I cried out in pain. The icy water felt like a hammer hitting the top of my head! Stunned, I needed a few minutes to recover. I nixed that method of rinsing out the shampoo. We proceeded to carefully pour water for each other so it wouldn't touch our scalps. We combed out the rest of the suds as best we could and agreed to pretend that any remaining soap residue might help keep the mosquitos away.

The mosquitos didn't normally bother us except at mealtimes. We usually ate our "homeless hummus" or "vulgar bulgur," as we came to nickname our food staples, each person standing on their own boulder in an attempt to avoid grouping our personal clouds of mosquitos. We also hoped, in vain, that this method would allow for a breeze to blow our personal swarms away. Some days we were more fortunate, when it was too cold even for the mosquitos. On those days we'd huddle together to eat and enjoy being able to converse without having to yell to each other across a field of rocks.

On July 14 we walked across the Arctic Circle. While the physical act of stepping across an imaginary line was relatively easy, I, like my fellow travellers, was thrilled to have completed this relatively rare feat. We celebrated with chocolate bars at the cairn that marked the line over the trail. However, the temperature had fallen below freezing and the frigid air kept us from lingering. Everyone dove into a nearby gully to get out of the wind. Pulling on extra layers, we huddled together to warm up again. Then we scoffed down the hot stew we cooked for dinner on the lightweight stoves we'd carried into the ditch with us. The food fuelled not only our bodies but our minds, giving us the mental energy to cope with the harsh environment. On full stomachs we could even appreciate the beauty of the world we were in.

We spent most of our evenings on quiet activities such as reading or playing cards. Charles avidly filled many rolls of film with photographs of every aspect of this unfamiliar world. André drew a caricature storybook of our adventures. I would pull out my sewing needle and embroidery floss, decorating first my shirt and eventually everyone else's as well. If the day was particularly cold, we would all squeeze into a couple of tents and share impressions of our adventure. Most of us spent some time under the midnight sun, recording the day's events in travel journals. These were the lightweight "entertainments" we had splurged on, stashing them in our packs where every gram mattered.

On the last day, a fishing boat picked us up from the base of Mount Overlord at the northeast end of Pangnirtung Fiord and ferried us about 30 kilometres westward, past icebergs and bergy bits, to the hamlet. We rode in silence, each of us lost in our own thoughts. This was the anticlimax of our expedition. As we arrived at the hamlet, our captain placed a plank of wood from the boat to the shore and helped us disembark. One of the guys missed his step when the boat shifted, and ended up with a soaker. No one cared anymore – we were back in civilization.

We pitched our tents, for the last time, in Pangnirtung's official campsite. Then we lined up to take our first showers in 15 days. As we had been outdoors, and always together, we hadn't noticed how rank we had all become. The hot water was plentiful and felt wonderful. Ahhh. As I finally washed the grease, dirt, soap scum and mosquitos out of my hair, I quietly murmured, "bye-bye, hat head."

Once presentable, we went to the lodge in town for a celebratory dinner. We sat down in chairs at tables, a civilized amenity we had become unaccustomed to, and were treated to a huge meal of delicious Arctic char, fresh vegetables and a salad. This was our first non-freeze-dried meal in over two weeks and we ate heartily.

Although while backpacking I had always eaten until I was full, and our meals consisted primarily of carbohydrates and proteins, I hadn't been able to consume enough calories to offset what I'd been burning.

I'd lost five kilograms on that trip. Note to self: backpacking is a good way to lose weight.

While I was pleased to be able to say I was physically and mentally able to cope with such a challenging adventure, I have to admit that on those last days, although the terrain was easier, I had tired from carrying all that weight. I had become cranky and had been spending a lot of extra energy suppressing my increasingly negative outlook. The expedition was no longer fun. I was thankful that the trip ended before I lost control of my emotions. I made another note to myself: any future backpacking trips were not to exceed seven days.

On my way home to southern Ontario, I stopped to visit my brother in Ottawa. When he picked me up from the airport that night, I was amazed at how dark the sky was! I couldn't see a thing, even under the street lights. As I was no longer used to the darkness, I managed to trip off the sidewalk. I had become night blind! What an interesting experience, I thought.

Furthermore, I found myself suffering from jet lag, despite not having crossed any time zones. I discovered that jet lag didn't have anything to do with jets or time zones; it's about when light and darkness happen versus when your body expects those. After such a long time in constant daylight, my body didn't know anymore to expect darkness. I needed several days to adjust.

37
Mealy Mountains Reserve

THE NORTH ATLANTIC COAST
SAGAS OF VIKINGS

I visited Mealy Mountains National Park Reserve in July 2016 while sailing with Adventure Canada on a small ship called the *Ocean Endeavour*. We were almost 200 passengers travelling from St. John's, Newfoundland, up the coast of Labrador and over to Greenland. On the scheduled morning, we were told we had arrived in Porcupine Cove, in the Park Reserve, about 800 kilometres north of St. John's. Despite a bright blue sky above, a thick grey fog enveloped us. We could see neither land nor sea. It seemed like we were adrift in a cloud.

While we prayed and waited for the fog to lift, we were shown Parks Canada's mandatory video on polar bear safety. There was a distinct possibility of encountering these carnivores on the coast. Most of us had mixed feelings about seeing polar bears. We wanted to see them, and yet if we did, it would be too dangerous to land in the park. However, as with the fog, the bears were beyond our control. We'd just have to make the best of whatever Mother Nature sent our way.

While we passengers were learning about bears, the Adventure Canada staff had used GPS to track a safe route through the fog to the beach. We were set to be shuttled there in inflatable boats. I was one of 10 people in the lead boat of a convoy of four. The fog was still dense: within minutes of leaving the *Ocean Endeavour*, we could no longer see the ship. Nor could we see any land. In fact, we couldn't see the last two inflatables of our own group! Our driver led us confidently, though, following the track on his hand-held GPS, the other three drivers staying in constant contact with us via their radios.

Fifteen minutes later the beach suddenly appeared, much closer than any of us expected. Other Adventure Canada staff were already there, waiting to help us off the inflatable boats. I took my first steps onto the Wonderstrands! This was the beach many believe to be the one referred to in the Icelandic sagas as the place where the Viking Leif Erikson may have set foot, around the year 1000.

The white sandy beach, about 20 metres wide, was split into two stretches: one about 45 kilometres long, the other a 20-kilometre section on the other side of Porcupine Point. The fog, blowing in waves from the sea, streamed onto the beach and rose over the land, where it dissipated. Looking inland past the long beach grasses, scraggly shrubs and clusters of stunted pine trees, I could see the low, green Mealy Mountains. A few patches of snow clung to the mountainsides. Although there were no trails, I yearned to hike through the brush and into those mountains, to feel the green.

However, Adventure Canada had set up a safety perimeter defined by point people in bright orange vests, carrying shotguns and rifles and watching for bears. We were to remain within the safety zone. So I contented myself with exploring the beach.

I walked a couple of kilometres down the beach, past piles of mussels and other seashells, bladder weed and kelp. I stopped to investigate three small perfect circles about 30 centimetres in diameter, drawn in the sand. "How odd," I thought, wondering how they might have been made. A slight breeze rustled the bits of grass growing in the sand, and that's how I noticed: each circle was centred by a single strand of beach grass. The central blades of grass had bent over so that the tips were touching the ground. The wind was blowing them around and around, like a compass, drawing those perfect circles in the sand. Nature has always inspired people, and I imagined that something like this might be where the idea for the first drawing compass had come from. Might the Vikings have used drawing compasses? I watched in awe at nature's perfection.

The air was cold and I was wearing my heavy jacket, woolly hat and gloves, but just wool socks in uninsulated rubber boots. The cold would creep into my feet if I stood around too long. But I'm hardy. I rolled my pant legs up over the tops of my boots and walked back through thick fluffy foam that had accumulated on the shallow water. Unexpectedly, the ocean sent a rogue wave washing over the tops of my boots and my feet were instantly sodden. Much to my surprise, the water was warmish. Okay, "tolerable." Or perhaps I was just being stubborn, wanting to experience as much of the park as I could in the short time I had on the beach. Ignoring my "soakers," I wandered along through deeper water – getting more water into my boots didn't matter anymore.

I found several of my fellow travellers at a small brook that meandered out of the forest, across the beach and into the ocean. They were inspecting several heavy timbers, blackened with age, pinned together with wooden pegs. A single long, square, rusty nail lay nearby in the water. My friends were theorizing on the origins of their find. An old bridge? Perhaps part of a ship wrecked on the beach long ago? Certainly not Viking – not that old! Despite the sagas, no actual traces of Leif Erikson had ever been found on this beach.

Our attention was diverted from the lumber by someone calling out from farther upstream: "Bear tracks!" We carefully walked single-file through the clear running water so as not to disturb any other possible tracks on the banks, to see what had been found. Oh yes, those were fresh polar bear tracks! "How long ago were they made?" we asked. "Was the bear still close by?" Our bear monitors assured us they had seen none all morning.

Back on the beach, a group of Nunatsiavut Inuit had just arrived in a small fishing boat from the nearby village of Cartwright. They had come to welcome us and teach us about their homeland. They had already set up a propane stove and were preparing "flummies" for us. Flummies are their version of bannock bread, made of flour, baking powder and water. They are deep fried like donuts, and served up with traditional purple partridgeberry jam, orange bakeapple jam and yellow rhubarb jam. We enjoyed these deliciously sweet treats while learning about the area from people who live there.

There are very few roads in Labrador. Most travelling is done by boat along the coast, as we were doing, or by air. But the easiest way to get around, we were told, was in the winter by snowmobile. We learned that people use their traditional unmarked routes through the mountains to visit their neighbours. The knowledge of where to go is passed down from generation to generation in these isolated yet tight-knit communities. To greet us on this summer day, though, our hosts had had to come by boat, a journey of a couple of hours along the foggy coastline. We appreciated their effort, their knowledge and of course the flummies they shared with us.

The fog had lifted over the course of the morning, and we were blessed with a perfectly sunny day. I, of course, wanting as much time as possible in the park, waited for the last boat. As I stood on the beach watching the inflatables shuttle people back to the *Ocean Endeavour*, I noticed the ship was anchored amid a group of coastal islands. And there were huge icebergs floating nearby! The realization that we had navigated safely into this bay, with zero visibility that morning, made me appreciate modern sonar and radar, and our captain's skill. I reboarded the ship with confidence, then watched the retreating coast with wonder as we sailed northward to explore more of the rugged Labrador coast.

Mother Nature had more marvels in store for us. We sailed into some of the deep, narrow fiords to explore the area, and at the very end of one of those inlets we found bears. Hidden in the long green weeds was a female polar bear. Her off-white fur made her look just like one of the yellowish boulders at the base of the cliffs. We only noticed her because she moved to look over her shoulder – at a pair of cubs that had been dozing in the sun! The trio glanced our way but decided to ignore us. They stretched and rolled over, made themselves more comfortable and went back to sleep. We sailed on.

38
Torngat Mountains

HIKING WITH ANCIENT SPIRITS

In 2016 I was travelling up the Atlantic coast on a small 200-passenger ship with Adventure Canada. We had stopped to explore Mealy Mountains National Park Reserve before heading north towards Torngat Mountains National Park. However, our coastal route had become hindered by fog-shrouded sea ice, and our ship, the *Ocean Endeavour*, was forced to circumnavigate the hazard. This meant an extra two days of sailing in the middle of the North Atlantic. With nothing but water to see, we occupied ourselves by studying the history of Labrador. When our ship finally found its way back to the coast, we discovered for ourselves "the place of spirits," Torngat Mountains National Park.

This Arctic park is at the northern tip of Labrador, well north of the treeline. The lack of major vegetation means that much of the 3.9 billion years of Earth's geological history is exposed in this part of the world. The land bears witness to repeated volcanic and glacial activity. Long, jagged fiords cut deep into the 1500-metre-high mountains. Ice and snow encrust the mountainsides, even in the summer. Although the winters are long, the abundance of natural resources both on the land and in the sea have rendered the Torngats very hospitable to people.

For as long as human memory, the Torngat Mountains have been the home of the Inuit and their forebears. Remnants of Maritime Archaic Indians, Pre-Dorset, Dorset Palaeo-Eskimos and Thule peoples' lives are scattered about the land. Their spirits still occupy this ancient world.

Our explorations started in Saglek Fiord at the south end of the park. We were shuttled in groups of 10 in inflatable boats from the *Ocean Endeavour* to the rocky beach at St. John's Harbour. I thought it odd that the province of Newfoundland and Labrador should have two places with the same name: this one in Labrador and another on the island of Newfoundland. Furthermore, the city on the island is the capital of the entire province. A quirk of history, was the explanation I was given. Of course, since St. John's (Labrador) is so very remote, there's little chance of anyone accidentally arriving at this site 1400 kilometres northwest of the capital city. There are no roads to Torngat; the only way to get here is by plane or boat, or perhaps a very long wilderness journey.

St. John's Harbour is where Parks Canada set up their base camp and research station. The few buildings at the site were still battened down for the winter when we arrived on July 6. The station and the beach on which it stood appeared abandoned and ghostly. The only signs of use were the few footpaths around the station, worn into the land by visitors in previous years.

Some of our group spent the afternoon exploring the beach at St. John's (Labrador), noting seashells and seaweed washed ashore and old caribou antlers and animal bones blown down from the mountains. However, most of us explored farther afield. Some hiked along a track to a thunderous waterfall, while others scrambled up along the ridgeline between the two arms of Saglek Fiord. I chose the challenging 1.5-kilometre climb up to an inukshuk at the top of a mountain, from which to overlook the entire area.

Twenty of us walked single file along an old footpath through a field of colourful wildflowers. After the trail petered out, we followed the lead of Derrick Pottle, our Inuit guide, trusting that he was selecting the easiest route. Following Derrick's example, several of us refilled our bottles with sweet cold water from a creek he led us along. Then we helped each other rock hop over that creek and then another brook that meandered through the sloped meadow. That slope became ever steeper as we approached the rocky base of the mountain; our pace slowed and our breathing quickened.

Then the real climbing began. We clambered hand and foot over and around huge boulders. We shimmied along narrow ledges on the cliff, our faces so close to the wall that we noticed the little things. For instance, there were woolly bears under the miniature plants that grew in the rocky crevices. These bushy brown caterpillars live up to 14 years, freezing solid in the winters and defrosting in the summers. After several summers of feeding, they become moths. Seeing these tiny creatures survive in the harsh Arctic climate made me ashamed to complain about the hardships of my short climb.

Every 15 minutes or so, our group would stop on a relatively level outcrop to catch our breath and admire the view. At first we could only see the cliff on the other side of the fiord, but eventually we were up high enough that we could see the mountaintops of the next range over. We spotted the group of hikers walking along the ridgeline far below us. Off in the distance we noted the tiny speck that was our ship, anchored in the fiord. Down on our right side, we could see a group of ant-sized people lounging by the waterfall.

After almost two hours of climbing, we finally arrived at the inukshuk that marks the summit. We had a 360-degree view of the world around us. Behind us were rugged mountains as far as we could see. There were classic glacier-carved, u-shaped valleys between many of those mountains. Snow and ice sparkled brightly on some of the mountainsides. In front of us, the fiord, like a crooked finger, pointed the way to the open ocean.

A few wisps of clouds hung over the fiord. Above it all shone a haloed sun. Called a 22-degree halo, a ring of light around the sun is created when light interacts with ice crystals suspended in the atmosphere. Some say the halo is an omen of bad weather, but that didn't seem to pertain to us. It wasn't even cold on the mountaintop. We lingered. I felt blessed. I thanked the Torngat spirits for this overwhelming experience.

I was one of the last people to leave the mountaintop. As I confidently scrambled down the rocks, I caught up to a woman who'd become petrified of the steep descent. Margaret couldn't move. Instinctively I offered to guide her, or was it the spirits directing me to help? Although Margaret didn't know me, she seemed to intuitively trust me to get her off the mountain. I stepped right in front of her to show the way. I set my pace so that she could place each of her footsteps in the exact spots I had just moved my feet out of. I guided her hands to hold on to the cliff-sides exactly as I did. A fellow climber, Ian, followed behind Margaret, encouraging her, distracting her from looking down off the precipice. Slowly, slowly we inched our way down the mountain, Ian and I patiently guiding her. Margaret was finally released from her fear when she stepped off the rocks and into the steep meadow. From there the three of us went skipping through the wildflowers, contentedly enjoying the day, all the way back down to the beach.

Amongst our team of explorers were Inuit from the nearby villages of Nain and Hopedale. While we were exploring the countryside, they had taken the opportunity to forage for wild edibles, "country food," to demonstrate the abundance of their land. Maria Dicker, an Inuit elder, collected seabeach sandwort, a succulent plant from the shoreline. The thick green leaves tasted like carrots. Maria explained that they are only so super-sweet early in the season. We also nibbled on a few wild partridgeberries that were just ripening in the meadow.

In the meantime, Billy Gauthier and Eli Merkuratsuk had caught 18 Arctic char. Right there on the beach I sampled a piece of the raw, pink, buttery flesh. It was delicious. The intense flavour lingered in my mouth for hours. Not even a good brushing back on board the ship could remove the pungent essence from my teeth. The spirits seemed to have become a part of me.

That evening we sailed deep into Saglek Fiord – a sunset cruise between the 900-metre-high cliffs. The corridor became ever narrower until there were only a few metres of clearance between our ship and the rock faces on either side. It was 10:30 when we reached the end of the fiord – a rock-strewn beach fronting a U-shaped valley. In the fading light, our captain executed a perfect 180-degree turn. Exhausted from the day's activities, I struggled to stay awake to admire this feat of navigation. The inky dark waters swirled around the hull of our ship, and sleep drifted into my head. I slunk off to my cabin and collapsed on my bed as we sailed back through the night.

I awoke the next day to find we were anchored in Ramah Bay. Refreshed from a good night's sleep and a hearty breakfast of smoked salmon on toasted rye bread, I was ready to go exploring again. The inflatable boats shuttled us to a pebble beach. We found that the flat stones were perfect for skipping – how many skips could we make? But I was distracted by the semi-translucent, whitish stones mixed in with the flat pebbles. These unique stones, I learned, were Ramah chert. There is evidence that Indigenous Peoples used these rare stones as flints, arrow heads, cutting tools and spiritual items as far back as 7,500 years ago. I rolled a piece in my hand, imagining some ancient person deciding what this fragment might be used for. Had they discarded it, tossing it back onto the beach as I just did?

I carefully walked around the tent rings (stones left behind to hold down circular tents) and remainders of sod houses on the low table-land. A small Inuit community had congregated around a Moravian Mission that had been set up here in the late 1800s. Partially due to lack of growth potential, the mission was dismantled in 1908 and the Inuit moved to join other communities in Labrador. Foundations of a few buildings still remain. Other odd items were also left behind such as iron stove bases, now lying upside down, their rusty legs sticking up in the air like some long-dead animals. Gravestones in the old cemetery still hark back to the Germanic names of the European spiritual leaders. Odd spirits definitely haunt this land.

Feeling the need to get grounded again, I wandered off to inspect the ancient sedimentary rocks around the edges of the plateau. The soft land has been sculpted by wind, rain and ice into bizarre formations. Giant rocky bowls and crescents remain where harder stones resisted the erosion. Uh-oh, there may be spirits sheltering in these alcoves. I moved on.

A brook flows from some unseen glacier in the mountains behind the rocky outcrops. The icy waters meander thought the meadow, over the bluff and down into the ocean. I clambered down to the base of the waterfall. Peering between the sparkling cascade and the under-cut bank, I saw our ship anchored in the deep bay. I joined my fellow travellers who were busy photographing the beautiful scenery: white-capped waves on the deep-blue sea, backed by grey, rocky, snow-crust-ed mountains, all topped with long, streaming clouds in a bright blue sky.

I was ambivalent about the presence of the two bright red Muskoka chairs near the waterfalls, overlooking the fiord. Parks Canada has placed such chairs in many of their parks, to indicate the location of some of the most spectacular vistas – as if we needed to be told these places are beautiful. Fair enough, the chairs did provide a bright, colourful contrast by which to gauge the remoteness of this park, and they definitely extended a friendly gesture: "Here, have a seat." On the other hand, the chairs seemed out of place in this remote part of the world. Nature also seemed to have decided that those chairs don't belong, having battered them with wind, ice and water. These chairs were not in good shape. Fortunately the park is big, and this small human element was set in just one tiny corner, easy to ignore if one chooses to. I chose to ignore it and did not sit down in the chairs.

Nearby was a large chunk of ice left over from the previous winter. With crevasses, caves and caverns, it looked like a miniature glacier. I couldn't resist – I got down on my belly and slithered into a tunnel under the ice. There, sunlight filtering down through the ice revealed splendid textures and shapes sculpted by meltwater: ridged pillars and blue-striped walls held up the stippled ceiling of this miniature cave. Rainbows of colours and shadows seemed to swirl as I rolled around to admire the contours. The spirits, I realized, were friendly. They were sharing the beauty of their world with me.

However, I am not of the spirit world – the reality of my frail physical nature was brought back to my attention by the cold. My coat had become soaked by the meltwater under the ice, and I was shivering. It was time for me to return to the shelter of our ship. Back on board, dry clothes and hot tea fortified my body so I could continue to explore and appreciate the Torngats.

We sailed farther north, up the rocky coast and into Nachvak Fiord. Steep mountains and cliffs edged the waterway. Black, jagged dikes and ancient, lava-filled crevasses scarred the mountainsides. Snow and ice clung to the shadowy crests. Small glaciers filled the hollows between the mountain peaks. Silver streams cascaded over rock faces, between green shrubby ledges and down to the sea. Another grassy u-shaped valley marked the end of the fiord.

And there, in the tall grasses, between the clusters of large light-grey rocks, we spotted some odd yellowy-white bulks. Our ship drew as near as the sea floor allowed. With binoculars we spotted them: three polar bears! A mother with two cubs were sleeping in the grass. But they were too far away to really appreciate them. So we scrambled into the inflatable boats and quietly (as quietly as the powerful motors could be) our flotilla slowly approached the shore for a closer look.

The low tide and shallow, pebbly beach kept our boats a safe distance from the grassy field. Still, we excitedly whispered to each other, pointing at the mother bear as she got up to have a look at us. Satisfied we weren't a threat, she lay down again, a yellowish bump in the grass. The cubs rolled over but took no notice of us. We lingered just off the shore, watching the family nap. Our patience paid off: the three bears got up and slowly wandered along the beach. Excitement rippled between the boats, everyone wanting to photograph this awesome sight. But as if camera-shy, the bears ambled off behind a mound of rocks and we never saw them again.

As our ship continued to ease through Nachvak Fiord, we spotted another polar bear. This one was swimming far from the shore. Its yellowy-white head distinguished it from the pure white of the waves and ice on the dark water. With binoculars we could discern the black tip of his nose. Did this polar bear embody the spirit of Torngarsoak, who controls the life of sea creatures? The ancient Inuit spirits certainly seemed to have granted us a wonderful visit into their world. I waved back to them as we departed, sailing off to the North Atlantic.

THE EAST COAST

39
Terra Nova

CAVE KAYAKING

I rented a car in St. John's, the capital of Newfoundland and Labrador, and drove westward from kilometre zero of the Trans-Canada Highway. For three hours, 240 kilometres, I drove in silence. I was travelling alone, taking in the landscape of rolling hills, windblown pines and a multitude of lakes and rushing rivers. Periodically I'd spot a pickup truck parked at the side of the highway, on the gravelled embankments of a bridge. The drivers were nowhere to be seen. I wondered what adventures they were on: fishing, hunting, hiking? I wondered what exploits awaited me in Terra Nova.

I booked into an efficiency unit at a motel in Charlottetown, Newfoundland – not the capital of Prince Edward Island – and settled in for the next few days. The only ways to get to Charlottetown are through the park or by sea. The hamlet is snuggled between the forested mountains, in Clode Sound, an arm of the North Atlantic. From the veranda of my room, I watched as a continuous line of dump trucks took away loads of road salt from a ship docked in the tiny port – preparations for the province's infamous winter snowfalls. Fortunately I was visiting during the very hot summer of 2014.

Terra Nova preserves a large chunk of the boreal forest, low mountains and waters of the island of Newfoundland. During my first hikes in this eastern wilderness, I realized these woods are similar to the "friendly forests" around Montreal, where I'd grown up. There is nothing in these woods that threatens humans, if treated with respect. I comfortably hiked alone on the well-defined trails that meandered under the trees, alongside the sea, through the humid valleys and up the mountains to windblown lookouts. Bunchberries blooming white, yellow lilies and a variety of other wildflowers create a welcoming garden on the forest floor. Squirrels and other small creatures rustled in the underbrush and songbirds added melody to the air. The air smelled of sweet, lush vegetation, interspersed with salty wafts from the sea.

My only bit of discomfort came from the usual hordes of mosquitos and blackflies. They forced me to pull the cuffs of my quick-dry hiking shirt down over my hands and button the collar high up my neck. In addition, I tied a large bandana over my head to keep the bugs out of my ears, and pulled my sun hat overtop.

As a result of all that clothing I was sweating buckets, attracting even more insects. However, I found that the alternative, a bug net over my hat, would trap the carbon dioxide of my exhalation under the net, creating the same result: overheating and attracting the bugs. There was no escape, so I hiked on with long, determined strides, hoping to outpace the mosquitos and blackflies.

The atmosphere changed completely as I climbed out from under the dark, hot, humid forest canopy, into the glaring bright sun and brisk winds on the mountaintops. The wind was so strong it threatened to blow me over. But I also relished with relief the wind that blew away the mosquitos and dried my perspiration-soaked clothes.

I took in the view: an endless carpet of forest covered the mountains as far inland as I could see. Seaward, in the jumble of the many green peninsulas and dark waterways, on the horizon sat several giant white blocks – so brilliantly white that they looked out of place. They seemed to be man-made, perhaps whitewashed warehouses on the distant seashore. No. They were icebergs, as the enhanced sight through my binoculars proved. I counted six of them. The unexpected contrast in colour stole my attention and held me in awe. Sitting in the leeward side of a large boulder on the crest of the mountain, taking in that vast view, I ate my lunch. The world was peaceful, all was as it should be and I fell asleep.

Later that day, I drove over to Sandy Pond. Park brochures promised that this small lake in the middle of the forest was a perfect place for a swim. Awkwardly I changed into my bikini in the back seat of my car before walking down the short path to the beach. There were lots of other vacationers there already, sunbathing. A few kids were playing with pool noodles in the water. I dropped my small bag with car keys and towel near the water's edge, where I might keep an eye on them, and waded into the water.

The tea-coloured water was warm. I kept on walking and walking, out a very long way into the pond. Still the water was only up to my shoulders. So I started to swim and suddenly realized that there was no one else around me anymore. I was in the middle of the lake. I reached my toe down to determine how deep the lake might be. I could just barely feel the mucky sand below me. I was safe. So I swam farther and farther, eventually traversing the entire 1-kilometre length of the long, narrow lake. Unfortunately the far end of the lake was full of reeds, so I couldn't get out of the water and walk back along the lakeside trail. I had to swim back to the beach. I took my time, knowing that if I grew tired, I could stop and stand up pretty much anywhere in the shallow pond.

The trail around Sandy Pond is an easy walk, with boardwalks much of the way. I strolled along the route to discover that much of the area around the pond is quite boggy, the reason I couldn't get out of the water anywhere but at the beach. But the bog did have its own special appeal: there were hundreds of pitcher plants, Newfoundland's floral emblem, growing out of the mud. These carnivorous plants, with their large dark-red blossoms hanging off of tall stalks, trap and devour mosquitos inside their pitcher-shaped leaves. I was happy about the reduction of the fly population that these pretty flowers provided, but also aware that their beauty is deceptive. Apparently they will also digest small vertebrates such as baby salamanders. My "friendly forests" might not be so peaceful after all.

On another bright day, I went on a tour by kayak from the hamlet of Happy Adventure, just outside the park. A young man, Chris, led our group to explore some nearby caves. With me was a family of four from Conception Bay, Newfoundland. We paddled out of the tiny harbour, along the high, sheer cliffs edging The Rock, towards the open sea. We were careful not to be bowled over by the rolling waves that rebounded off the massive boulders along the shoreline. Those ragged dark blocks had long ago (hopefully) fallen off the high walls to our left. As I was an experienced paddler, Chris let me explore a bit more on my own. I paddled into a narrow inlet that led into a low cave. Of course I had to go in, carefully. The clearance on either side of my kayak was only a few inches – not enough room to use my paddle. I laid the paddle along the deck and pulled myself forward by "walking" my hands along the ceiling of the low cave. There was a slurping noise coming from the rear of the cave. I strained to peer into the darkness to determine whether the sound came from a hole waiting to suck me down. I found only a small pile of black sand at the end of the cave, the echoing effect of the narrow passageway distorting the sound of small waves sloshing over the sand. I paused in this underground hideaway, wondering what secrets people might have hidden in it.

After I rejoined my group, we went on to explore "The Dungeon," a huge cavern with such a narrow watery entrance that only one boat could enter at a time. The inside of the cave was very dark and we hadn't brought flashlights with us. Our eyes adjusted to the darkness. There was a sliver of light emanating from the mouth of the cave, reflecting in the water below us, enabling us to just barely see each other. Although there was space for several boats, our kayaks bumped into each other and into the walls of the cave as we negotiated the gloom. Images of pirate hideaways and sheltering weather-weary fishermen filled our heads.

Single file we paddled back out of the cave, shielding our eyes from the bright sun reflecting off the open ocean. The wind had picked up and the sea was now rougher, so we stopped for a rest on the beach at Sandy Cove. We were very tempted to stay on that warm sunny beach with the other sunbathers. However, we all agreed we should finish what we had started: we'd paddle, instead of hail a ride, back to Happy Adventure.

Timing the incoming surf, we carefully, safely got all our kayaks back into the water. Unfortunately, as we paddled away from the beach, the dad got side-swiped by a rogue wave and rolled over. He was okay but distraught because he had his daughter's iPad under his life vest – it was ruined, and the pictures they had taken were lost. I worked with Chris to right the kayak and get dad back into it.

We paddled on in silence with me leading the way, skimming along the wind-sheltered sides of the many coves. Chris, at the back of our group, was "sweep" so he could see if anyone in front of him was having any further difficulties. We made it back to Happy Adventure without further incident. I later emailed the family the pictures I had taken, so at least they would have some souvenirs of our happy adventure.

A few days later I rented a kayak in the park, intending to explore the waters of Terra Nova. Chris joined me. We paddled across the narrows of Newman Sound, around small islands and into tiny, protected coves and inlets. The shallow waters were crystal clear. I commented on how tasty those mussels down there, just knee deep below us, would be. Chris reminded me that collecting anything in a national park was illegal – I complied, feigning regret. A few minutes later we were paddling through schools of capelin, and it was Chris's turn to sadly leave the tempting seafood behind. The sea is definitely bountiful, even if not harvestable in the park. That night, I sated my appetite with a dinner of garlic and wine steamed mussels (and lots of fresh-baked bread to mop up the sauce) at the restaurant in Clode Sound.

40
Gros Morne

THE NORTHERN APPALACHIANS
HIKING FROM SEA TO SUMMIT

My visit to Gros Morne National Park occurred in July of 1995. I'd flown 2100 kilometres from Toronto to St. John's, Newfoundland, and then on to Deer Lake, where I rented a car for the rest of my journey. I wound my way northwest up the highway, through the forested mountains, to Rocky Harbour, a small community within the park. There I booked into a bed and breakfast and immediately set out to explore the park.

This was an unusually hot summer, with temperatures above 30°C. I therefore chose easier walks, starting with a two-kilometre stroll around Berry Head Pond. The air was heavy and quiet except for the bugs that swarmed thick around the bog. Along the marshy edges of the pond were pitcher plants, Newfoundland's provincial flower. This was the first time I'd seen these pretty, dark-red flowers. Their beauty belies the murderous nature of the plants, which devour insects within their cupped leaves. I couldn't help but wish they'd eat just a few more mosquitos.

I did a second hike that afternoon: 10 kilometres through the dark forest and over boardwalks to the spectacular Bakers Brook Falls and back again. There were moose hoofprints all over the damp sod path. If these giant beasts were around, they were well camouflaged – I didn't see a one. The highlight of the walk was, of course, the broad waterfall. The river falls over several limestone ledges and pools surrounded by soft balsam firs. If it hadn't been for the mosquitos, I thought, this would have been a lovely spot for a picnic. However, in the hot, humid forest, sweating under my bug hat and the long sleeves needed to keep the mosquitos at bay, I wasn't interested in lingering. On my way back to the trailhead, I found that if I walked very fast, I could outpace the bugs. So by the time I got back, I was totally soaked from heat- and action-induced perspiration.

I couldn't imagine doing any major hikes in that extreme heat, so I opted instead for the boat tour on Western Brook Pond. I chose well: on the small boat I was able to sit back and enjoy a bit of breeze and cooler air. The Pond is actually a lake in an inland fiord, with steep cliffs rising 650 metres up on either side. Numerous small waterfalls cascaded down those walls. At the far end of the lake, the cliffs give way to a valley extending into the mountains. Like everyone else on board, I went wild taking photographs of the wilderness that surrounded us.

After the two-hour boat tour, I slowly walked the long way, via Shallow Bay, back to my car. Exhausted from the heat, I found a shady spot overlooking the beach at Shallow Bay, for a picnic. There were many people sunbathing and beachcombing, and even a few brave enough to wade into the frigid water. The temperature difference between the icy Atlantic and the extreme heat of the day was too much for me to go for a swim; I conceded defeat.

As I couldn't go on hiking in the heat, I took a short break from the park for a multi-day, 370-kilometre drive up the breezy west coast of Newfoundland. I was hoping the heat wave would be over by the time I returned from the northern end of "The Rock."

I discovered I'd given up one challenge for another: driving in a thick fog along a narrow, winding road with just a low guardrail between me and a tumble down to the ocean. I learned to start my drives later in the morning, after the fog had lifted. Then I had to be careful not to let the awesome ocean vista, with whales blowing and icebergs floating by, distract my attention from the winding road. I made many stops to gawk at the views.

At the very northern tip of the island lies L'Anse aux Meadows. I wandered in amazement through this 1,000-year-old Viking village site, with its archaeological remains and replica sod longhouses. The Viking cloak pin that had been found on this site, now displayed in the nearby museum, was the most poignant sign that Europeans had been to North America long before Christopher Columbus "discovered" America.

Might this pin have belonged to Leif Erikson? This is truly Canada's most historic of historic sites, at least from a European perspective. It is also appropriately designated as a UNESCO World Heritage Site.

There were several other tourists driving the same route at the same pace. We got to know each other at the lookouts en route. As I was driving on my own, I was happy for the company. At Port aux Choix, we did a car shuttle together. We left two cars at one end of a five-kilometre seaside trail, and drove together in a third car to the other end of the trail. We hiked back down the easy trail, enjoying the views, and stopped at the archaeological sites along the way. Several artifacts from the extinct Dorset peoples who had lived here over 3,000 years ago had been found in this location. While most of what's left of these sites is not obvious to non-scientists like me, the display boards and the museum in the town at the trailhead offered fabulous insights to this national historic site.

Back on my southbound drive, I made a slight detour, taking the ferry across to Quebec and driving the 80 kilometres north to Red Bay, Labrador. There the remains of a 500-year-old Basque whaling station are preserved and conserved to remind us of where Europeans had gotten their lamp oil from. I could only imagine what a hellhole this must have been: the heavy ocean fog holding down the smoke from the firepits used to render the whale blubber, and soaking up the stench of rotting carcasses. I tried to be generous by looking for something positive about the place. Perhaps the smoke had kept the mosquitos from being attracted to the rot. Perhaps the heat of the fires had offset the cold of the Labrador winter. Perhaps Red Bay had been more comfortable than the squalor of 16th century Europe. Or perhaps not: maybe the whalers were stuck here once they'd arrived. Not me. I left this mosquito-infested national historic site after just one day.

Back in Gros Morne National Park, the temperature had moderated somewhat – much better for longer hikes. On the 16-kilometre James Callaghan Trail to the summit of Gros Morne Mountain I met Reverend Paul. He too was travelling alone and was happy for the company. We climbed together, encouraging each other over the rougher section of the climb. At 806 metres, this mountain is the highest in the park. We spent more than three hours climbing the steep, loose scree through Ferry Gulch: two steps up and one sliding step back down. I was happy I wasn't alone on this arduous venture. Paul graciously helped me up the steepest sections of the slope.

From the rock-strewn plateau we got a spectacular 360° view of the park: forest-covered mountains and valleys right to the horizon. There were dozens of dark-blue lakes to be seen, including the oddly shaped Ten Mile Pond. So many more places to explore, I thought. We were so engrossed with the vista that a rock ptarmigan hen startled us when it scooted out of a bush and fluttered across our path. Looking closer, we spotted seven fluffy chicks huddled in a nest between the rocks, safely out of the wind. I shouldn't have been surprised to see Arctic birds in this chilly alpine environment. They are well adapted to Arctic-like conditions.

Due to its many switchbacks, the descending section of the trail is longer than the ascending section. These meanders in the path provided a gentler slope that was meant to ease the descent, but my knees ached anyway. On our way we accidentally flushed a mountain hare out of the bush – that was one big bunny! I happily paused to watch the hare and made other stops to view the forested valley below us, my knees complaining the entire way down the long descent.

When we finally got back down to sea level, we found a couple of moose wandering by the trailhead. They didn't pay any attention to us when we stopped to stare. They just quietly disappeared into the forest. We drove off to town, contented with the day's adventures.

I don't know why I do these things, but despite my sore, protesting muscles, I pushed myself the next day to do another big hike: Green Gardens Trail. I arrived alone at the parking lot early in the morning – it was foggy and there was no one else around. Undeterred by my presence, a cow moose crossed my path as I wandered across the tableland steppe. The fog had begun to lift as I entered the forest, where the friendly sounds of songbirds kept me company until I got to the beach. All alone again, I explored a massive lava pillow on the sand, an oddly rounded giant boulder left over from ancient lava flows. I carefully stepped through the driftwood- and seaweed-strewn beach and discovered a hidden waterfall by a sea stack. Due to the high tide I could not continue along the trail to explore the caves described in the guidebook I carried. However, I had had such a full morning of exploration that I was content to backtrack along the 4.5 kilometres I had come, to my car.

There were so many more trails to explore, but I had spent all my energy and was ready to go home for a rest. I needed a vacation from my vacation! I needed time to digest the wonderful things I'd seen and learned about in Newfoundland and Labrador.

41
Mingan Archipelago Reserve

SHARING BOUNTIES WITH NOUVEAUX AMIS

Mingan Archipelago is in Quebec, 200 kilometres from the end of the road, and another 320 kilometres south of the Labrador boundary. Low, bald granite hills with scrubby conifers, blueberry shrubs and mosquitos are the main features of the mainland. The park was created to protect the contrasting limestone-based islands just a short distance offshore in the Gulf of St. Lawrence. Only 1,000 or so islands of this 100-kilometre-long archipelago are part of the park, though; the mainland and even the waters between the islands are outside the park.

Some islands of the park boast dense, mossy forests over low hills, with cliffs plunging straight down into the sea. Others are low, shrubby protrusions, and some are just bald, rocky islets. There are sandy beaches and campsites in protected coves. Weather-eroded flowerpot monoliths are the main attraction, along with lighthouses, puffin colonies and fossils of long-extinct sea creatures.

My visit to Mingan Archipelago in 2014 was to make up for an earlier, failed visit. In September 2000 Martin and I had driven some 870 kilometres from Quebec City to Mingan, exploring the remote North Shore along the way. However, upon arrival at Parks Canada's visitor centre in Longue-Pointe-de-Mingan, we discovered that tours of the islands and most of the park facilities had closed for the winter, in late August! We could not go onto the islands, and therefore I hadn't actually been in the park. So, to make good on my tally of the Canadian national parks I'd visited, I had to return and actually set foot on the islands.

Using Aeroplan miles, I flew Air Canada to Sept Îles, rented a car and drove up Highway 138 again, but this time I was on my own. The long stretches of forest at the start of the drive dissipated into a scrubby landscape as I drove northeast towards Havre-Saint-Pierre. There were just a handful of seaside villages and only one service station in over 200 kilometres of narrow, winding highway.

Besides being the main entry point to the national park reserve, Havre-Saint-Pierre is a town with an active fishery and a working seaport. Awaiting shipment to faraway refineries were mounds of titanium and iron ore under the tall, trellised rail terminus. Locals and tourists alike strolled, jogged and cycled down the lovely, broad Promenade des Anciens boardwalk along a segment of the endless sandy beach.

I walked barefoot over four kilometres down that beach, way past the last cottage and the last road, to where the low land meets the tree-crested cliffs. And still the narrow beach stretched endlessly before me, farther than I could ever follow. The unreachable horizon shimmered in the hot, humid air, taunting me. Only bird footprints, mussel and lobster shells, crab legs and ropy giant kelp marked the sand. If there'd been anyone else there before me, the tide had long since washed away any sign of them. I was alone on the coast of this expanse of the Atlantic Ocean. I found myself being drawn into the waters by some great force, or was it by the heat of the day? I stripped off my T-shirt and shorts, and dove in bare. The clear, calm water was cold and refreshing, washing the perspiration off my sunburnt skin. The rocky sea floor disappeared under me as I swam farther out. I became a mere speck in the ocean, somewhere between the cliffs of a dense, impenetrable forest and the distant islands in the Gulf of St. Lawrence. Those are the islands of the park, the reason I was there! The guillemots were calling me to join them over there.

The only way into the park – that is, onto any of the islands – is by boat. There are no bridges and indeed no roads or vehicles on the islands. I booked a tour with Services Maritimes Boréale. Most people here speak some English, but I wanted to immerse myself in the Québécois culture and refamiliarize myself with the language of my home province. While waiting for the tour to start, I befriended Denise, from Gatineau, on the other side of Quebec – whose primary language is

French. She helped me interpret some technical information provided by the park wardens.

Together Denise and I explored Île Quarry first. We found this coastal boreal forest filled with moss and lichen-draped conifers. There were colourless Indian pipe plants in the shadow of unexpected inland "flowerpots," carnivorous pitcher plants in the bogs, and ghostly white calcium ponds. In the centre of the island was an old, exposed gravel seabed that looked like bulldozers had been preparing a road. Very odd. On the far side of the island, we discovered tall, monumental flowerpots, like stone sentinels looking out to the open sea. These monoliths had been, and still are being, eroded out of the islands by wind, winter ice and sea. So much variety on such a small island! Within 10 minutes we had followed the trails back to the floating dock where our inflatable boat awaited to whisk us over to the next island.

On the rocky-ledged coast of the only island with any elevation, Île Niapiskau, we explored odd crevices and cracks, and numerous fossils of long-extinct sea creatures. Denise and I laughed at the imaginations of previous visitors who had seen and tagged several of the towering limestone monoliths with names such as "owl," "eagle" and even a "dame."

One possible derivation of the name Mingan is thought to be from the Breton for "white rock." Passing Île du Fantôme on our way back to the mainland, I was inclined to concur with this guess. We gawked at the low, white, rounded monoliths. They looked like stacks of giant vanilla macaroons slipping off one another, in danger of sliding into the sea. "Quick, catch them before they fall off!" I wanted to call out. Our imaginations too had been sparked!

Over a fresh lobster dinner in a restaurant with an ocean view, Denise and I excitedly relived our adventures. The information overload of the day, the delicious dinner, the fresh sea air and the French immersion had all exhausted me. We toasted the day and our new friendship, and then bid each other farewell and safe travels.

A good night's rest and I was ready to explore the park some more. From Longue-Pointe-de-Mingan, I took the tour with Les Excursions du Phare, run by la famille Vibert. Denise had recommended this tour of some of the other islands in the park.

The puffins had fledged and were either sitting on the water or flying around us on the aptly named Île aux Perroquets. Our small group of seven tourists followed the park warden on a tour of the lighthouse there. I translated as best I could for an anglophone couple of cyclists who were touring the Maritimes. This was the first English I'd spoken in almost a week, and it was a challenge to go back and forth between the languages. Fortunately the story of isolation of the lighthouse keepers was also presented in English on the Parks information boards. I left the island sure that I would never have volunteered to work a lighthouse on such a tiny island with no place to stretch my legs.

Our young, handsome captain guided our boat past Île du Wreck and L'îlot on the way to see the stone monoliths standing in the sea around the treeless Île Nue de Mingan. The tops of several of those monoliths were still attached to the islands' clifftops, creating holes and gaps in the rock and "elephant trunks" extending down into the sea. We let our imaginations run.

Minke whales glided silently by our boat. We stopped to laugh at the seals diving and slapping the water around us. The ocean was alive!

We'd been told our guide would use a "mop" to scoop up sea urchins for us. I was sure this was mistranslated – that they had meant "net." But no, our captain used an actual floor-washing mop to sweep the flat rocks beneath the boat, catching the spiny sea urchins in its woollen strands. As the waters around the islands are not part of the park, we were allowed to harvest these creatures, cut them open and eat the five clusters of salty, raw, orange roe. Our cyclists provided rustic bread to go with these delicacies. Yum. An eager photographer on board our boat recorded our feast for future promotional materials for the area.

As I stepped off the boat onto the beach at Longue-Pointe-de-Mingan, Danielle, the daughter of the last lighthouse keeper on Île aux Perroquets, who runs the tour desk, came running out. "Vous-là!" she commanded me. In English she continued: "You are not allowed to leave! I've been commissioned to keep you here." Everyone stood staring at me in shock, until she broke out in a huge grin. Apparently Denise had heard I was here and had asked that I wait until she returned from a shopping trip. Five minutes later Denise and I were hugging each other in greeting. She was thrilled I'd experienced the same adventures as she had done a few days earlier. After much chatter with everyone, including the others from my tour and our hosts, the Vibert family, I had to say goodbye to my new friends. My time in Mingan had come to an end. I had a long drive back to Sept Îles to catch my flight home, alone.

42
Forillon

FRIENDLY QUÉBÉCOISE CULTURE ON THE TRAILS

In September 2000 Martin and I toured Eastern Quebec, including La Gaspésie. Our drive around the circumference of the Gaspé Peninsula started at the ferry terminal at Matane, on the south side of the St. Lawrence River. This peninsula, jutting out into the Gulf of St. Lawrence, is the northern part of the Appalachian mountain range. These Canadian peaks, up to 1200 metres high, live up to the reputation of the famous US Appalachians, with their narrow, densely forested valleys and steep, barren, rocky peaks – total wilderness.

Our exploration of La Gaspésie started with a long, winding drive from sea level on the St. Lawrence up into the Chic-Choc Mountains in le Parc de la Gaspésie, a provincial park. From the main road across the peninsula we turned onto a switchbacking dirt road to the head of the Pic du Brûlé trail. We continued our climb on foot for another six kilometres through small, fern-filled valleys and up to the summit of Mont Ernest-Ménard, about 869 metres.

On the mountaintop, Martin and I ducked under one of the few tenacious, weatherbeaten balsam firs for protection from the strong wind. Huddled in our little shelter, bundled in layers of clothing, we ate our sandwiches and admired the view. The panorama was definitely worth the effort to get to this summit. There was a small lake tucked into the mountains, and forests extending as far as we could see. The vista reminded me yet again of how immense the natural world is, and how insignificant humanity's fleeting existence is.

My contemplations proved proportionally brief when survival instincts kicked in: the wind had become wickedly cold and distant storm clouds were barrelling towards us. We had to go. Other hikers fleeing the impending storm joined us on the descent. Two of us translated between French and English, for Martin who spoke no French, and the rest who spoke no English. Despite the language barrier, we shared stories of our wonderful impressions of these mountains. And then the rain started. The trail quickly became treacherous, the boulders slick, the ground muddy. Everyone helped one another along the slippery steep sections. Some parts of the trail were impossible to walk down, so we slid down on our rears. Our rain pants and coats quickly became sodden with mud and forest debris. Still, working together as a team, we were in high spirits and we laughed at the insanity of the mess we'd found ourselves in.

Finally back at the trailhead, we joined in an impromptu fête with our new Quebec friends, enjoying wine and cheese under a canopy of opened van-tailgates and umbrellas. Other hikers arrived off the mountains. Someone opened a bottle of cognac, someone else passed around a baguette, and I offered up the fruit I'd purchased before our drive. I'm not sure where all the various cups, plates and knives came from, but everyone pitched in something towards this party. A bit of bad weather doesn't dampen Quebecers' joie de vivre.

With this introduction to the Gaspésie, Martin and I drove into le Parc National Forillon, at the very tip of the peninsula and the end of the exposed Appalachian range. From there on, the mountain range runs underwater, rearing up as the French islands of Saint-Pierre-et-Miquelon and again in Newfoundland. We were there to see the Quebec end.

To our surprise, the first thing we came upon in the park was a fort from the Second World War: Fort-Péninsule. This fully preserved installation includes artillery and an underground network of munitions bunkers meant to protect North American shores. Despite 23 ships having been sunk by German U-boats in these waters, no shots were ever fired from this fort. Martin was fascinated and took his time reading all the information panels; I read a few, but big guns are not really that interesting to me. Instead, I watched the sea for the spouts from whales.

We spent another hour touring the historic buildings of Grande-Grave, an old fishing village. The name "Grave" refers to the dead fish, cod to be exact, that used to be dried on racks on the pebble beaches. The exhibits depict the lives of the fishermen and their love of fishing, over a hundred years ago – a rather romanticized story. As I wandered through the old Hyman & Sons General Store and warehouse, my mind turned to compassion for those working people who were forever indebted to the company store. That must have been a tough life, but perhaps better than the alternatives.

Martin and I, on the other hand, were having an easy life as we picnicked on fresh lobster-salad sandwiches at Anse-aux-Sauvages, overlooking the sea. The salty air blew through my hair and the sun burnt our faces. Gulls sailed overhead and a whale spouted in the distance. So peaceful, so picturesque.

The one-kilometre hike to La Chute took us down a set of stairs and through a forest. There was so much to enjoy on such a short trail. The leaves of many of the maples and other hardwood trees had already changed colours. We were walking under a canopy of bright reds, oranges and yellows beneath a brilliant blue sky. A perfect autumn day. The colours almost outshone the beauty of a pretty five-metre-high waterfall, the highlight of the trail. At the top of the waterfall, a dark-green moss-covered "stairway" of rapids was perfectly cast against the golden forest.

A longer, eight-kilometre hike to Cap-Gaspé, the very pinnacle of the peninsula, was just as interesting. Martin and I started out along the beach. The trail ascended onto a ridge and merged with a bicycle trail. From that higher level I took way too many photographs of the rocky seashore: glimpses through the trees, of small beaches, coves and cliffs.

The trail descended into a clearing where a Quebec TV mini-series had been filmed. The set consisted of several houses and facades of buildings scattered about the meadow in an obviously picturesque manner. As I wandered through the tall grass, I got stung by a bee – my cue to leave? I applied bit of ointment from the first aid kit I always carry in my day pack, and exited the scene.

Martin and I followed the trail farther along the narrowing ridge of the peninsula. We could see the ocean through the thin line of trees alongside the path. Eventually we arrived at a small meadow with a nine-metre-tall lighthouse on the point. The signal was originally built in 1873 as a warning for sailing ships going into and out of the Gulf of St. Lawrence. Due to fire and exposure to high winds and storms, the lighthouse had been rebuilt a few times and finally was completely automated.

The trail ends at the bottom of the 95-metre cliff at the Atlantic Ocean. This is "Land's End," the northern terminus of the Appalachian Trail. Only 4,450 miles to go, southbound. "Not today," I thought. This was a good place to end our exploration of Forillon. We retraced our steps to our car and drove on along the south coast of La Gaspésie.

43
Kouchibouguac

THE MARITIMES

SKINNY DIPPING

In July 2012 I gave up. I was emotionally exhausted from taking care of my dying father and then his estate. At the same time, corporate HR had decided that after more than 25 years of service, I'd become redundant. Family were unsupportive, and I didn't want to burden my friends by dumping my sorrows and frustrations on them. But I could no longer pretend I was alright. So I went to my place of healing: the friendly forests of Eastern Canada. Under the protective forest of Kouchibouguac National Park, in New Brunswick, I shed my woes and began my emotional recovery. I found myself again, in the wilderness.

I rented a tiny one-bedroom clapboard cottage just outside the park. No phone, no TV, no internet – yeah! There was just enough space next to the picnic table outside to park my rented car. A narrow stretch of mowed lawn separated the cul-de-sac in front of my cottage from the cliff down to the sea. There was a narrow set of stairs to the debris-strewn beach. On clear days, from the small table at my kitchen window, I could see clear across Northumberland Strait to the wind turbines on Prince Edward Island. On other mornings I would sit back and watch the sea fog roll by and the ensuing torrential rains. The monotonous sound of the surf, always present, seemed to wash over me. Finally, I cried. My tears seemed to merge with the waves, unnoticed by anyone.

Each day, rain or shine, I staunchly drove the short distance down the nearly empty highway and into Kouchibouguac National Park to accomplish my escape. There I spent hours wandering through the forest, reflecting, contemplating, meditating. I paddled, cycled and walked out the anger and sadness that had enveloped me. The trees were like protective walls around me, a sanctuary in which I could confront my jumble of emotions. And there was no one around I might risk disturbing.

As the weather forecast on my first day in the park was for a sunny 28^0C and then rain the next day, I adjusted my usual approach to visiting national parks. Instead of orienting myself on foot (which can be done in the rain), I decided to explore by boat. I rented a kayak.

Wearing just a bikini and a sun hat, and of course sunscreen, I paddled up Major Kollock Creek. The route was more of an estuary, choked with grassy sandbanks that I had to carefully navigate around. Eventually I beached my boat on a deserted strand and went for a swim.

The tide was out and the water was shallow. I was able to stand on the sandy, hilly ocean bottom, but had to take care not to get entangled in the seaweed-choked hollows between the underwater dunes. The water was warm and I had nowhere to be, so I took my time. I wallowed. I came across a poor beached jellyfish, and it occurred to me that I was faring far better than it was. I did not have to wait for fate to decide what would become of me; I could decide for myself.

With renewed energy, I hopped back into my kayak and paddled back out of the estuary. Along the seashore were a few other kayakers who were aiming to paddle up the north arm of the Kouchibouguac River. I followed them into the "river of long tides" and almost floated upstream with the incoming tide.

The cool, shady hardwood forest through which the river flowed provided a wonderful relief from the heat of the sun-exposed estuary. But I was here to do my own thing and stop doing what everyone else wanted. So when the other kayakers turned back, I continued paddling upstream. I just paddled mindlessly, allowing the tranquility of the forest to permeate my mood. Eventually, somewhere after passing under a bridge (or two?), time dictated that I return. I'd paddled longer than I'd planned, and I had to get my boat back to the rental shop before it closed for the day.

One of my old bosses once described me as "tenacious"; that's a nice way of saying "stubborn." The forecasted rain that night, and the drizzly morning after, had brought on a migraine. True to form, I was not willing to let this affliction dictate my life. With determination I went back into the park to amble along several shorter trails in the rain. As the weather cleared, hundreds of mosquitos joined my wanderings.

I walked the short Tweedie Trail, over broken boardwalks and through marshy open fields filled with wildflowers. There were also mounds of poison ivy that I mindfully avoided. As I returned to my car at the trailhead, I noticed a beat-up old car with two men in it. I had obviously interrupted their party. Upon seeing me they quickly tossed several beer cans out their windows and drove off. How could people throw out their garbage like that in pristine wilderness, in a national park?! And to boot, they were drinking and driving! There was just so much wrong with this. I wanted desperately to yell at them to pick up their litter, but as a woman alone in the wilderness, I thought it safer to keep quiet. These slobs, and the mosquitos, all so frustrating! I collected their garbage and threw it into the trash can at the edge of the parking lot. Then I stomped off, looking for another trail to walk off my anger.

Still irritated, I questioned why the path through a spruce and balsam forest was called "Pine Trail." I didn't get far down that trail before I saw them: several giant, century-old pine trees. These were the few descendants of the largest, straightest white pines which European loggers had taken for the masts of sailing ships. These survivors reminded me that nature will, eventually, prevail. I started to feel better about the world.

My last hike that afternoon was the five-kilometre Osprey Trail. The track hadn't been used for a while and was heavily overgrown. Stubbornly, I bushwhacked through a forested section and sloshed through low-lying, boggy mudholes. I was wearing just shorts and a T-shirt because the day had become hot and dry, so the underbrush scratched at my arms and gashed legs. I climbed over and under downed trees and around overgrown wild blueberry bushes (the fruit was not yet ripe). My thrashing through the bush raised clouds of mosquitos and alarms from the local chipmunks. Far above me, songbirds serenaded in the canopy – too bad, I thought, that they didn't eat more of these annoying mosquitos.

By the time I arrived at the tip of the Black River peninsula, I was soaked in sweat and itchy all over. I stood there on the small, sandy beach, taking in the view of the saltwater Kouchibouguac Lagoon. The placid pond was protected from the violence of the open ocean by the North Kouchibouguac Dune. I couldn't see beyond that sandy natural breakwater. A fishing boat was anchored at the other end of the lagoon, so far away I could barely ascertain that there were two people on board.

I figured that the fishermen wouldn't have been able to see me against my forest backdrop. And surely, I rationalized, no one else would be as stubborn as me to bushwhack to this remote point. I was alone. So why waste such a perfect opportunity? I stripped down and slowly walked into the cool shallow water, wading out a long way until the water got deep enough to swim in.

The salt stung the open wounds on my bared skin, but it felt good. Cleansing. A natural spa. I let my body float, staring up at the endless blue sky. My mind emptied as I drifted with the current. I let myself be comforted and taken away… until the cold penetrated and brought me back to physical reality. I suddenly realized I was covered in goosebumps, and I was a long way from where I'd walked into the lagoon. With a bit of urgency, and a strong breast stroke, I swam directly to the shore. Happy to be back on safe ground, I quietly walked back along the deserted beach and around the point to my pile of clothes. The warm breeze had dried me off before I got dressed. Peacefully, I followed the path I had earlier bashed open, back to the trailhead. I slept well that night.

The following day, I rented a bicycle with the intention of pedalling the 25-kilometre trail/roadway loop in the park. The man renting the bikes from his private business within the park pumped up the tires before setting me off on my ride. Like all the bicycles on his lot, mine was a refurbished old coaster bike: no gears; backpedal to stop. I felt rather silly in my hi-tech cycling shorts and jersey on such a simple bike. But hey, if I wanted to cycle that day, this bike was my only option. Yup, I was tenacious.

I hadn't ridden a coaster bike since I was a kid. Memories of my first one, a red "boy's bike," rushed back to me. My dad had taught me to ride. He had taught me so much. I missed him. The memories saddened me. But he was gone, I sighed. I continued, as I must, on my own. I bravely got on the ancient bike and was distracted from my sorrows by the challenges of relearning how to ride this style of bike. True, I discovered, "you never forget…" But coaster brakes sure are awkward.

I cycled the looped route counterclockwise, first on the hard-packed trail, then on the unpaved road by the river I had paddled along the other day. I breathed in the green air – I call it green because it smelled of green: trees, leaves and wild roses – mixed with the salt of the sea. A few gusts rustled the leaves as I coasted under the trees. Or was that the sound of waves lapping over the nearby pebbly beach? I was present, fully aware of the world around me. I was content.

Unfortunately a slow leak and eventual flat tire interrupted my bliss. I had to walk the bicycle nine kilometres back, through the shady forest, to the rental shop to get the tire fixed. While I wanted to be frustrated, the cool forest trail was tranquilizing. I came to the realization that I really didn't have to cycle to enjoy the day. I surrendered to the walk. It was already late in the afternoon when I set out again with a repaired tire. To see the complete circuit, I cycled the opposite way around the loop on my second attempt.

This clockwise direction started alongside the sandy shore of the St. Louis Lagoon. After three kilometres of sand-blown paved path, the trail turned inland, following alongside the main park road and through dense deciduous forest. Although I was happy to be out of the blazing sun, I was motivated to pedal fast, faster than the mosquitos could fly. The farther I got from the beach, the fewer people I met. I was, in fact, the only cyclist that day.

Eventually the forest gave way to open, shrubby land where the sun beat down again. The heat reflected back off the dry earth. I applied more sunscreen and finished the water I had brought along. I had pedalled until my legs ached from working up the inclines without gears. However, the heat and dehydration eventually forced me to turn back. I had almost made it as far as the point where I'd gotten the flat.

With fatigue setting in, I took the shortcut back along the main park road. I was relieved to find it was primarily downhill, so I could still cycle at a good clip. A few kilometres from the rental shop I finally settled into a more leisurely pace. I stopped at the beach snack shop for an ice cream, to refill my water bottle and watch children playing in the sand. I had cycled 34 kilometres and gotten to see most of the park.

Having seen and done most everything I had wanted to in the park, I spent my last afternoon at Kellys Beach. A one-kilometre boardwalk high over the dunes and salt marshes leads to the main beach on a 14-kilometre-long sandspit called South Kouchibouguac Dune, which protects the St. Louis Lagoon from the Atlantic Ocean. As it was midweek, there were only a few families around. I found my spot, laid out my towel and ate my picnic lunch. With sunscreen lathered, I laid myself back to read a novel. But I'm not a beach person. Within 15 minutes I became restless and I went for a swim. I stayed in the water until rainclouds rolled in overhead. I was happy. "It's good to be alive," I wrote in my journal that night.

By the time I arrived at my cottage, the storm had come and gone. I discovered that, for the first time that week, I had neighbours: all the cottages were occupied for a family reunion. Members from all over New Brunswick had come. I felt a bit odd, barbecuing my dinner all by myself with this huge group of people all around me, so I ate my dinner inside my cottage. However, Maritimers are very friendly people and these had noticed how awkward I had felt. They invited me to their bonfire that night, and I accepted.

A couple of hours later I brought the only things I had that could be shared: a bottle of wine and a large bag of potato chips, and joined the party on the beach below the cliff. I enjoyed the company, the first conversations I'd had in several days. We shared the wine, bottles of beer, and various snacks as the fire crackled up to the stars above us. A full moon rose over the ocean, its reflection in the calm water lighting up the night. Yes, it had been a good day; a good week.

The party had been a nice, short foray back into civilization, but I wasn't ready yet to return full time to society. Therefore I was thankful the next morning that while my week in Kouchibouguac had come to an end, my second week of vacation was about to start in Fundy National Park. I said goodbye to my new friends and drove off.

44
Fundy

15-METRE HIGH TIDES

After going to Kouchibouguac National Park to grieve the loss of my father in 2012, I spent a day driving. I took the long road, 300 kilometres around the scenic New Brunswick coast, through Acadian fishing villages, by the giant lobster statue in the town of Shediac, past the Confederation Bridge to PEI, along the New Brunswick/Nova Scotia boundary, through logged forests, by the salt marshes at Moncton and into Fundy National Park. While the sites along the way were interesting distractions, I was targeting Fundy as much to explore the vicinity as for the sanctuary of the woods. I needed healing.

I set up house in an efficiency unit in a motel within the park. The room had satellite TV but no internet or cell phone access – I would have to drive 40 kilometres to connect with my husband and friends. As I had picked up groceries on my way into the park, I was self-sufficient for the next few days. The relative isolation suited me just fine.

My motel was situated near the top of a steep mountain. From the picnic table outside my room, across the lawn and through a narrow gap between the trees, I could barely discern the Nova Scotia coast on the southeast side of the vast Bay of Fundy. Far below my temporary home lay the bay itself, boasting the highest tides in the world. The park showcases these 15-metre tides as well as the rivers, waterfalls and forests of the Caledonia Highlands.

I started my explorations of this park by hiking some of the shorter but very scenic trails: I spent 2½ hours on the rugged cliff edge above the ocean on the Matthews Head Trail. The trail meandered in and out of the forest and onto spectacular clifftop lookouts. From one of these vantage points I could see many giant flowerpots – monolithic pillars of red rock exposed by the low tide – dotting the coast all the way to the broad mud flats at the end of the Bay of Fundy. I needed to get closer.

I carefully climbed 250 metres down an unofficial path on the cliff face. At the base I found a jumble of huge seaweed-covered boulders that I had to clamber over to reach the water. There I found seashells and snails stranded in the pools of water left behind by the receding tide. There were even some tiny fish left amongst the seaweeds on the muddy bottom. Everything, it seemed, was patiently waiting for the water to return. I of course could not be down there for the incoming tide. There's about six hours between low and high tides, that is, between 0 and 15 metres of seawater. Not having tide tables with me, I had no idea where the cycle currently was, but I could see the water rising towards me even as I retreated to the boulders at the base of the precipice. Quickly I climbed, hand and foot, back up the vertical cliff of rock and loose soil to the safety of the main trail.

The heat of the day had quietened the forest, and the mild sea breeze kept the mosquitos away. I was at peace as I walked alone through the forest at the edge of the ocean. At the point overlooking "Squaw's Cap," a taller-than-wide rocky island, I took a short break. As I stood there photographing the beautiful site, two young women who were hiking the entire Coastal Route came up behind me. We were all surprised at having met someone else on the trail that mid-week day. After exchanging friendly greetings, we continued on our independent ways, respectful of each other's space.

On my way back to the trailhead, I stopped to snack on tiny wild strawberries growing in the field by the parking lot. Then I sat down at a picnic table near my car and I ate the fresh, sweet lobster-salad-filled hotdog bun I'd purchased that morning in the town of Alma. Lobster rolls are a special treat I like to savour when I'm in the Maritimes. They're so simple, yet so delicious.

In the afternoon I walked the short, picturesque Dickson Falls Trail. This boardwalked route leads through a mixed forest of hardwood and conifer trees. The air is cool and damp under the canopy, and the rocky ground is carpeted with thick green mosses. Birds sing overhead and chipmunks run underfoot. The highlight of this trail is of course the waterfall of Dickson Brook, splashing down over the emerald algae that covers the rocky cliffs dropping towards the sea. The entire scene is like something out of a storybook – I was half expecting fairies and mythical creatures to appear from the rays of sunlight that pierced down between the trees.

Unfortunately, what I found instead were several beer cans down below the high boardwalk. How appalling! How could anyone even think to sully such a heavenly garden?! They don't "think," I supposed – that's the only excuse I could fathom. So I jumped over the railing, climbed down one of the boardwalk's footings and collected the cans. Some other tourists who'd just arrived on the scene, raised their eyebrows when they saw me trespassing off the boardwalk. Then they saw the garbage I'd brought back up to the trail with me, and they gave me a thumbs-up. Satisfied, I chucked the trash in a garbage can back in the parking lot. I'd done my part; the beauty of Dickson Falls had been restored.

Before returning to my room, I explored a bit more by driving the 42-kilometre segment of Highway 114 that bisects the park. The forested two-lane route is very hilly and absolutely gorgeous. When I arrived at the junction with Route 1 in the hamlet of Springdale, my cell phone chirped back to life. Obviously other park visitors had also discovered this phone access point: there were several cars parked on the side of the road, all with people talking or texting on their phones. I joined the lineup and made a quick call home to let everyone know I was still alive.

My driving exploration of the park included a venture down to Point Wolfe. The road passed through a quaint, red, covered bridge. Roofs and walls are said to have been built on such bridges to protect people from the elements when crossing the river. That reason seems insufficient to me because people wouldn't have had any protection along the rest of the roadway. So my guess is that the coverings were traditionally built to obscure the view of rushing rivers far below – a potentially scary vision for people riding in open horse-drawn carriages.

I parked at a trailhead near the bridge. From there a short, wooded path led me to a wild, rocky, driftwood-strewn beach. The picturesque scene, however, belied a destructive past. Leftover wooden pylons stood rotting in the water off Point Wolfe. This was where a wharf serving the logging industry used to stand long ago. Just inland I found other signs of the local resource-based economy that used to thrive in this region. A steep hike up a two-kilometre trail revealed remnants of a copper mine, one of many that once scarred this land. Fortunately much of the man-made damage has been healed by a dense second growth of forest in the park. This evidence of the strength of nature gave me hope for the future.

I drove over to see Bennett Lake, a long, narrow freshwater lake with a very nice sandy beach and swimming area. I put on my bathing suit in one of the wooden changing cabins. It was late in the day when I walked across the deserted beach strewn with forgotten toys and went for a leisurely swim. The water was comfortably warm. I swam over the buoyed rope marking the end of the safe area, and made my way to and around a small island with a few trees and shrubs growing on it. Off the far side of the island, the water was covered with a mass of lily pads and crisp white flowers. As I swam through this "garden" I had to guard against a slight inkling towards panic when the ropey stems drifted over my body, twining around my limbs and my neck. Retaining my composure, I slowly breast-stroked, keeping my head out of the water, back towards the beach. Having conquering my fear, I followed this same route every day thereafter, either first thing in the morning or last thing in the evening, when there were no crowds.

Adding to my enjoyment of Bennett Lake one evening, the resident loon popped up next to me. The bird was probably checking that I wasn't going to be a threat to its territory. The loon escorted me back to the buoys where it left me to swim the rest of the way back to the beach on my own, me with a big happy grin on my face.

After having completed the easy explorations of Fundy early in the week, I moved on to some more-challenging hikes. The first was the narrow, five-kilometre Moosehorn Trail, which largely followed along the Upper Salmon River. There are several cascades and inviting pools between long, broad stretches of fast-running water. I'd come prepared for a swim, so I sat down on a sun-warmed boulder and changed into my bathing suit. Then I slowly eased myself over the large rounded rocks and into a pool that was just large enough for a few strokes. I found a submerged "armchair" carved into the rocks where the water was still and warm – perfect. I settled in, closed my eyes and almost drifted off.

As I was drying myself off after my dip, a couple of other hikers arrived at the pool. Besides being envious that they hadn't brought swimwear, John and Mary were happy to find another person in the middle of the woods. They'd been having difficulty locating the trail in the thick underbrush. Since I had a map, they asked to join me as I continued my way up the trail. Together the three of us bushwhacked along the overgrown riverbank.

We eventually found the connecting path to the Laverty Falls Trail and within a few minutes we were admiring the 12-metre-high waterfall. There were several people sitting under the curtain of the falls. Scratched up, overheated and itchy from the bushwhacking, I eagerly hopped into the river. The cool water was refreshing. This swimming hole was the real reason I'd brought along my bathing suit.

With much regret, John and Mary wouldn't come in for a swim, and continued along the well-defined path up to the parking lot. After soaking for half an hour, I followed them up the 2.5-kilometre Laverty Trail, by the reed-choked Laverty Lake, to the trailhead where I'd left my rental car. I had really enjoyed this eight-kilometre loop and was looking forward to another hike the next day.

The Third Vault Falls Trail meanders for 2.5 kilometres, gently descending through the humid Acadian forest. Sets of wooden staircases ease the way down the steeper sections. The farther I went, the rockier the trail became. Tiny streams trickled down between the boulders and around lush green ferns. Water seeped through the thick, shaggy mosses that draped down to the steep forest floor. I stopped for a moment in this verdant wilderness and glanced back over my left shoulder.

Through a stand of tall trees in narrow ravine, I spotted the waterfalls. I followed a switchback leading into the crevasse and was suddenly accosted by the deafening roar of Third Vault Falls. As the long, narrow waterfall crashed over several ledges on its way down, the steep cliffs echoed and amplified the clamour, belying the relatively small amount of water.

I rock-hopped to the pool at the base of the falls, found a comfortable spot with a good view and sat down on the perfect boulder to enjoy my lunch.

There was no one else at the falls when I'd arrived but eventually a young couple came and then another couple. The guys were showing off in front of their girlfriends. One of the guys climbed the moss- and algae-covered rocks up the side of the waterfall. The other guy, not wanting to be outdone, dove off a boulder halfway up, into a pool below. The first guy slipped and slid all the way down, scraping his bare chest on the sharp rocks. The second guy climbed out of the water holding one of his feet. As a result, the girlfriends started fawning over their injured boys, much to the boys' delight.

Then the one couple started to panic – the injury had been more than they could handle. From the other side of the pond, I held up my first aid kit and pointed to it. They couldn't hear me for the roar of the falls, but understood my offer. The guy saw me and nodded. I made my way over to him and found that he had a very deep gash in the sole of his foot. I too couldn't stop the bleeding. So I put on antiseptic and bandaged him up, instructing him to get proper medical care – there would probably be algae from the rock he'd hit, deep inside the wound. While I was doctoring the one guy, the other came to me for the antiseptic cream and bandages to patch up his scrapes and cuts. After I attended to the wounds, the girls helped their guys hobble out of the forest. I never saw any of them again.

Alone in the forest again, I became contemplative. I thought about the foolish things young people do to impress each other. Then I waded into the icy water of the lowest pool, intent on a quick dip, and it occurred to me that I too was taking risks. There I was, at age 50, exploring the wilderness all by myself. I supposed that if we managed to survive the risks we took, we learned, and we took on new risks – that's how we grow.

I spent my last days at the Bay of Fundy exploring the bay itself. I drove out of the park and over to the Hopewell Rocks. At high tide the rocks look like small islands dotting the bay, but when the 15-metre tide goes out, the full height of the rocks is revealed. They are massive red pillars of hard sandstone, the surrounding softer ground having been eroded away by the tides. With trees and shrubs growing atop the pillars these natural features look somewhat like vases when the tide is out, hence their common name "flowerpots."

I joined hundreds of other people at this tourist attraction. At low tide, we climbed down the stairs that are pinned to the steep cliffside and went for a walk on the exposed bottom of the ocean. The area the low tide had made available to us was so large that I never felt crowded by my fellow tourists. I took my time, about three hours, exploring this temporarily water-free site.

I had to watch my footing on the exposed sea floor, which was wet and slippery in some places yet sandy in other. I wandered around, admiring the wonderful shapes eroded into the bases of the flowerpots. There were swirls, ledges, caverns and holes. I could walk right through some of the pillars, the gaps were that big. While gawking through a heart-shaped hole in one of the towers, I accidentally stepped into a pool of ankle-deep mud. Others had obviously experienced the same fate and we all laughed at our common folly.

Children squealed with glee as they discovered the various sea creatures in the shallow pools left behind by the receding tide. I too delighted in squishing the water out of some of the bulbous seaweed that clung to the sides of the flowerpots, rock arches and caves. So this is what it's like at the bottom of the sea – only the fish were missing!

Although it was impossible to get a photograph without people in it, most people courteously avoided walking directly through the field of vision of others' cameras. In fact, everyone was so enthused and excited to share the experience, that we comfortably exchanged cameras to photograph one another in front of the oddest shaped rocks. I also noted that actually having other people in my photographs provided human perspective to the incredible size of the rocks.

To complete my experience, I wanted to kayak at high tide over the same places I had walked. However, I found that the tours offered at the tourist attraction were geared towards novice paddlers and were also quite expensive. So I joined a small group of six seasoned paddlers, renting kayaks from a tour operator in the national park. On a high tide, with two guides, we paddled from the village of Alma, at the Salmon River estuary, towards Matthews Head.

Even with about 15 metres of water beneath us, the tower-islands loomed far above. We craned our necks to see the forest-topped cliffs as we paddled along the shoreline. Somewhere up there was where I'd hiked a few days ago. How interesting the different perspective from down at sea level was. I couldn't see Nova Scotia on the other side of the bay. From the water, it seemed like I was kayaking on the vast open ocean.

The water was choppy with white-capped waves and we had a stiff headwind – a hard paddle. Eventually we took a short break at a small, rocky beach. We took this opportunity to clamber over the large boulders that had fallen from the cliffs – a long time ago, we hoped – and inspect the hollows in the high walls. The caves were too shallow for any hidden treasures we might have hoped for, natural or man-made. I chuckled as it occurred to me that finding nothing is part of exploration.

A thick fog had started to roll in from the mouth of the bay when we got back into our kayaks. We could no longer see Matthews Head. Sadly that meant it was too dangerous for us to continue. We had to turn back. While the less experienced kayakers paddled out over deeper water, a couple of us had fun darting along the coastline, in and out of tiny coves and between giant boulders just off the shore.

As the tide was almost out by the time we got back, we could not take out over the newly exposed, barnacle- and limpet-covered rocks. We had to paddle farther, to a small bay near the park's swimming pool, for a safe place to land. Once off the water, we clamoured on about having experienced some of the winds, waves, fog and tides that were part of typical seaside life. I was aware that, fortunately, we hadn't had to face anything really too dramatic.

I found that not only was I enjoying the scenery and learning about this awesome place, but I was also enjoying the company of other people again. I was ready to go home, to my family and work. I had recovered myself in the national parks.

45
Prince Edward Island

A MARITIME ISLAND

WINDY BEACHES

As the province of Prince Edward Island (or simply PEI) is less than 6000 square kilometres in size, Prince Edward Island National Park is significant in highlighting the coastal features of this island province. In 1977 this was one of the first national parks I'd ever visited; and I did so as a Girl Guide, as part of a tour of the Maritimes. Our group arrived by coach from New Brunswick.

We took the ferry from Cape Tormentine, New Brunswick, to Borden, PEI. The Confederation Bridge connecting the island to the mainland would only be built 20 years later, replacing the ferry service. The hour or so ferry ride was exciting for our group of 15-year-old girls. After hours of sitting on the bus, we got to get off the coach and stretch our legs, inhale the salty air and feel the sea wind whip our hair. Our heads were filled with notions of romantic ocean crossings. As we approached the island, the renowned red-soil cliffs of PEI grew ever more distinct, contrasting against the blue ocean and the whitewashed houses that dotted the shoreline. We waved at the welcoming parties we imagined were awaiting our arrival.

I was excited to finally be seeing the place where the British North America Act, creating the Dominion of Canada, our country, had been signed. This was also the province where potatoes came from, and the home of Anne (of Green Gables) – all things I had learned about in school. I later learned that prior to being named in honour of the 18th century King George III's son, the island had been known as Epekwitk, or "lying on the water," by the Mi'kmaw people.

The wind had grown progressively stronger through the day as our coach drove off the ferry and headed to the park on the other side of the island. By the time we arrived at Cavendish Beach in Prince Edward Island National Park, a storm was brewing. Sadly, the campground, or at least the group camping area we were assigned to, was an open grassy field bordered by tall, wildly swaying trees at the far end. We'd have no protection from the storm. We struggled to set up our tents in the gale. One tent was immediately lost to the treetops because the sandy soil under the thin layer of sod couldn't hold the tent pegs. The wind simply blew the tent away like a giant orange balloon. A few girls would have to sleep on the bus.

We were grateful for the picnic shelter under which we ate our dinner. Our gas lanterns swung wildly in the howling wind, casting eerie shadows. The setting was perfect for the ghost stories we scared each other with. Oh, we had so much fun playing up the dangers of the storm we were living through. Finally, exhausted, we tumbled into our sleeping bags, those of us in the remaining tents adding our weight to keep these tents from flying away also. As the storm raged through the night, several of us wished we too were sleeping on the bus.

Possibly due to the high winds, the storm passed quickly and the Island was calm the following day. Set for a swim in the ocean, we walked along a leaf-strewn path through the narrow strip of trees. On the other side of the woods, the trail meandered between high sandy dunes and out to the beach. Obediently (because we were Girl Guides) we complied with the Parks signs requesting that we not climb onto the dunes. Other placards at the beach informed us that a very special type of grass had been planted to help keep the dunes from blowing away into the sea during storms. Storms like the one we had just experienced, we assumed.

On the beach we discovered that the storm had stirred up too much sand in the water to allow for swimming. Still, we stripped off our Girl Guide regulation blue-checkered shirts that we put on over our bathing suits, and waded into the ocean. We laughed as we jumped over the remaining small breakers that were washing onto the shore. We posed all grown-up-like in our bikinis for the pictures we took of each other using our first ever, brand new Instamatic cameras. We had each been given several cartridges of film to record our adventures, and we were having fun pretending to be famous photographers and movie stars.

A day tour was sufficient for us to visit some of the major attractions on PEI. Our bus took us by too many kilometres of potato fields – not particularly interesting to a bunch of young teenagers – to Green Gables and the house in which Lucy Maud Montgomery had written her famous book. The reality of the stuffy, old-fashioned house, with its sprawling, perfectly mowed lawn, was a bit of a disappointment for me. I had been expecting, unrealistically, a bubbly, lively environment that mirrored Anne's nature. I sadly discovered that, of course, the girl's character was intended to be a juxtaposition to the place in which she "lived." That evening, however, we got to experience some Anne of Green Gables liveliness in a stage play at the theater in Charlottetown, the provincial capital. My need to meet a "kindred spirit" was thereby finally fulfilled, and I was a happy camper again.

On this, my first time in the Maritimes, I had had the opportunity to explore so many of the places I'd learned about in my Canadian geography and history classes. Back at home, I was surprised at how meaningful these experiences had been for me, and I longed for more. My thirst to get to know more of my country, and the world, had been whetted. My journey of exploration had begun.

46
Cape Breton Highlands

DRIVING ALONG THE EDGE

This was my first big trip away from home without my parents. I was 15, travelling with a group from the Montreal area to a Girl Guide International Camp hosted by our friends in Nova Scotia. The jamboree was being held in Cape Breton Highlands National Park. We were an impressive group, I thought, always in our uniforms of light blue blouses and navy skirts. I had bought into the military discipline of the dress code, which, by design, made me feel like I belonged. I was thrilled to be part of this well-respected international organization, and proud to be seen in my uniform.

We, like all teenagers, talked too loudly, believing what we had to say was very important and interesting to everyone around us. Didn't everyone want to hear our gossip about boys and our complaints about parents and teachers? We sang never-ending circle songs that drove our leaders and our bus driver crazy. We taunted one poor leader who was particularly upset about deceptively inappropriate songs such as "The Farmer and the Maid." We believed we were grown up. We were, after all, on our way to take part in a very important international event!

Covering some 3000 kilometres by coach, our route took us through Quebec City, where we overnighted in sleeping bags in a church basement. The following day my high school Canadian history lessons were brought to life when we walked around the Quebec Citadel (designated as a national historic site in 1981) and down the 300-year-old Promenade des Gouverneurs to the Chateau Frontenac. For me, Old Quebec was no longer merely the setting of some abstract stories related in dusty textbooks. This trip was living up to its promise of teaching us something about our country.

The next day, our coach crossed into New Brunswick. The highlight of our drive through the province was our stop at Magnetic Hill. Basically, there is a rural road running through nondescript farmland near Moncton that contains a natural optical illusion: a steep incline on which vehicles appear to roll uphill. We were excited to test this. Did it work for everyone? Would anyone not see the bizarre effect? Would the "magnet" be strong enough to pull our heavy coach, with some two dozen girls on board, up the hill? Our bus queued up behind several other vehicles waiting their turn to experience the "miracle." Our driver put the bus in neutral, and sure enough, we started rolling uphill! We cheered wildly!

Looking backwards, we appeared to be in a valley which moved forward with us as we travelled through the farmscape. Every inch of road that was declining behind us was inclining ahead of us. When we reached the "top" of the hill and looked back, we could see the reality that we just had rolled downhill, following the rules of physics. This was pretty cool.

Then onwards down never-ending highways we drove, past all varieties of farms and through forests. We tried to do the right thing and pay attention to the scenery we knew we were privileged to be passing through, but the monotonous rocking of the bus lulled us to sleep. The awareness that our leaders too had been nodding off comforted me – I was like the adults, not offending anyone by sleeping through the important landscapes we were passing.

The Girl Guide International Camp was being held at a group campsite in the national park. Our group, however, could not officially register to camp with the other girls from around the world, because the campsite was full. Instead we were to "camp" in four rooms of a consolidated school in the nearby town of Marion Bridge. The community, we found, had its own attractions. We girls discovered the local boys jumping off an old bridge into the Mira River. The boys, playing up to us, dared each other into ever more fanciful dives. We were enchanted. Our leaders were not so amused, and soon we were herded into the school and out of sight. Poop.

At the camp in the park, girls from various countries were performing their native dances for each other. While we all enjoyed the shows, the event was overshadowed by the news that some poor girl from India had fallen into a latrine. We suppressed guilty giggles at the thought of the mess. We felt so bad for the girl, who we'd been told was accustomed to standing on blocks on either side of small wells that were the toilets where she came from. She hadn't known to sit on the seat. Instead the poor girl had tried to stand on the seat, lost her balance, and fell through the hole. Pee-hew! These international camps are intended for girls to learn about other cultures and ways of living, but this was an awfully unfortunate way for us to learn how some basic things are done differently in other countries.

My group spent another day in the national park driving along the famous Cabot Trail. Once out of the dark, dense forest, the two-lane highway hugged the rugged cliff edge overlooking the Atlantic Ocean. We pressed our noses to the seaside windows, squealing as our bus rounded the tight curves along the narrow highway. We took turns sitting on the land side of the bus, just to be sure our combined weight wouldn't tip the coach over the steep cliffs and into the ocean! Our driver ignored our childish worries, and calmly drove on down the winding road. At each designated scenic lookout, we climbed off the bus to gaze at the sea. We were looking for whales but saw only seagulls and foamy ocean out to the horizon. Back on our coach, the rhythmic sound of the waves breaking on the cliffs below us, the cool, fresh sea air and the motion of the bus put us to sleep again. I suspected our leaders were torn between relief at the resulting peace and frustration about our apparent disinterest.

My interest was piqued again when we stopped to visit the Alexander Graham Bell National Historic Site in Baddeck, on the way back to our schoolhouse. This was the first museum I had ever really taken an interest in: the drawings, photographs and samples of kite-based flying machines made my imagination soar. Then there was the iron lung Bell invented. "How did he come up with that idea?" I wondered. And surprise: the world's first telephone call, I learned, had been made in Canada – Ontario, to be exact!

The museum is housed in what had been Alexander Graham Bell's artsy-type home on a pretty little lake hidden among the forested hills of Cape Breton Island. This is where the great inventor toyed, literally, with the principles of physics. I had never considered that famous inventors might have lived and come up with their brilliant ideas in such remote wilderness settings. I had always associated inventiveness with big cities and staid universities where theories could be exchanged – the Industrial Revolution. Here, however, I began to comprehend that segregation from the bounds of social expectations and academic norms could allow for play, experimentation and brand-new ideas. My perceptions were changing, growing.

I was awed, inspired, and wanted to spend more time learning in this museum! Alas, I was the last girl of our group still reading the information boards when I got dragged back onto the bus. Time to go. The other girls were bored and didn't understand how mechanics and engineering could so fascinate me. They teased me about being a nerd. Perhaps I inherited this interest from my maternal grandfather. My father had probably further instilled it in me. Both men had been auto mechanics by trade. My grandfather had been the master mechanic, my dad his apprentice. So, like them, I love to know how things are made and why they work. Or sometimes don't. I felt an intense appreciation of those museum displays of Bell's experiments.

Our last stop in Cape Breton was at the Fortress of Louisbourg, the French-built, English-conquered fortress that is now a national historic site. Not wanting to be treated like children, we teenagers felt silly answering "Friend" to the period-uniformed "guard" at the gate of the fortress. He had demanded to know whether we were friend or foe before allowing us in. Other period-costumed guides depicted the life of 18th century Europeans in the New World as being so simple, innocent and rosy. My maturing thoughts ran more along the lines of how tough life must have been back then. The ladies' long skirts would be heavy with mud on rainy days, their hands would be callused from hard work, their lives painful and short due to illness, infection and disease. And would they have considered themselves lucky to have drafty outhouses buried in snowdrifts, instead of just using holes in the ground? Which brought to my mind: How did women manage with petticoats? "Nope!" I thought. "I would not want to have been living at that time." I was very happy with my lifestyle and luxuries. And I wasn't going to be at risk of falling into any old-time latrines!

47
Kejimkujik

FUN IN THE SUN

I visited Kejimkujik, pronounced keji-meh-'kujik, or just "Keji" as the locals call it, late in the summer of 2014. The park is just a 200-kilometre drive from Halifax, after a 1300-kilometre flight from Toronto. When I arrived mid-afternoon, I was told that recent days had been unusually hot for that late in the season. Expecting cold rainy weather, I hadn't come prepared to camp in this southwestern Nova Scotia forest. So instead I checked into a pretty little inn just outside the park. That would be my home base from which to discover Keji's secrets.

The first thing that hit me was how damp and humid the endless conifer forest was; the heat seemed to stifle all living things. The songbirds were quiet; only a few blue jays sounded off like creaky door hinges. A sole merganser flew along the dark Mersey River that meanders through the park. Otherwise the forest was still. Although it was midday, I met no one as I walked the trails. Only the occasional late-season mosquito buzzed around to bother me. I walked under hemlocks heavily draped in mosses and lichens. Various mushrooms grew on the fallen trees strewn over the forest floor. Red bunchberries lined the trail. I was alone, blissful in this fairy-tale forest.

After a very peaceful night at the inn, I re-entered the park early in the morning. The air was still cool, refreshing after the heat of the previous day. I rented a small kayak and paddled out into the vast, islanded Kejimkujik Lake. The water was as peaceful as the low hills surrounding it. The paddling was easy that day. I went in close to the shoreline so I could admire the way the rounded granite rocks and beefy tree roots held fast to the water's edge. The air smelled "green" – there was life.

As I approached the edge of the Mi'kmaw traditional homeland, I noted the white-signed buoys requesting boaters to maintain a respectful distance. With my binoculars I peered from my kayak, looking for the petroglyph paintings I'd been told were on the flat rocks lining the lake. I shouldn't be peeping into someone else's home, but I guiltily did so anyways. With some imagination, I thought I could make out the outline of a white canoe with a paddle sticking out, Then again, I also saw wonderful shapes in the clouds. And up there, beneath the few fluffy clouds, a hawk settled onto the top branch of a tall hemlock. The sentinel bird watched me from its perch, as if ensuring I wouldn't invade this private space any further. I tucked away my spyglass and paddled on.

The tranquility of the park was wonderful, but I ached to expel the excess energy that had built up in me over the previous days of travelling. I found release that afternoon, when I rented a mountain bike at Jakes Landing. I tore up the trails, cycling through the narrow, winding Slapfoot Trail to Meadow Beach, then along the campsite road to the paved park road, and back along the gravelled Mersey River trail.

As my comfort with the suspensioned bike increased, so did my speed. My eyes were glued to the route – over protruding rocks and roots, between trees, through mudholes and over tilted boardwalks. I had only just enough time for quick judgments on where to steer and when to brake or accelerate over and around the obstacles immediately in my path. I revelled in the control I could exert over the bike as I pushed my limits. I was high on the adrenalin rush!

While I was concentrating on the features of the trail directly ahead of me, I did have a niggling thought that perhaps I should be paying more attention to the broader world around me. I had been having so much fun tearing up the trails that I hadn't even noticed whether there had been anyone else around. So twice I forced myself to stop and look out over the river I was cycling along – but only very short stops, just long enough to gulp down some water. My heart and lungs were pumping and my legs insisted on matching the pace. I raced on!

I arrived back at Jakes, sunburnt, my face dripping with sweat and my T-shirt mud splattered. I was grinning from ear to ear with the pleasure of having released all that pent-up energy. The cute young guy at the rental booth smiled knowingly at me. I turned and walked away. My cardiovascular system settled and I was content.

I topped off my adventures in Kejimkujik with a late evening trip to Merrymakedge Beach – a small stretch of sand looking out onto Kejimkujik Lake. As the change rooms were locked up for the season, and there was no one around, I changed into my bikini in my car. In my rear-view mirror I saw a couple with a dog hiking by along the beach, but they never noticed me. They walked off down the trail into the woods, and I was alone again. The beach was mine.

Swimming in the tranquil lake, I stretching out my muscles, releasing the aches from the days of hiking, kayaking and cycling. A loon floated by; it too stretched out its wings, then disappeared down into the dark, deeper end of the lake. Back and forth I swam in the clear water, between the reeds at one end of the bay and the lily pads at the other. I could see the rocks beneath me, just out of reach. Due to the shallowness of the lake, and the peat bogs, the water was warm and brown. I felt like I was swimming in a lukewarm cup of tea; it was sweet. I was in no hurry to leave.

After a few days exploring the forest, I drove out of the park, almost 100 kilometres southeast to the separate Seaside Adjunct of Kejimkujik National Park. This smaller part of the park highlights the Nova Scotia seashore. I spent a quiet couple of hours there walking the Port Joli Head trail, a nine-kilometre return hike.

The trail starts in a small coastal forest, then winds on boardwalks over a seemingly endless bog. Insect-eating pitcher plants alongside the trail seemed to be doing their jobs – there were relatively few insects disturbing me in what should have been a bug-infested marsh. The tall grasses swayed in the salty breeze sweeping across the boardwalk. Gulls, riding the winds, cried above me. Eventually the bog gave way to the open ocean: nothing but water out to the horizon.

Ah, but in those waters I saw the spray of whales – too far off to identify what kind, but I saw whales! They entertained me and kept me company. I was not alone in this park after all.

Under the hot sun, I sat down on a grey, weathered wooden bench on a viewing platform. There, with the ocean world before me, I silently ate my picnic lunch. I leaned back and the crash of the surf on the rocks below lulled me to sleep. What a laid-back kind of place.

I went home deeply tanned and calmed.

48
Sable Island Reserve

SKIRMISH OF WILD HORSES

Sable Island is just a crescent of sand more than 160 kilometres off the coast of Nova Scotia, though its exact position and size are constantly changing, being pushed around by the winds and currents. The island, with its hidden underwater sandbars and criss-crossing currents, is infamous for causing over 350 shipwrecks. I arrived on the 101-metre MV *Sea Adventurer*, on a tour arranged by Adventure Canada, in June of 2014. Our captain joked about how ships are warned to steer clear of this area of the Atlantic, and yet here he was taking his ship right up to and anchoring at the dreaded island. Despite all concerns, the ocean was calm and eerily quiet during the four days of our visit. We wondered why.

I was travelling with a seasoned group of approximately 90 research scientists, photographers, authors, people from *Canadian Geographic* and *Canadian Gardening* magazines, horse enthusiasts, birders and adventure travellers. We were only the second group of tourists to visit Sable Island since it was designated as a national park, and we were keenly aware that we were to be the last until Parks Canada assessed our impact on the fragile environment. We had to be on our best behaviour.

Each day, we were allowed only a half day on the island and were transferred there in inflatable Zodiac boats from the ship. As I stumbled off the Zodiac that first day, a new friend winked at me, and offered his hand to help me through the surf and onto the beach. Steve and I would go on to explore together.

Our large group was split up into four, each under the supervision of one or two Parks personnel. They introduced us to the island's history and current situation before leading us single file along the horse trails to see for ourselves. We carefully followed, avoiding stepping on the fragile vegetation.

The walking was difficult on the loosely mounded sands, in the valleys and over the dunes. Although the island is only about 1.5 kilometres across at its widest point, the sea could not be heard from between the dunes. Except for the mouse-like squeaking sounds of our own footsteps in the sand, there was no noise at all. We trekked between and over the dunes and then along endless driftwood-strewn beaches.

Although treeless, Sable Island does boast a good variety of shrubs, including wild roses and blueberries. We explored the freshwater ponds: bright-yellow-cupped bullhead lilies floated among the mirrored images of wispy clouds above us. The blossoms of blue flag iris and grass pink orchids rimmed the ponds, contributing to the pretty, meadow-like scene. Our expert guides described how the various plants interact with each other, the land and the animals and birds.

We watched Ipswich sparrows, which don't nest anywhere else in the world but here, flitting about. Terns, feigning broken wings, hobbled along, distracting us from their nests. In the background, between the tangle of low shrubs, giant predatory black-backed gull chicks squawked to be fed.

And then there were the horses. Wild horses, gone feral from the days of the Acadian deportations in the mid-1700s, were always near us, on the beach or just behind the next sand dune. Over 500 of them roam freely on Sable Island. These small horses, so resilient in this unexpected island in the Atlantic Ocean, live their lives free from any human interference or provisions. They live, reproduce and die as nature sees fit. These facts were revealed to us as we walked by the occasional decomposing horse carcass. Steve pointed at some old bleached horse bones we passed on our way to visiting with their descendants.

Steve and I watched the feral horses from a respectable distance, our binoculars bringing their images closer to us. With their long, dreadlocked manes blowing in the breeze, small herds grazed, gradually wearing down their teeth on the tough marram grass. Several foals, running amuck, scrutinized us as curiously as they looked at everything else in their new world. The mares and stallions simply ignored us; we humans had no purpose in their lives.

When we weren't exploring the island on foot, we were observing it from the sea. From our small, manoeuvrable Zodiacs we saw both grey and harbour seals lounging on the beaches. We had to be careful not to approach too close or these mammals, so clumsy on land, would abandon the warm, sunny shore for the comfort of the sea. Those that were in the water around us would pop their heads out, periscope-like, to check us out: "friend or foe?" Their playful antics entertained us as we strived to take photographs from our bobbing boats. The movement of the sea, the boats and the seals rendered a good photograph a lucky shot.

Our best experience at Sable was saved for our last day. We weren't even on the island, but sitting in our Zodiacs heading for the far end of it. We saw a stallion pushing his herd of mares and a foal across a long, narrow spit of sand between two shrub-covered dunes. The sea and sky behind silhouetted the scene, making it look like we were watching a giant silver screen. We shut off our engines and silently watched.

Behind this small herd, another stallion trotted along the waterline to catch up to them. Stallion 1 turned and raced to chase stallion 2 back into the shrubs. The mares weren't really interested in moving forward, so they stopped and waited until stallion 1 returned. He ran full speed back to his herd and nudged them onwards. Stallion 2 then made a second attempt, trotting through the water this time, to catch up to the herd. For his efforts, stallion 2 received a rear hoof to his head from stallion 1. This back and forth faceoff between the two stallions continued down the length of the sandspit, the horses running farther and farther each time. Each time, the mares just waited and watched the males duke it out.

As the herd slowly progressed along the sandspit, we too had to move our Zodiacs farther along, like reparking for a better vantage point at a drive-in movie. In the final episode we were privileged to witness, the two stallions rose up against each other and then galloped off into the wilderness. We floated silently, awed by what we had just seen. This was nature in the raw, unscripted and untamed.

We were further blessed that evening as we wandered along the western shore of Sable for the last time: Mother Nature treated us to a golden sunset over the icy-blue ocean. It was the perfect ending to a perfect visit. We celebrated with glasses of sparkling wine. Steve and I nudged each other, grinning in mutual admiration of this world that had been revealed to us.

On our two-day journey back to St. John's, Newfoundland, we stopped to do some research over The Gully, located on the edge of the North American continental shelf, 200 kilometres off the coast of Nova Scotia. At about 65 kilometres long by up to 1 kilometre deep, The Gully is the largest submerged canyon in the western Atlantic Ocean. This underwater fiord is home to a large diversity of marine life and is the subject of much study.

We were fortunate that the sun was shining when we arrived at The Gully, and that we had permission from Fisheries and Oceans Canada to sail over the area. The calm seas allowed the *Sea Adventurer* to follow a zigzag route along the length of The Gully, as prescribed by the scientists. The ornithologist on board busied himself with identifying and counting the seabirds we passed. For the rest of us, our job as designated citizen scientists was to spot any and all marine life along the way. We shouted out with great delight our sightings of endangered bottlenose whales, dolphins and a multitude of birds. I was particularly happy for the opportunity to contribute to the scientific work in this Marine Protected Area. Not only was I enjoying the natural beauty of our country but I was helping with its conservation.

A DREAM REALIZED

Wow! After so many years, I've done it: I've visited all the Canadian national parks! I "bagged" them all.

My goal of visiting every one of the Canadian national parks has taken most of my adult life to complete. Major factors included the need to earn a living and support my family, and the challenges of physically getting to some of the parks. In addition, I needed to build the mental fortitude to complete such a huge project.

I'd used part-time jobs and student loans to get through university. That education led me to a well-paying career, which in turn provided the funding to get to parks in the distant reaches of this huge country. Strategically, I used my vacations to travel, alternating years between getting to know Canada and exploring the rest of the world. Of course, family and friends always took priority over exploration, but then they were often dragged along with me on my crazy adventures. And when no one wanted to accompany me, I tenaciously went on my own.

Getting to some of the parks will always be a challenge, for anyone. Canada is so large that it's costly to get to a park on the other side of the country. Natural disasters, weather and sea conditions also dictate how and when travel to some parks, such as those in the Arctic, can be done. Patience and planning (and persistence at the right times) have enabled me to realize my dreams.

The opportunity to see and learn about places I haven't been to before, and the anticipation of sharing what I've learned after my exploits, always excites me. Then the hard reality of just how to execute the trips hits me, and nervousness sets in. I flip-flop anxiously between these emotions, but I carry on, having learned from past travels that everything will fall into place – I just need to plan carefully. My trick is not to ignore or get overwhelmed by my racing imagination. I methodically find ways to overcome the obstacles and mitigate the risks. And then I sit back and enjoy the ride.

I'm now sitting at my desk at home, reflecting on my experiences and writing my stories. The expression "getting there is half the fun" might suggest that the other half is "being there." But I've come to believe that enjoyment is divvied up into three: "getting there is a *third* of the fun, being there is a third of the fun and reminiscing is a third of the fun." That last part may rank even greater because I tend to discount the severity of the really bad episodes. I revel in memories of the best experiences. I enjoy sharing tales of my adventures, and I get immense satisfaction out of inspiring others. The Canadian national parks have given me so much enjoyment, knowledge and appreciation of this country.

The variety of my experiences ran parallel with the diversity of the land protected by the parks, and thus I've seen first-hand that the parks have something for all abilities and interests. The opportunities range from very laid-back to extremely challenging. Visitors can enjoy everything from a luxurious spa in a first-class hotel to a polar dip in the Arctic Ocean. Casual sightseers can appreciate the wilderness stretched out before them at a roadside scenic lookout, and exceptionally active people can enjoy the vistas from remote mountaintops. Park visitors can vacation with others, meditate all by themselves or become immersed through books and movies. Regardless of how one chooses to experience the parks, I think all visitors learn something about this huge country: its geography, flora, fauna and of course its Indigenous Peoples.

Parks Canada's continuous challenge is to find and maintain the balance:

> To protect for all time representative natural areas of Canadian significance in a system of national parks, and to encourage public understanding, appreciation and enjoyment of this natural heritage so as to leave it unimpaired for future generations.

I truly hope that Parks Canada devises ways of ensuring that the parks never become over-developed, and that there will always be areas to challenge people who enjoy extreme exploration, as well as places accessible for casual vacationers.

Although there are 39 regions, there are already 48 parks (including an urban one) because for historical or political reasons some regions have more than one park. For example, Banff, Jasper, Waterton, Yoho and Kootenay are all in the same region. In 2020 there are still a few regions with no parks to represent them. I look forward to seeing what beauty lies in those regions, and to helping to protect them for the future.

I sincerely hope also that by sharing my adventures, I might inspire others to seek out their own exploits and come to appreciate the natural Canadian wilderness as much as I have.

AFTERTHOUGHTS

Whenever I travel, I keep a journal in which I record what I was doing, where and when. I also record my thoughts, inspirations and trepidations. At the end of each trip, when I get home, I add one last section entitled "Afterthoughts" to my journal. This postscript is where I write down the elements of the journey that most intrigued me, and reminders and learnings to consider during future adventures.

The writing of this book and the inherent reliving of my adventures has been its own journey. Therefore as with all my travels, I log the following "afterthoughts" about the creation of Park Bagger:

- Yes, our Canadian national parks definitely provided me not only with education about my country but also with adventure, understanding of mankind and discovery of myself.
- Canada is so large, the second-largest country in the world, area wise. Over such a large expanse, it is inevitable that each region would be so vastly different and distinct from any other. This is why I cannot offer up a "favourite" park. Each one is special. My opinion is of course moulded by Parks Canada's mandate to preserve, conserve and highlight something that represents the best of each part of the country. I think Parks has largely succeeded in this.
- In my travels I've seen many wildernesses that are inhospitable to people, where perhaps we don't seem to belong. Yet human beings are a natural part of this planet and it's in our nature to explore, learn and make ourselves comfortable. Our mere existence is at once impacted by, and impacting on, the environment. I'm aware that my going to and reporting on our remote parks will affect them – a form of the "observer effect." I hope, however, that learning about the beauty and value of "uncivilized" places will give us reason to

continue to preserve and protect some of the wilderness. The challenge to each of us is to enjoy without destroying these amazing resources.

- Unfortunately, climate change is real – I've seen it for myself, particularly in parks in the far North. Temperatures in the high 20s and even 30°C in the Arctic, defrosting permafrost, slumping riverbanks, retreating glaciers, flooding, droughts, major forest fires and changes in the number and kinds of insects, birds, fish and mammals were all clearly visible to me.

  Climate change may be due to human activity or natural environmental cycles or a combination of things. Whatever the causes are, it seems to me that we humans shouldn't be sullying this beautiful planet. Beliefs that climate change is primarily a cyclical event or that minimizing pollution hinders economic advancement, together with blatant indifference, are not excuses for people to pollute this beautiful world.

  No one wants to live in shit.

- I am not particularly religious, but I am very spiritual. I have found the greatest spiritual strength in the giving and taking and sharing of energy with the natural world. I feel an especially acute energy from trees. Forests are therefore my sanctuary.

  I like to tick things off lists, such as how many parks I've visited. The act of counting what I've done makes me feel like I've accomplished something and inspires me to complete what I set out to do. Documenting and reviewing my accomplishments reminds me that I have done something with my life. So, among other things, I've been to all the national parks of Canada!

- I really enjoy sharing my stories, both orally and in writing, in the hope of inspiring others.

- I've truly enjoyed writing this book. The stories just ran out of my mind and onto the page. I hope my accounts are as interesting and fun to read as they were to write.

- My photographs and journals have been great memory assistants, particularly in the creation of this book.

I'm so thankful to Jack Blonk, the father of one of my best friends, who inspired my teenage self to pay attention to the composition of my photographs, even when I only had a simple point-and-shoot camera with film cartridges. His words guided me to improving my photographic ability through SLR cameras with zoom lenses, DSLR cameras, and smart phones, which can now produce excellent photos. Over the years, technology has taken care of the science of photography – but the art of photography is still mine!

Journaling too has evolved from pen-and-paper to word processors. However, looking back at my handwritten journals, I've noticed that the tightness or looseness, pressure, slant and other characteristics of my script (including the odd bloody fingerprint and occasional squashed mosquito under the ink on the pages) added dimension to my words. Technology has taken care of spelling and grammar, but composition and physical writing remain human art forms.

Friends have described me as "driven." Perhaps I am. My favourite experiences, or memories after the fact, are of things I did outside my comfort zone. While some experiences may have been difficult (too cold, wet, tiring, hot, new…), the feeling of accomplishment afterward is what I love the most. This is what drives me! This is why I pushed myself to do awesome things in each park I visited and to write this book. I must not give in to the temptation of lethargy!

May the adventures, explorations, learnings, conservation and preservation of this great country and its peoples continue!

TERRITORIAL ACKNOWLEDGEMENT

We would like to also take this opportunity to acknowledge the traditional territories upon which we live and work. In Calgary, Alberta, we acknowledge the Niitsítapi (Blackfoot) and the people of the Treaty 7 region in Southern Alberta, which includes the Siksika, the Piikuni, the Kainai, the Tsuut'ina, and the Stoney Nakoda First Nations, including Chiniki, Bearpaw, and Wesley First Nations. The City of Calgary is also home to Métis Nation of Alberta, Region III. In Victoria, British Columbia, we acknowledge the traditional territories of the Lkwungen (Esquimalt and Songhees), Malahat, Pacheedaht, Scia'new, T'Sou-ke, and W̱SÁNEĆ (Pauquachin, Tsartlip, Tsawout, Tseycum) peoples.